Ephemeral Histories

Ephemeral Histories

Public Art, Politics, and the Struggle for the Streets in Chile

CAMILO D. TRUMPER

University of California Press

University of California Press, one of the most distinguished university presses in the United States, enriches lives around the world by advancing scholarship in the humanities, social sciences, and natural sciences. Its activities are supported by the UC Press Foundation and by philanthropic contributions from individuals and institutions. For more information, visit www.ucpress.edu.

University of California Press
Oakland, California

Library of Congress Cataloging-in-Publication Data

Names: Trumper, Camilo D., 1977– author.
Title: Ephemeral histories : public art, politics, and the struggle for the streets in Chile / Camilo D. Trumper.
Description: Oakland, California : University of California Press, [2016] | Includes index.
Identifiers: LCCN 2016012001| ISBN 9780520289901 (cloth : alk. paper) | ISBN 9780520289918 (pbk. : alk. paper) | ISBN 9780520964303 (ebook)
Subjects: LCSH: Art—Political aspects—Chile. | Politics in art. | Politics in motion pictures.
Classification: LCC N72.P6 T78 2016 | DDC 700.983—dc23
LC record available at http://lccn.loc.gov/2016012001

Manufactured in the United States of America
25   24   23   22   21   20   19   18   17   16
10   9   8   7   6   5   4   3   2   1

In keeping with a commitment to support environmentally responsible and sustainable printing practices, UC Press has printed this book on Natures Natural, a fiber that contains 30% post-consumer waste and meets the minimum requirements of ANSI/NISO z39.48–1992 (R 1997) (Permanence of Paper).

A mis padres. This is their history.

Contents

Acknowledgments

This book is the product of a long, collaborative effort. I have had the privilege to learn from committed scholars and teachers throughout my academic career. My undergraduate education at the University of British Columbia shaped me deeply. Ernie Hamm, Thomas Kemple, Blanca Muratorio, Clint Burnham, Joy Dixon, Anne Gorsuch, and Alan Sinel were early and enduring influences. William E. French, my undergraduate adviser and mentor, with his inventive, wry approach to cultural history, carries much of the blame for my decision to become a historian.

I began work on this project in earnest while surrounded by colleagues and mentors in the University of California, Berkeley, Department of History. Mary Ryan, David Henkin, and James Vernon were particularly inspiring. Mary's and David's courses on urban history indelibly marked how I think about the city. James's intellectual curiosity made me imagine the practice of writing and teaching in new ways. Mark Healey's timely arrival and his willingness to read and comment on early drafts greatly enhanced this book. Patrick Barr-Melej and James Cane-Carrasco offered sage guidance and support as insightful scholars of Chile and the Southern Cone in early days, and do so to this day. Margaret Chowning continues to be a thoughtful and encouraging mentor. Margaret read and improved countless drafts, offered intellectual guidance and practical advice, and modeled serious archival scholarship. My thesis adviser, William B. Taylor, enthusiastically shepherded this project through its various incarnations. A generous, inspiring scholar and committed teacher, his influence can be felt here in concrete and ephemeral forms: in my attempt to restlessly contextualize, to sit with apparent paradox, to be open yet critical about archives and sources, to develop synoptic approaches, and to write and teach about the past in all its richness carefully and ethically.

Many librarians and archivists helped me build this book. I am particularly grateful to the archivists at the Biblioteca Nacional de Chile's (BNC's) Salon Investigadores and Hemeroteca, the Archivo Nacional de la Administración (ARNAD), the Universidad Católica's Centro de Información y Documentación Sergio Larraín García-Moreno and its Archivo de Prensa, the Museo Histórico Nacional de Chile and the Universidad de Chile's Archivos Fotográficos, and the Ministerio de la Educación de Chile's Centro de Documentación. Other institutions throughout the Americas provided invaluable assistance, including the Casa de las Americas and Biblioteca Nacional de Cuba, the Hemeroteca Nacional and Archivo Gráfico at the UNAM and the Instituto Mora in Mexico City; the New York Public Library, Columbia University Library, and the NACLA Archive of Latin Americana at the New School for Social Research in New York City; the Center for the Study of Political Graphics in Los Angeles; and especially the Bancroft Library in Berkeley and the Hoover Institute and Special Collections at Stanford University. Walter Brem, who introduced generations of prospective Berkeley historians to the richness of archival possibility, deserves special thanks.

I cannot express the depths of my gratitude to the many people who opened their personal archives and shared their memories and views with me. Special thanks to Pedro Chaskel, Antonio Larrea, Vicente Larrea, Marcelo Montecino, and Brigada Ramona Parra members Alejandro "Mono" González, Juan "Chin Chin" Tralma, Boris and Beto, all of whom were indescribably helpful. Vicente and Antonio Larrea, Luis Albornoz, and Waldo González spoke with me numerous times and opened their professional and personal archives without hesitation. Pedro Chaskel, the first person I spoke with in Chile, not only facilitated all these other conversations, but continued to talk and share with me over the years, and I cannot thank him enough. Mono shared his memories, his personal archive, and was willing to entertain, discuss, and debate for hours on end. Chin Chin and his wife opened their home for many conversations over *té con canela* and delicious *pan amasado*. Both invited me to paint with them and take photographs of their work. This book would not be what it is without them. I hope these pages do justice to their insight and generosity. The filmmakers and artists José Balmes, Francisco Brugnoli, Manuel Calvelo, Leonardo Céspedes, José Donoso, Luz Donoso, Carlos Flores, Francisco Gedda, Alvaro Hoppe, Douglas Hübner, Hector Lopez, Pedro Millar, Hector Marotta, Samuel Mena, Álvaro Ramírez, Federico Salzman, Domingo Ulloa and Faride Zerán took hours out of their days to speak with me; even when I fail to refer to them directly here, their insights buoy these pages.

This book is deeply influenced by the pathbreaking work of Chilean scholars who not only welcomed me but also shaped my way of seeing art, politics, and the city. Eduardo Castillo, Alejandro Godoy, Gonzalo Leiva, David Maulen de los Reyes, Patricio Rodríguez-Plaza, and Mauricio Vico pioneered the study of Chilean posters and murals. Eduardo continues to generously share his personal archive and deep insights into the era's visual culture. Claudio Rolle and Alberto Harambour's scholarship have taught me much about the social and cultural history of Chile. Rolf Foester not only walked me to his favorite stops in Franklin but also helped me with archives and sources over the years. Sonia Montecino has always been supportive and generous. Claudia Mora helped me arrange research and transcriptions across the miles. Gonzalo Cáceres shared early, significant contacts. And Rodrigo Detwyller spoke with me at length about the history of housing in Chile and offered affiliation with the Universidad Católica when I was beginning my research.

Alicia Partnoy's magnificent analysis of theory and testimony has been truly inspiring; she is one of those rare few who are brilliant scholars yet even more impressive people, and I value her friendship, and that of Antonio, greatly because of it. The influence of conversations with Pablo Piccato regarding the public sphere can be felt throughout these pages. Heidi Tinsman has read and shared invaluable insight and guidance from very early days. Ray Craib has been an inspiration and generous supporter. I have enjoyed fruitful conversations with an exciting group of scholars of Southern Cone politics, including Alison J. Bruey, Brenda Elsey, Edward D. Melillo, Edward Murphy, Marian Schlotterbeck, and Jessica Stites Mor, whose work and generosity is evidenced in these pages. A dynamic group of visual studies scholars, including Natalia Brizuela, Mary Coffey, Claire Fox, Esther Gabara, and Roberto Tejada, invited me to join their ongoing conversations as I was completing this work, conversations that have greatly enriched my analysis of images, visual practice, and archives. Peter Winn, whose written work had already influenced me profoundly, offered incisive advice and encouragement at a crucial stage. Michael Needham and the team at Humanities First edited and shaped an early version of this book, and it is better for it. My experience at the University of California Press has been exceptional. Many thanks to Kate Marshall for seeing promise in this project; to Zuha Khan, Rose Vekony, Jessica Ling, Sheila Berg, and Ryan Furtkamp and Susan Storch for their care and professionalism; and to the anonymous readers who offered time, insights, and advice that made this book immeasurably richer.

This project has been generously funded by the Tinker Foundation; UC Berkeley's Department of History; a Loyola Marymout pre-dissertation grant; a SUNY Faculty Diversity Program Award; a United University

Professionals' Faculty Development grant; and the University at Buffalo's Julian Park Publication Fund, Baldy Center for Law and Social Policy and Humanities Institute. The University at Buffalo's Humanities Institute has provided the resource of time for thinking and writing, which is invaluable at the later stages of any project. I cannot thank Tim Dean, Carrie Braemen, Erik Seaman, and Libby Otto enough. Welcome support from a National Endowment of the Humanities Summer Stipend made it possible to finish this project on time.

My debts at the University at Buffalo are too many to name. I have space only to remark on the generosity of my mentors, Michael Frisch and Monroe Eagles, and Mariella Bacigalupo, David Hertzberg, Keith Griffler, Theresa McCarthy, LaKisha Simmons, Gwynn Thomas, Carl Nightingale, Victoria Wolcott, Jason Young, and Jim Bono, all of whom have read countless drafts and offered counsel and support that have improved this book. Deborah Pierce-Tate and Karen Reinard were invariably helpful and kind over the years. John Burdick, Dzheni Dilcheva, and Fernanda Glaser helped immensely with research assistance and thoughtful criticism. Hal Langfur merits special mention as a trusted colleague and cherished friend who has shared sage guidance, advice, and, along with Kerry Reynolds, welcome mornings of waffles, shirred eggs, and warm conversation. Ellen Berrey, Steve Hoffman, Jordan Geiger, Miriam Paeslack, and Eric Walker became lifelong friends in the lowest of times and continue to shine in the best of them.

My view of the world has been most deeply shaped by friends and family. Joy Horan, David Henderson-Hean, and Eli Silver continue to inspire. Kevin Adams, Chris Agee, David Granger, Alan Mikhail, Kalil Oldham, Tim Rose, and the rest of Berkeley's historian-*fútbolistas* made years of Saturdays memorable. I am proud to have built a friendship with Jason Sokol on scholarship, barbecue, and basketball. I cannot help but smile when I think of Jose Refugio de la Torre's deep thinking, deceptively open mind, and unrivaled love for tacos and tortas. I was captivated by Jessica Delgado from the very first moments I heard her speak in class, and she has offered new ways of seeing (and talking) about countless things ever since. Anne Marie Nicpon Farley, Hien Nguyen, and David Commins not only helped me regain perspective while writing early iterations of this book, but continue to visit and reach out across the distance. I have been particularly lucky to build lasting family ties through the years of research and writing. My love to my family in Chile, including *mis tías y primos*, who welcomed me warmly over the years, and to Dalia Justo, Tina, Dulce, Crisanta, and my adoptive godparents, Isa and Jorge, and cousin Jimena.

My grandmothers, Berta (Mamy), Elena (Nena), and Raquel (Raca), have a very special place at the very root of my love for Chile. Mamy and Nena quite literally fed my love for cooking, eating, and Santiago. Raca met me with a gruff hug, meaty French fries, and crushingly strong Pisco Sour(s). These strong, sharp, funny, and loving women indelibly shaped who I am. Celso Castilho became family as we wrote, revised, discussed, and debated history, politics, and *fútbol*. Many thanks to my brother, Jorge, my earliest influence, who brought my beautiful and funny niece and nephew, Rayén and Nahuel, into my life. And to Lucie, who has not only been generous and loving but also helped me develop my intellectual interest in photography and the city.

I dedicate this book to my parents. Their curiosity, kindness, and devotion has influenced me in too many ways to address here. They have also shaped this book in too many ways to fully appreciate. They have shared their memories and insights, talked over ideas, read multiple drafts, and helped me each and every day. This book would not exist without them.

I must express my deepest gratitude to Dalia Muller, who has helped this book develop from its inception. Kind, caring, adventurous, brilliant, and funny, Dalia is at the center of it all. I can only try to convey my joy in and love for our little ones. I pause as I write here to mark and feel the memory of Emiliano Salvador. And to dedicate too few words to the incomparable Amaya Elena and Simón Santiago Emilio: their sleepless nights, the warmth of their hugs, and their brilliant, surprising ways of seeing the world radically changed my outlook on absolutely everything. *Los quiero con todo.*

Introduction

The Politics of the Streets

Álvaro Ramírez's documentary short, *Brigada Ramona Parra*, is a synesthetic exploration of urban politics in Chile. The folkloric group Quilapayun's memorable interpretation of the Nicolás Guillén poem *La Muralla*, set to music in the late 1960s, initially dominates the movie's soundscape. But the sound is jagged, cutting suddenly as the filmmakers follow members of the Communist Youth's Brigada Ramona Parra (BRP) muralist "brigades." Quilapayun gives way to the sounds of the young members' chants, the rumble of the street, interviews, and everyday conversations that contextualize the grainy images of the Brigada. Ramírez's camera stays with the *brigadistas* as they cover Santiago city walls with graffiti (*rayados*) and slogans (*consignas*) on the eve of Salvador Allende's presidential election on September 4, 1970. The documentary is built upon rare, handheld footage of brigade members as they perfect their technique: one young member quickly traces the rough outlines of the candidate's name in black over an existing drawing; others dart in, painting inside and around the outline in color; a final pass in black sharpens the lines, making the letters stand out from the relief and giving the Brigada's iconography a characteristic style. When it is finished, someone calls to his colleagues and, in seconds, the group piles into an open-bed truck and disappears.

Ramírez's film affords the viewer an almost tangible sense of a kinetic politics—of the contest over public spaces, the corporeal rituals of street art, and the transformation of city streets and walls by ephemeral acts of public writing. The filmmakers follow brigade members as they hoist wooden contraptions that allow them to glue posters far beyond their reach without the aid of a ladder. Others run along buses pulling away from stops, pasting posters on the vehicles' sides and backs as they pick up speed. Another group of brigadistas returns to existing BRP slogans that have been painted

1

over or defaced, covering them with new posters and slogans or answering with their own simple rayados. These actions appear as different ways of engaging in an ongoing physical and symbolic struggle over the shape, form, and limits of public expression and public debate. The documentary ends suddenly as it follows BRP members to a march in support of Allende, where the president's words compel his "young" supporters to continue to act in the "decisive conflict" between "a people that refuse to be shackled" and their oppressors.

The film, then, is a rare document that captures the ephemeral roots of political practice, revealing that evanescent public art can be a significant means of shaping the city into an arena of fraught political debate. Brigadistas may have claimed a particular wall for only an hour or a day before their graffiti, slogans, and posters were torn down or painted over, but their work is no less significant because of its impermanence. In fact, ephemeral urban acts, ranging from public protest to public art, transformed the city into a contested public arena where political discourse was made material, written in text and image directly on streets and walls. This type of urban practice or performance was one of the distinctive markers of Chilean politics under Allende, and one of the first targets of repression by the military regime that deposed him.

The September 11, 1973, coup that toppled Allende's democratically elected government fundamentally altered Chilean political landscape and political history. The military junta held power for nearly two decades. In this time, it killed or disappeared some 4,500 citizens and detained and tortured another 150,000 to 200,000. It sent military forces into city centers, shantytowns, mines, and factories and farms that had been occupied by workers and peasants, with the objective of detaining or disappearing "subversives."[1] In Santiago, the junta bombed the presidential palace from the sky. It occupied government buildings, union halls, and worker-run industries. It fired on apartment buildings, sending families to hide from bullets in bathtubs and bedrooms. It deployed tanks, officers, and cadets to patrol the streets and set up barricades and checkpoints where it could stop, search, and detain citizens. It outlawed public gatherings, political association of any kind, and the practice of elections "even in social organizations such as youth clubs and labor unions."[2] It burned books, records, and posters in downtown city streets. *Santiaguinos* themselves hid, buried, or destroyed "[political] paraphernalia [including] party identity cards, posters and banners, certificates from workshops and meetings, and pamphlets and books."[3]

Chile's newspaper of record—*El Mercurio*—published ghostly images of empty streets in the days after the coup. Photographers captured citizens painting over graffiti and murals at gunpoint. These images made a national spectacle of the fledgling military regime's efforts to erase the vestiges of art and writing that had covered every public surface during Allende's presidency, silencing what scholars have called a "shout inscribed on city walls."[4]

The bombing of the presidential palace on the morning of the coup may have been the most spectacular display of martial power, and the ongoing state of siege a continued reminder of military control over everyday life, but the Mapocho River basin became a main stage upon which a far more insidious theater of repression played out. The junta abandoned the mutilated bodies of the "disappeared" in the river where it snaked through the downtown core, leaving them to float through the city in a silent but macabre reminder of the dangers of political activism. The stone and concrete walls of the Mapocho River embankment had long been one of the most significant arenas of ephemeral public artistic production. Artists, muralists, and shantytown residents had painted complex evocative visual narratives that went on for blocks and blocks along the riverbed walls. These murals were quickly expunged. Yet, after the coup and under the very real threat of disappearance, torture, and death, santiaguinos returned again and again to participate in fleeting but persistent acts of political resistance. Performance art groups unfurled banners proclaiming "No +," or "No More," followed by a blank space, inviting the passerby walking along the river to complete the sentiment of charged political disaffection before disappearing into the crowd. Many more wrote and drew on embankment walls, covering them again and again with slogans and arguments against repression, images of murdered figures like Allende and the folklorist Victor Jara, and times and dates of clandestine political rallies.[5]

Public expression was as meaningful as it was jarring in a whitewashed urban realm governed by the military. The obstinate presence of public art and public writing highlighted the potential resurgence of a type of political dialogue that appeared to be erased by military repression. These "resistant practices progressively opened space for new possibilities for political organization that led to the rebuilding of networks of sociability and political resistance."[6] Even though they were quickly covered again, these tenuous, evanescent visual essays were more lasting and significant than anyone could have imagined. Public expression remained a political act, a sign of continued resistance, and a means of reestablishing political association.

How had these forms of public art and public expression become so significant? How do we write a political history that takes these ephemeral entries and practices as essential sources of analysis? How do we explain the violence with which the military clamped down on political expression and the continued repression that marked everyday life in Chile during seventeen years of dictatorship? *Ephemeral Histories* pairs political and urban history to answer these driving questions.

STREETS, WALLS, CITIZENS: EVERYDAY URBANISM AND THE HISTORY OF CHILEAN POLITICS

Historians mark a turning point in Chilean politics in the early twentieth century, with the passing of the 1925 Constitution and the 1932 election of Arturo Alessandri, whose presidency reinaugurated a sustained period of constitutional government.[7] This period was characterized by a "gradual opening" in which a more diverse range of actors, including historically disenfranchised groups, entered into national politics. Between 1920 and 1970 the Chilean electorate was transformed. The numbers of registered voters expanded to 36 percent of a population that in 1970 reached 9.7 million. Women gained suffrage in municipal elections in 1935 and in national elections in 1949. Other electoral reforms were introduced in this period. In 1958 a single, official, and secret ballot was implemented. Legislation made voter registration obligatory and permanent in 1962.[8] Until then, the landed aristocracy had manipulated rural votes under a system known as *cohecho,* which allowed them to gain sway over 30 to 40 percent of the national vote.[9]

Changes in suffrage and electoral trends in turn gradually altered national politics. In 1958 Salvador Allende came close to winning the presidential elections, reflecting an overall rise of the Left in postwar electoral politics. The candidate of the Right, Jorge Alessandri Rodriguez, won by only around 35,000 votes in an election in which 1,235,000 people voted. In the following contest, six years later, the Right was forced to support Eduardo Frei Montalva, the candidate of the Christian Democratic Party. Frei won the election. His *Revolución en Libertad* was predicated on a series of political programs that aimed at ameliorating the most salient social inequities. Frei's regime provided a measure of political opening and a language of reform but proved unable to contain the demands of an increasingly urban, politicized citizenry.[10]

These transformations in electoral politics went hand in hand with shifts in the country's economy and urban geography. Import substitution programs placed emphasis on industrialization. Chileans flocked to the nation's cities in the mid-twentieth century. By 1970, 70 percent of Chile's population was urban. One-third settled in Santiago alone, making it the country's unrivaled demographic, economic, and political center. Roughly a quarter of all santiaguinos lived in shantytowns along the city's edges, packed into two-room houses with limited access to electricity and drinking water.[11] Basic needs, including medical care and food, were rarely met. Social inequality was written on the fabric of the city and on residents' bodies. While one quarter of the residents consumed 2,100 calories a day, half of the residents took in only 1,600. Elite Chileans rivaled their counterparts in the United States in height and weight. Nutritional deprivation assured the majority did not.[12]

Yet migration, industrialization, and urbanization lent political power to a growing industrial working class and a burgeoning middle class supported by state employment. Santiago's newest inhabitants were a historically itinerant population profoundly influenced by the battles they and their families had waged to expand labor rights in the nation's nitrate and copper mines, to extend political suffrage to women and rural workers, and to assure equitable political representation for all citizens.[13] As new urban residents, they soon developed original tactics of political action and began to assert their rights to the city in innovative ways. They called for a secure place to live, shared authority in the workplace, and equal rights in a city that had historically been riven by class and gender inequities. Under Frei, they challenged the state's attempt to mollify their demands and continued to influence national policy. Shantytowns became particularly well organized and militant in this period and turned to public action in order to achieve their political goals. Strikes and work stoppages almost doubled under the Frei government (and grew exponentially under his successor): rural and urban land seizures grew from 16 in 1968 to 369 in 1970; factory takeovers, from 5 to 133.[14]

This increasingly politicized urban citizenry mobilized in support of Allende, who again ran for president in 1970, now at the head of a Unidad Popular, or Popular Unity, coalition led by the Communist and Socialist Parties. Allende promised a radical, nationalist "road to socialism" that stressed large-scale structural changes in politics, economics, and society of the kind that Frei's regime did not deliver; substantive gains in the standard of living for workers, peasants, and *pobladores,* or shantytown residents; and political representation for historically marginalized groups. Unprecedented mobilization and coalition building in the last months and weeks of Allende's final presidential campaign made up "in grassroots strength what the Allende campaign lacked in funds, sophistication, and dynamism at the top." While his rivals controlled traditional arenas of political association, "Allende had the walls, streets, and slums of Chile."[15] These grassroots organizations effectively took over the campaign in its final stages.[16] Youth groups developed an innovative strategy, blanketing streets, walls, and public spaces in visual and material manifestations of popular support.[17] "Pasted on crumbling walls and plastered over public buildings in working-class districts, painted on construction sites and along the river walls and park walks," Winn evocatively remembers, "the message of the Allende campaign seemed to be everywhere. . . . By September, it was clear that Allende had won the battle of the poster and the paintbrush, while the election had become too close to call."[18]

After the election, Allende supporters built on these creative strategies and practices of urban politics. Workers, women, students, artists, sectors of the middle class, and shantytown residents supported the new government and simultaneously challenged the Popular Unity to fulfill its promises. Their tactics included protests, marches, and strikes; political art and graffiti; and documentary film and street photography. In turn, the opposition to the Popular Unity crafted their own innovative urban programs to supplement traditional means of political conflict. Politics was felt and fought on the streets, especially the streets of the city center. Winn recalls a conversation with a "well dressed woman that looked upon an ex-Yarur worker march in downtown Santiago" with fear that "her world was turned upside down": "What scares me the most is that the *rotos* [the poor, the broken ones] are taking control of the city's core."[19]

Under Allende, then, Santiago became a contested political arena. Friends and foes of the Popular Unity occupied public spaces in ways that appear fleeting or mundane but that ultimately reshaped the very form of political conflict and debate in Chile in the late twentieth century. Evanescent urban action allowed urban residents to carve out spaces of political mobilization and create languages of political analysis through which they could fashion themselves into active citizens. Seizing city spaces, even if only for a moment or a day, santiaguinos created "an entire mode of thinking" about the city and about "lived urban space" as a site of democratic political practice, contest, and exchange.[20] This was a "new politics in the service of an old politician, but all for a New Chile."[21]

Ephemeral Histories examines how different actors grasped the opportunity offered by a fractured democratic state to create new modes of political expression by taking to and taking over city streets and walls. Both left- and right-wing actors engaged in ongoing struggle over public space that led to a deeper transformation in where and, more significantly, how politics was done. Residents fought over control of city streets and walls, made urban action political, and made themselves into political citizens. "Everyday urbanism," those quotidian forms of urban practice that included protests and marches, posters, murals, graffiti, street photography, and urban documentary film, became part of a broader political repertoire by which a wide range of santiaguinos entered into and shaped political debate.

This book places culture, especially urban and visual culture, at the center of this investigation and finds a large variety of materials key sources for a history of political change over time.[22] It begins with the premise that space is not static or natural but instead made and remade through social and political struggle.[23] Critical geographers remind us that city space is a "work of appropriation" on the part of citizens in search of a political voice and an appropriate idiom and vehicle of political participation.[24] Spatial practice, the ways in which people envisioned, planned, and inhabited the city, became political practice: laying claim to city spaces became an imaginative political act by which social space and political citizenship are produced together.[25]

This is the city as stage and site of political practice, as "context for creative action *and* a product of that creative act," and the dynamic relationship between urban and visual practice as a key part of this inventive process.[26] In Allende's Chile, urban and visual practice became a means of seizing and shaping city spaces into a contested arena. The relationship between city plans and maps, and the material and visual practices through which peoples engaged and transformed this "ideal" city, helped fashion a unique field of play in which politics was done and debated. Experts' infrastructures and plans and laypeople's mundane actions, the formal and the informal, were part of the same fluid process by which cities and social relations were made and remade together.[27] My investigation demonstrates that ephemeral forms of urban and visual practice were creative acts that generated a new way of acting on and thinking about the city as a democratic space.[28] The struggle over public space, to "win the battle for the street," or *ganar la calle*, was a messy and often violent conflict between different groups over the boundaries, terms, and languages of politics that affected the very "rules of the political game."[29]

Ephemeral Histories engages the politics of the streets by coupling this analysis of space with a reinterpretation of the public sphere.[30] Feminist scholars have developed a compelling critique of Habermas's original hypothesis that the forceful entry of previously marginal groups into the public would tear asunder the ideal public sphere of rational debate. They argue that the very concepts of reason and rational communication are illusions that effectively function to exclude a range of political practices and peoples as irrational or illegitimate, and that power, conflict, and inequality are built into and ultimately define the terms of inclusion and exclusion from the public sphere.[31]

Historians of nineteenth- and twentieth-century Latin American public spheres illustrate how marginalized groups challenged their historical exclusion from politics and created novel forms of political participation. Students of gender and the public sphere pay particular attention to the role that political violence played in defining the limits of "legitimate" political action in the hemisphere.[32] Placing works on the public sphere and communicative action in direct conversation with studies of hegemony and power, these authors revise Habermas's unitary public in favor of a characterization of multiple open, unfinished public spheres in which the language of political communication and modes of political citizenship are continually being formed through varied processes of dialogue, debate, and contest. They focus especially on the tension between publics and counterpublics as a means of highlighting the importance of power and conflict in shaping a conflictive, fractured public sphere.

But, as Pablo Piccato notes, emphasizing the fractured, contested nature of the public sphere threatens to leave us with a series of related "plots" that do not afford an examination of larger structures, narratives, and questions concerning political change over time.[33] One way to avoid this pitfall is to locate the formation of the public sphere and the constitutions of publics in both time and space. Mary Ryan, for one, explores the relationship between the production of space, the construction of multiple public spheres, and the making of gendered political citizenship in an early, influential monograph.[34] Ryan proposes a suggestive thesis regarding the benefits of locating the public sphere in situ. "Public opinion," she suggests, "was formed in the streets, in the struggles of political parties, and in popular press"; the "most febrile public debate and decisive public action took place outside the voting booths and the halls of government."[35]

Suffrage and elections establish the frame but do not fill out the full story of political citizenship. Hilda Sabato finds that "public spheres were sites for the exercise of and negotiation around rights, and for the constitution of citizens. . . . [I]n many cases, the development of new webs of sociability and collective action, as well as the creation of new forms of dialogue and communication, contributed to the disruption and the modification of social and cultural traditions."[36] In this context, Sabato points out, public sphere scholars must "decipher" the different "codes" of political communication, which can include architecture, urban practices, and visual languages that myriad actors formulated in order to enter into political debate.[37] If Ryan locates the contest over the public sphere in the street to expand the geography of political conflict, Sabato studies this grounded public sphere in a way that lays the foundation for an interdisciplinary method of analysis that crosses urban, visual, and political studies.

The connection between spatial and political practice holds special potential for a rethinking of late twentieth-century Chilean political history. Influenced by the twin lenses of public space and the public sphere, *Ephemeral Histories* proposes an interdisciplinary political history that focuses on the strategies and tactics through which santiaguinos across traditional political divides refashioned themselves into political citizens. They seized city streets, walls, and other public spaces. They made claims *to* the city rather than directly *on* the state that were significant in their own right.[38] Politicians, architects, urban planners, industrial designers, artists, marchers, protesters, and passersby all engaged in the struggle over city spaces, over the rules and limits of the public sphere, and over who could define the form and language of legitimate political conflict. In seizing public space as a means of developing political citizenship, they fashioned political action and debate in unexpected places and surprising forms. They ultimately reshaped the *mode* of political contest.[39] In fact, this critical and cross-disciplinary perspective on the public sphere has the potential to move us past neat dichotomies and narratives of polarization and schism and closer to a rich understanding of how and where politics was done in the late twentieth century and suggests new means and methods for studying this complex political conflict.

PALIMPSEST AS HISTORICAL METHOD

Placing urbanism at the center of political history, I bring together seemingly diverse political practices and highlight the unforeseen connections between them. This unique and deeply interdisciplinary way of research ties architecture, urban planning, industrial design, political protest, and visual practice into a coherent narrative.[40] I build and analyze a heterogeneous collection of practices and materials whose juxtaposition reveals the complex interconnections between urban, material, and visual practices.[41] This approach allows me to unearth and engage an unconventional range of sources. It turns palimpsest into historical method.[42]

My aim is to produce a "post-documentary sensibility" by juxtaposing urban action, visual practice, and oral history.[43] The post-documentary perspective integrates multiple media in radically fluid ways, making possible a nonlinear orientation that encourages productive tensions, surprising connections, and new relationships between materials that are usually the purview of different disciplinary experts.[44] This is the documentary as product displaced by documentary as process—"as an ongoing, contextually contingent, fluid construction of meaning."[45] The processual sensibility expresses the potential of multiple perspectives and nonhierarchical relationships fostered by and between multimedia materials. This is ultimately a meditation on history as discipline and practice and on how text, oral histories, and visual culture can reciprocally inform each other. Taking everyday urbanism as a prism for the study of politics and examining urban platforms, processes, and practices through which residents claimed new political spaces and new political identities, *Ephemeral Histories* unravels the complexity of a single site, Santiago's city center in a short but fraught period of time, over the breadth of the *long durée*. In so doing, it opens up a discussion of interdisciplinary methodology for political scholarship that draws from visual, urban, and oral histories.

Thinking about methods is particularly important in light of the legacies of political repression. The history of Chilean politics in the 1970s is haunted by erasure: the military whitewashing murals, ripping down posters, and burning books in the streets; the collections of the Ministry of the Interior mostly destroyed in the bombing of the presidential palace; other state records effectively buried by willful indifference. Essentially uncataloged, many of the boxes of the state archives announce only the length, in kilometers, of documents that each collection holds. Municipal records, criminal records, and others are similarly inaccessible, and oral histories of this period are informed by fear and omission.

Recognizing that archives and memory are both shaped by and reproduce historical silences, this book intertwines political, cultural, urban, and oral history to find the sometimes surprising, quotidian forms, places, and practices that people used to express their political concepts and concerns.[46] This evidence survives, and it can be found in the records that have not been thoroughly redacted precisely because they are not outwardly or clearly "political" in a traditional sense. The Ministry of Housing and Urbanism (MINVU) records, for instance, hold the traces of urban reform plans that give insight into the politicization of urban planning and public space. Congressional records hint at the stakes of national politics and the language of national debates, but they also collect testimonies and evidence regarding the period's central issues. Magazines, domestic journals, and architectural and planning papers all provide evidence of the politicization of everyday life, urban practice, and the state. Personal collections contain the remnants and records of ephemeral urban and visual practice. Oral histories may only partially fill the gaps left by erasure, but even the omissions or mistakes that stud these narratives reveal much about the ways in which official stories are structured, what must be left unsaid, and where nodes of contradiction coalesce.[47]

Studying these different sources concurrently allows us to analyze urban practice and visual materials not as isolated objects or as finished, fixed forms of visual and political expression but as part of a longer process of public political contest.[48] This book is therefore willfully eclectic in structure, method, and material; it integrates analysis of archival documents (including press, letters, government records, speeches, and congressional debates), urban and visual culture (including fleeting urban acts and aesthetic practices), and oral history (including the collection and interpretations of formal and semistructured interviews) and weaves these together around an analysis of diverse forms of urban politics in myriad sites around Santiago's city center. In a way that is reminiscent of how santiaguinos layered walls with traces of an ongoing public dialogue, each chapter of this book engages, alters, and builds on the last. In so doing, the book takes advantage of the tensions generated by juxtaposition to cultivate a sense of the different forms of political practice. *Ephemeral Histories* rests one chapter on another, gaining insight from the overlap and contradiction between different forms of analyzing political practice, turning palimpsest into a method of scholarly analysis and critical writing.[49]

The project's assessment of the transformations in the shape and form of urban politics and political citizenship ultimately contextualizes the radical, state-sponsored violence that characterized the military regimes in Chile and throughout the Southern Cone from the 1960s through the 1980. It offers an avenue through which to study democracy and dictatorship together. The gaps in the historical record that this palimpsestic methodology addresses have led scholars to imagine the coup as an unthinkable and unbridgeable moment of rupture, an event that marked an irreconcilable break between two seemingly separate and incommensurable regimes. My research suggests that the regime's violence did not represent a clean break with the past but a brutal engagement with the history of urban politics under Allende.[50] A deeply contextualized view of urban politics that pays attention to changing modes of political debate ultimately allows us to understand the military's spectacular crackdown on public forms of expression and association as a means by which to censure the public spheres and political practices developed in democracy. It also sheds light on the myriad ways in which politicized actors re-created strategies and tactics of political association and debate even in the moments of most dire repression.[51]

ORGANIZATION AND OUTLINE

Ephemeral Histories mobilizes a multiplicity of methodologies and materials and highlights the relationship, tension, and even contradictions between them. It presents both the massive popular mobilizations and the everyday ways in which peoples across the political spectrum took to city streets and walls as complex acts that stitched together seemingly dissimilar tropes and discourses and created new political languages that transformed everyday sites into new spaces of political sociability. It concludes that both supporters and enemies of Allende opened up new sites of political association and new ways of imagining themselves as self-consciously political citizens based on revised notions of gender, class, and place that often challenged, transcended, or intersected uneasily with traditional party identities. These practices were reimagined and honed under a brutal military dictatorship marked by the pervasive threat of violence. Perfected in democracy, urban actions became some of the only available means by which shantytown residents, students, muralists, performance artists, and others were able to stitch together new political associations, networks, and connections and fashion new languages and tactics of political dissent. This study sees everyday urbanism "not merely as a spatial formation but as a way of doing things," a way of both making and interpreting the world.[52] It treats embodied forms of urban and visual practice as "an episteme and a praxis," a locus of analysis and a way of fashioning political identity.[53]

The book is organized in five chapters and a conclusion and epilogue, which together address different forms of urban contest in the capital city of Santiago, using interlocking methodologies. Chapter 1 examines the connections between urban planning and political theory, with particular attention to how the state's urbanization and industrial design programs of the 1960s and 1970s shed light on the era's political debates over citizenship. The archives of the Ministry of Housing and Urban Planning and records culled from planning and architectural design competitions to "remake the city center" under Allende shed light on state policy and political theory. I also draw on state documents, urban planners' writings, sketches, and objects, architectural magazines, and the press. I look especially closely at the work of the state-sponsored industrial design team that was charged with reshaping both everyday objects like spoons, plates, and chairs and the larger processes that underwrote the integration of industry into a national socialist economy. Its most representative design may have been an effort to transform the simple spoon used daily by thousands to measure the half liter of milk Allende promised to every Chilean child. This project articulated a clear argument regarding the political significance of "useful" design and its ability to inform the practice of socialist citizenship. Ultimately, this chapter offers a unique view into multilayered visions for an "ideal" socialist city. It reveals a new vision of the role that maps, objects, and spaces were meant to play in remaking codes of urban behavior and political practice, and in building a socialist modernity.

The second and third chapters examine the ways in which a broad range of people made this "ideal" city their own—how those on the Left and the Right alike crafted political narratives that made new sense of these idealized views of the city and of citizenship. Chapter 2 analyzes the December 1, 1971, "march of the empty pots." In an effort to fashion political opposition to Allende, women organized around the specter of food shortages, scarcity, and price inflation. Circulating information and organizing meetings in the press, supermarkets, food queues, and hair salons, they politicized traditionally "apolitical" places and created new possibilities for political association and debate. Marchers also made a gendered spectacle of "reclaiming the streets" from Allende supporters. They marched into the city center banging empty pots and pans, arguing that they were forced out of their domestic worlds by the "dire" lack of subsistence goods and into the contested space of urban politics. Paying close attention to the march itself—its trajectory through the city, the meaning of participants' chants and placards, and the visual and aural symbolism of clashing empty pots—reveals how the ephemeral political practice of protest fashioned "new repertoires of contention."[54] In this case, protesters drew attention to gendered tropes and to the political significance of consumption: They wove together discourses of "proper" femininity, masculinity, and citizenship in novel ways. The march was, in essence, a public act that stitched together gendered and political languages and transformed conservative gendered identities into bases for political organization.

Chapter 3 rounds out this analysis by investigating the monthlong October 1972 transportation strike. It looks at how this mobilization in opposition to Allende created new sites, forms, and identities of political conflict in factories, soup kitchens, and sidewalks; how it challenged traditional lines of political allegiance on the streets and in Congress; and, ultimately, how it set in motion a chain of events that shaped the September 1973 coup. My attention to protest in opposition to Allende allows me to examine urban and political mobilization across the political spectrum, placing public practices on the Left and the Right in the same analytical frame. Investigating the contests over public space allows me to show how the ongoing effort to win the battle for the streets changed the way in which participants understood the potential limits of political citizenship across political divides and expanded their sense of the role they could play in politics. Residents occupied spaces in the city, sometimes for as little as an hour, a day, or a month, as a means of reimagining and reconstructing complex political identities; these overlapping sites and forms of political conflict transformed city streets into arenas where participants could redefine what it meant to be *allendistas* or anti-*allendistas* and where they could politicize the categories and identities of poblador, worker, middle-class entrepreneur, housewife, or artist in new ways. Read together, chapters 2 and 3 illustrate how the act of claiming public spaces became essential political practice and how these acts fundamentally reshaped the city's political geography. They marry urban studies to gender and masculinity to explore how urban acts transformed the shape and limits of political and gendered citizenship.[55]

Chapters 4 and 5, along with the conclusion and epilogue, turn to visual culture as a potent avenue for political change and a new source for historians of politics and citizenship. In chapter 4, I utilize public archives, published primary documents, private collections, and oral histories to study ephemeral forms of public art. Posters, murals, and graffiti were part and product of the battle over the streets. They changed streets and walls in the city center, shantytowns, and factories alike into spaces for political debate.

The political significance that this public art held was rooted in its very ephemerality. It was meant to last for an hour or a day. Often posters, murals, and graffiti were only partially ripped or painted over, new attempts layered over older pieces, creating palimpsests of political debate. They generated a visual style that allowed a host of actors who had been politically marginalized to enter into public political debate and articulate an intricate, ever-changing political discourse. Pasted and painted in the busiest intersections of the city center but also on the walls of the poorest shantytowns, they transformed city walls into arenas of dialogue and brought their viewers into a space of wider political analysis. They simultaneously commented on and constituted a public sphere of political debate rooted in urban practices that claimed and transformed public spaces. They served as vehicles of and metaphors for the fluid, relentless political exchanges that characterized the three years of Allende's presidency, and they ultimately remade the city into a political arena and rewrote the terms and limits of political citizenship in the postwar period.

Chapter 5 examines documentary films as rich historical documents and creative political exercises. Chilean documentarians turned their attention to the streets in order to reconcile cinematic form and political commitment.

Their films were visual experiments that constituted part of the ongoing attempt to redefine the terms and forms of political citizenship emblematic of postwar Latin American politics. They produced a documentary aesthetic that could record and reveal the everyday experiences and material worlds of those peoples and places rendered socially and spatially "marginal" to national politics and society, yet remained flexible and creative enough to form subjective narratives crafted out of the building blocks of these sights and sounds. These films emerge as key sources for political history; I read them as emblematic of the complex and reciprocal relationship between political and aesthetic modes and as evidence that styles and forms of political participation were rapidly and radically changing, together, in the 1960s and 1970s. I also propose that filmmakers and photographers fashioned a distinct visual language that played on the objectivity of the lens without losing sight of the creative play that characterized Popular Unity–era visual practice. This visual practice built on actions and languages honed in democracy but reimagined in response to military violence and the instabilities engendered by widespread terror and disappearance.[56]

The conclusion charts these concurrent transformations in political and visual practice after the coup. It returns to the book's different strands and studies how they assumed new shapes during and after the military coup that deposed Allende and sought to eradicate and remake national politics and everyday lives simultaneously. It finds that citizens responded to political violence by reimagining the tactics of political conflict they had developed in democracy into a rich visual and material culture of political resistance. It approaches photography as a case study for transformation and continuity in political practice and visual culture as the hallmark of a political history that addresses democracy and dictatorship. It shows how photographers responded to political repression by fashioning a visual language that played on the "objectivity" of the lens and the "transparency" of the image, fashioning an innovative genre of "creative testimony." They ultimately turned images into the preeminent medium around which they could organize an active resistance movement. Those who recorded the whitewashing of the Mapocho riverbed's iconic wall art and documented the bodies of the victims of the dictatorship floating through downtown Santiago were actively engaged in setting the terms for critique of the military regime and an emergent language of international human rights. They played especially important roles in defining how old forms of public politics functioned amid the new context of dictatorship.

Photographers charted how, in the first year of the military dictatorship, Chileans living under the threat of violence, curfew, and a brutally repressive regime struggled to maintain a public presence by turning again to the ephemeral practices they had honed under Allende. They scrawled slogans and images on buildings, distributed leaflets, acted out fleeting forms of furtive political street theater, and crashed empty pots and pans as an ongoing form of aural protest. In the absence of generalized armed conflict, ephemeral acts and visual culture became the most effective form of political engagement and resistance in Chile. Developed in democracy but reimagined under dictatorship, they were essential to the creation of clandestine networks of political association and organization after the coup. My conclusion turns to photography as a means of tracing, commenting on, and participating in clandestine political conflict and, simultaneously, reimagining the historiographic approach that finds continuity within change, that opens the political history of democratic practice to include and broach the study of dictatorship and repression.

My epilogue assesses how the military sought to eliminate the public practice of political debate. It returns to the Mapocho River as a complex site of urban conflict, visual practice, and political citizenship in democracy and dictatorship. The murals along the Mapocho riverbed that opened this book shed light on this process. Public artists were so successful that after the coup murals, posters, and graffiti were specifically targeted for erasure. Murals were often made with whatever was at hand, including domestic materials and supplies cobbled from factories. Recycled materials lent these ephemeral murals an unexpected, obstinate persistence. Made with burnt oil, house paint, or industrial dyes, they often outlasted the thin layers of whitewash, which washed away in heavy rains and periodic floods or simply faded in the hot sun. Each layer of whitewash was not an end but only another point in an ongoing story of political conflict that connected two seemingly dissimilar periods. The power of ephemeral political art only grew under repression. The persistence of ephemeral visual art reveals that whitewash, erasure, and silence were effective but incomplete. In studying these often-overlooked forms rooted in democracy but remade in response to radical repression, this book illustrates how clandestine visual practices ultimately helped a range of citizens maintain and re-create networks of political association and identity that had been shattered by continued political violence. The military's cover-up, its unfinished attempt to silence these emergent forms of debate, adds another layer that we must peel back and examine as part of a complex process of political contest and change over time. But, as this book suggests, we can only do so if we fully understand the means by which streets and walls became complex public spheres of political action.

1. Of Spoons and Other Political Things
The Design of Socialist Citizenship

The destruction of the Diego Portales building in downtown Santiago was spectacular but not without precedent. Flames engulfed the lower section of the two-part structure in the early afternoon hours of March 5, 2006. The squat lower edifice was gutted. Its roof collapsed. Its exposed metallic skeleton was charred. The adjacent tower was left standing, only partially damaged. The fire was only the latest of a series of transformations. Though it was made of concrete, metal, and glass, the complex was remarkably malleable. It had been fluidly reimagined and reinvented over its forty-five years.

The structure was originally erected to house the Third United Nations Congress on Trade and Development, or UNCTAD III, in April 1972. Faced with the nearly impossible task of planning and building a conference site in less than one year, Popular Unity agents turned to the Urban Development Corporation (CORMU) leaders Miguel Lawner and Jorge Wong to coordinate various state organizations, industries, and workers to complete the project on time. The project's advisory committee decided on a site along the Alameda, Santiago's main axis, that was adjacent to the "Parque Forestal, Museum of Fine Arts, National Library, Municipal Theater, and one of Santiago's main universities."[1] This location had a number of advantages, not least of which was the fact that it was already part of the CORMU's citywide San Borja social housing project. The residential building already on site could be easily appropriated as an office tower, immediately connecting the UNCTAD project to the state's broader reinvention of the city's architectural and social topography. Making use of the ready-built tower, the team could instead focus on the construction of the lower structure. Modeled in part on the UN building in New York and developed in loose consultation between UN architects and an interdisciplinary team in Chile, the lower structure was made of "reinforced concrete and prefabricated

metal building housed under a 97,000 sq. ft. metal roof supported by six-
teen oversized reinforced concrete pillars." Under this roof, Daniel Talesnik
writes, the building featured "a 2,300-seat plenary assembly room, several
large conference rooms, as well as two dining areas seating 600 and 200
people respectively. Shops, bank branches, travel agencies, a post office,
communications room, delegates' halls, and a myriad of minor services
were also distributed throughout the four-story low-rise structure."[2] Over
a total of 260,000 square feet, the dyad of "low-rise and [twenty-two-story]
tower—a combination utilized in existing UN organizational buildings,
such as UNESCO in Paris and the UN headquarters in New York—were
connected by service bridges on three levels."[3] The structure was designed
with multiple entry points, removable walls, and modifiable floor plans that
enabled flexible layouts and malleable spaces. The structure was variously
described as a plaza, a gallery, and a pedestrian passageway.[4]

The multidisciplinary team that designed the building was composed of
architects, designers, workers, and artists. Original artworks were commissioned and designed for the building and built directly into its structure.
"The most prominent local artists and artisans were included in the design
process, not only in the creation of close to forty artworks that were distributed throughout the building," Talesnik writes, but also in "the design of
the lighting, furnishing, ventilation, and acoustics of the building."[5] The
sculptor Juan Egenau designed doors in aluminum and bronze that opened
into the two conference rooms; Felix Maruenda painted the exposed ventilation system bright red; Guillermo Nuñez, Jose Balmes, Gracia Barrios,
Luz Donoso, Pedro Millar, and José Venturelli created murals in acrylic,
wood, and cloth; Bernardo Trumper devised the building's illumination system; and Gui Bonsiepe, who led the CORMU's Industrial Design team,
developed a coherent set of symbols that would direct the multilingual
cadre of visitors seamlessly through the structure.[6] These projects turned
foundational and practical objects—air ducts, lights and door handles,
woods and fabrics—into creative works, influencing the experience visitors
would have when moving through it. The architect Jose Covacevich suggests that "artists came to define certain technical and tectonic conditions of
the building" by embedding their works in it and thereby achieved what he
called an "integrated design."[7] Miguel Lawner remembers the construction
as "an unprecedented and unparalleled accomplishment, a model of how to
integrate art and architecture."[8] Allende proposed that the building would
"become the material base of the great Institute of National Culture."[9]

The building formed part of a larger, nascent plan to engineer a "modern"
socialist city center and a modern socialist experience and interaction. It was

praised at the time as "one of the most important Chilean contributions to Latin American modernism."[10] Following the example of modernist architecture in Europe and the Americas, the construction unified public and private, street and interior into an ideal of uninterrupted and egalitarian circulation.[11] Strolling past and through the UNCTAD became "santiaguinos' favorite pastime," a daily ritual that crossed class lines.[12] According to Talesnik, "the building became a gathering point, a pole of urban attraction, where one could suppose that social differences could be set aside. Social equality had a theater in this building, a stage for a daily performance of an idealized country."[13] After the conference had run its course, the building was rechristened the Gabriela Mistral Cultural Center (GAM) and served as a showroom for the national Social Housing Exposition (VIEXPO), a fledgling art center, and a gathering place for lunches in dining halls that catered expressly to patrons of all class backgrounds.

The structure's place in the urban and political imagination was radically altered from the inaugural moments of the dictatorship's almost seventeen-year reign, as part of an attempt to first "sanitize" Popular Unity's aesthetic as well as political production and then institutionalize military rule.[14] Unable to inhabit a presidential palace in ruins and having dissolved Congress and outlawed political parties and suffrage, the junta occupied the Gabriela Mistral structure in the hours and days following the bloody coup that toppled Allende. It transformed the low-rise into the seat of the executive and the tower into the headquarters of the Ministry of Defense, the symbol of military authority in the very heart of the city. It sheathed the structure's windows in metal grates, erected fences, and posted guards at every fortified entrance, modifications that utterly transformed "the original transparent relationship with Alameda Avenue"; "the windowed façade at the plinth level was blocked with masonry[,] . . . isolated both visually and physically from its surroundings." The open plaza and gathering space that connected the structure and the residential Villavicencio neighborhood was shuttered.[15] Egenau's side door was sealed. The "cafeteria was closed, and all public circulation through the building was banned, radically changing its civic character."[16]

The junta enacted a series of more symbolic if no less subtle changes. It renamed the structure "Diego Portales" in line with a broad attempt to write a nationalist military history that included "heroes" of independence struggles and the early republic into the urban landscape. Maruenda's ventilation shafts were painted army green. Artworks were removed or destroyed, replaced with busts of the military and nationalist figures O'Higgins, Prats, and Merino.[17] Milton Friedman, one of the ideologues of the military's experiment with economic neoliberalism, delivered a lecture titled "Chile and Its Economic Take-Off" in the building in May 1975, and Henry Kissinger, then U.S. secretary of state, remarked on the beauty of the building to Pinochet when he visited as part of the Organization of American States' general conference. Though the executive returned to the Presidential Palace in 1981, the structure endured as the control center for the Minister of Internal Affairs and the headquarters of the Ministry of Defense. Ironically, the building's monumental nature, its symbolic weight, and the flexibility and adaptability built into its design made it a perfect target for a regime intent on the reinvention and legitimation of tradition.[18] Yet the "return to democracy" did little to change this. The building retained the role it had played during the dictatorship into the early 1990s, when it was rented out as a convention center and the press hub for the plebiscite and first elections in the first years after Augusto Pinochet's ouster. The National Council of Culture oversaw a public competition for its design and reconstruction in the wake of the 2006 fire. It was reinaugurated in 2010 as the Gabriela Mistral Cultural Center.

The 2006 blaze set in motion an impassioned public debate regarding the relationship between politics, architecture, and design that lasted well into the twenty-first century.[19] In a series of opinion pieces published in *El Mercurio*'s Architecture section, leading Chilean professionals maligned the UNCTAD's architectural and aesthetic value.[20] The director of the School of Architects went as far as to lament that the once-lauded building had not in fact been completely destroyed in the fire. A former national prize-winning architect, Christian De Groote, advocated razing the building. Lawner, director of the CORMU under Allende, entered the public debate. He argued that these professionals' assault was emblematic of the neoliberal moment.[21] Those who leveled these critiques were the architects and planners who were swayed into betraying their political and social ideals by the "multinational corporations" for whom they worked. He interpreted his contemporaries' wishes for demolition as a gesture toward erasure and silence, an attempt to demolish the "historical memory" of "the emblematic architectural works of the Allende period" and the "collective effort by workers, artisans, professionals and artists." This silence was, Lawner argued, directly parallel to what the military "had attempted with the disappearance of people."[22] The debate was therefore a sign of the triumph of the military's long-term repressive project, in which the threat of violence simultaneously censured political freedoms, restricted access to public spaces, and shattered long-standing political and social connections between individuals.[23]

The UNCTAD's successive transformations over time opens a window into the many ways in which public space became political in democracy and in dictatorship. This chapter investigates the UNCTAD building and its physical and symbolic place in Chile's changing urban and political landscape to address the broader themes and tensions that underwrite this debate, treating the struggle over public space as a creative act that transformed both the language and the form of political debate. It explores the connections between the public sphere, the production of space, and the rhythms of political change. It studies the ongoing and overlapping attempts to define and redefine legitimate languages of political conflict that occurred simultaneously in parallel sites and spheres and that remade politics "from above" and "from below." Grounding an analysis of the form and function of the public sphere in public spaces opens unexpected sites and sources of political debate and political history. The study of urban planning and design has untapped potential for Chilean political history. Examining the state's role in the production of space allows us to reconsider some of the basic assumptions that shape this historiography. Most significantly, it prompts us to contextualize Allende's socialist project in a longer history of political thought. It allows us to study politics "from above" and "from below" and on the Left and Right together. Finally, it suggests that we can study political citizenship as it was practiced in the everyday—in quotidian, often ephemeral, urban encounters. I focus below on chairs, spoons, buildings, walls, and streets as significant players in a complex political contest.

CITY VISIONS: STATE PROJECTIONS OF SOCIAL SPACE

After decades of conflict over rights, workers, women, and campesinos successfully gained universal suffrage in the 1940s and 1950s. But the expanded electoral rights told only part of a larger story. Waves of Chileans migrated permanently to the capital in search of new industrial jobs and, as the historian Mario Garcés Durán has argued, quickly began to make demands for fair housing. They expressed their needs through the vote, courts, and, ultimately, land seizures.[24] Grassroots urban groups were able to effect significant change in their everyday lives from the ground up. They engaged in direct action, often seizing lands and building communities and then demanding that the state support their efforts or provide basic needs, including sanitation, lighting, and housing.[25] The Christian Democratic Party (PDC) attempted to bring these new political subjects into the fold in the early years of Eduardo Frei's presidency, but residents' challenges soon outstripped the government's offers. They ultimately forced the state to establish projects, policies, and institutional structures that amounted to a reappraisal of the relationship between state and citizen.

The PDC responded to the pressures of this emergent citizenry by intervening directly in the landscape of urban planning.[26] The Frei regime, through the CORMU, oversaw a "vast program of urban change that promised an important transformation of Santiago's urban landscape."[27] Though much of this program was ultimately frustrated, the state's plan reveals an attempt by the PDC to rearticulate the role of the state vis-à-vis its citizens, filtering the state's influence ever more through its ability to act on the city.

A close reading of its role in urban planning and design suggests that it would be a mistake to see "the state" as a single or unified actor in the field.[28] Rather, multiple state agencies proposed contrasting, sometimes complementary, projects and visions of Chilean urban policy.[29] The CORMU developed a concept of urban design that drew on and developed alternative renditions of hemispheric urban projects and sparked innovative understandings and practices of space and social relations that ran contrary to overarching ideas in urban planning and party politics.[30] Grassroots urban groups shaped this vision to an extent: reflecting the growing role of "marginal" groups, the Frei regime proposed a vision of the city that drew heavily from hemispheric modernist projects that aimed to ameliorate the largest social discrepancies and glaring social differences marking Chilean society. State making was increasingly tethered to new strategies and policies of urban design, and Santiago was transformed into a laboratory for novel forms of urbanism.

The San Borja and San Luis housing projects illustrate the Frei government's vision of the politics of urban planning and social housing. The San Borja plan included forty-five high-density towers on eighteen hectares to house some eighteen thousand residents. It envisioned a ring of residential buildings placed throughout and integrated into the city, and that included a large swath of parks and recreational areas.[31] Authorities saw the San Borja towers as the CORMU's "emblematic achievement" in the period—the cornerstone of a larger urban renewal project that would transform the city's urban and social landscape in its design and its breadth.[32] The "megaproject" was nevertheless only a first step; it became the inspiration for a "more drastic, radical and unprecedented construction: the Parque San Luis."[33]

Whereas San Borja was touted as a "re-modeling" of the urban fabric, San Luis was to achieve the creation of an entire city-within-a-city built virtually ex nihilo. It was planned as a new metropolitan hub of approximately fifty hectares and seventy thousand residents in eastern Santiago,

intended to answer growing political pressures and ameliorate social inequalities by providing quality housing for workers within city bounds. In its
size and scale, it paralleled the larger urban projects inspired by Le Corbusier
and the modernist Congrès International d'Architecture Moderne (CIAM)
and brought Santiago into a hemispheric if not global conversation.[34]

Popular Unity urbanism was indebted to but promised a substantial shift
away from this program of urban design. It radically circumscribed existing, Frei-era projects. Instead, it aimed to fundamentally restructure the
urban landscape as part of its overall strategy to radically alter Chilean
economics and society. Housing was not meant to simply improve social
conditions but to transform social relations.

The Popular Unity's 1971 housing plan promised "the implementation of
an extensive model for the construction of housing," with the explicit goal
of "providing Chilean workers access to dignified living by fully integrating
them into the social fabric." State agencies imagined themselves as the
brokers not only of social housing, but of social housing as a means by
which "the infrastructure of the social is treated as a dynamic relationship
between . . . the integration of *poblador* into a life rich in human and political
capital [on the one hand] and the buildings and spaces in which this life
occurs [on the other]."[35] They also championed the need to incorporate input
from workers into the design and construction of their own housing. Social
housing agencies saw direct "contact with shantytown residents" as a source
of deeper knowledge of their "reality and pressing needs" and as a way of
eventually giving decision-making roles to workers and pobladores.[36]
Housing was, in short, a means by which to remake political citizens and the
city in which they lived.[37]

Urban planning in general, and social housing in particular, would therefore be an important tool for crafting new, equitable social, economic, and
urban worlds alongside active, authoritative, and productive citizens.[38] In
turn, "temporary" camp residents "themselves worked to transform the
state's housing policy" by progressively "seizing, expropriating and building on public and private lands."[39] By 1972, Allende would affirm that "we
have already taken the first steps in redistributing members of different
socioeconomic classes in the city."[40] But the strongest evidence of this
model of urban planning as social and political project can be gleaned from
an international competition for the renewal of the city center.

The competition was sponsored by the state and the International Union
of Architects (UIA) as part of the 1972 Social Housing Exposition, or
VIEXPO, which was, not coincidentally, hosted in the new UNCTAD building in downtown Santiago.[41] Organizers saw the competition as a means of

gauging the "state of contemporary urban design" and how it addressed the needs of the state's "revolutionary project." They collected eighty-seven applications from twenty-five countries. Judges looked for a few fundamental tenets or categories of evaluation that shed light on the theoretical underpinning of the period's urban design. They preferred projects that fit the city's flow of vehicular and pedestrian traffic and addressed the relationship between housing, services, and public spaces.[42] Urban scholars have since studied the winning bids as "a fairly representative sample of some of the tendencies of urban modernization that could be applicable to contemporary Chilean reality."[43]

The winning project explored the architecture of "alternative urban forms" that wove principles of fluidity and integration into a novel form of modern socialist urbanism.[44] Judges favored the bid because of its integration of scale, volume, and verticality. It proposed four "superblocks," relatively self-contained neighborhood units separated by the metro along the north-south axis and by existing thoroughfares and commercial sectors along the east-west axis.[45] The plan integrated three planes. A sunken, subterranean level encouraged automobile and metro transit, making possible an uninterrupted flow of people and goods. A passageway elevated above street level encouraged seamless pedestrian traffic. Four-story structures were interspersed among larger towers that alternated every two square blocks. These towers held medical facilities, schools, solaria, gyms, and residential areas. Each was connected directly to the metro by express elevators. This plan proposed a vision of modern life that was defined by the seamless assimilation of residence, leisure, and labor. It reimagined the core of the city center (along the city's north-south axis and between Agustinas, Almirante Barroso, Santo Domingo, and Amunátegui Streets) as an integrated arena, a zone of mixed use and of social integration and exchange that would bring those people who now lived in the city's most precarious housing along its peripheries into the downtown core where the majority of services were concentrated.

The proposal was not particularly innovative for its time. The winning project drew heavily from extant modernist principles and precedents (including, most notably, Brasília and the plan for Guyana City) in an effort to translate these principles into architectural practice. Yet it is significant as a document of political history precisely because it drew on, engaged, and reinterpreted modernist urban theory to articulate the shape of a particularly Chilean socialist modernity. This rearticulation of what were in the 1970s relatively well-trod principles became a vehicle through which to articulate and develop the language and design of socialist modernity. If the Popular

Unity government could present the possibility for a "break with the past and the construction of a new model of society," architecture, urban planning, and material culture would be the vehicle by which the Chilean state could shape a novel form of socialist society and of socialist citizenship.[46]

THE POLITICS OF THINGS

Between 1970 and 1973, the Popular Unity coalition proposed a global vision under the stewardship of a handful of overlapping, sometimes complementary institutions. Under Allende, these players came together to rationalize systems of production and patterns of consumption in an effort to fashion a "project for an alternative material culture" to buttress Chilean socialism.[47] Popular Unity state policies, informed by economic theory, emphasized programs that could raise workers' wages and purchasing power and in turn stimulate demand for local consumer goods. The state's development agency, the Corporación de Fomento (CORFO), sought to quickly increase national production. For instance, it sponsored attempts to design, manufacture, and eventually mass-produce low-cost consumer goods in order to reinvigorate production and allow "poor Chileans and members of working classes" access to "products and services previously reserved for the elite."[48] It supported the production of a Citroën car, the Yagán, which was made in a northern town of Arica, and an affordable black-and-white television set called the IRT Antú.[49] This developmentalist aspect of the state's economic policy has been well documented, but it had both tangible and symbolic repercussions at a local level that have not received sufficient attention. The Instituto de Tecnología de Chile (INTEC) would go on to design a range of inexpensive products ranging from calculators and record players to electronic machinery for sowing and harvesting under the Agrarian Reform and "a collection of inexpensive, durable furniture for use in public housing and playgrounds."[50]

The CORFO played a key role in this project to "change Chilean material culture to reflect the goals of Chilean socialism."[51] It was CORFO's director, Fernando Flores, who helped create INTEC and its Grupo de Diseño Industrial (Industrial Design Group) to further these goals. *INTEC Magazine*'s mission statement clearly delineated the way in which the group understood the role "industrial design" and the "material culture of everyday objects" could have in Popular Unity's project of political and social transformation. It proposed that the "myth of an aseptic neutrality of technology has been destroyed." And it instead recognized that the dialectical relationship between "society" and "technology" was a concretely "political" one.[52] José Valenzuela argued that the potential for "political change that the Popular Unity represents, and its determined efforts to establish a Socialist society," requires "that the group interpret the Government's plans . . . [and] generate technologies in conjunction with state organisms in charge of planning and industry."[53]

In the next issue of *INTEC Magazine*, in an article that "traced the promise of design in general and of industrial design" in particular, Gui Bonsiepe argued that Chilean political change required a radical redefinition of the goals, methods, and practices of the field of industrial design. "It might very well be that the much expected transition from a society disfigured by the sores of dependent development towards a more promising alternative," Bonsiepe wrote, "will require an examination of both the policies and the methodologies of design, because the latter is not totally independent from the context where it is going to be applied."[54] INTEC members saw themselves as part of Popular Unity projects to spur political, economic, and social change; they mobilized the principles and strategies of modernist design to transform relations of production and the experience of consumption, to reshape institutional structures and everyday experiences and practices.

The Industrial Design Group aimed both to revolutionize the "relations of production" and to establish "everyday practices" that were neither "imported from the metropolis" nor legacies of "dependent underdevelopment."[55] José Valenzuela's discussion of INTEC's role and structure furthered Bonsiepe's vision: "Technology is not an end in itself; it is rather a means to achieve social goals. . . . It is necessary to achieve a high level of technological development[,] . . . not to follow the path set by or close the gap with other nations, but to break with different forms of technological and cultural domination and to do so through choices arrived at freely and according to local values."[56] Technological transformation could lead the state to achieve real social and political change.

The relationship between design and political change that the INTEC championed in its everyday objects became clearest in the government's tumultuous final years.[57] Responding to a crisis that threatened the state's ability to foster the production and efficient distribution of essential foodstuffs, the Industrial Design Group turned its attention to networks of distribution and the design of containers in which to transport goods, such as fish and milk, more efficiently.[58] Prompted by the Popular Unity's attempt to encourage consumption of fish and fish protein, the team strove to replace the ad hoc collection of individual, makeshift or artisan containers in which fish was transported and sold. Its new plastic crates would be light, flat, and smooth. They would be standard, economically assembled, efficiently stackable, hold more produce, be easier to clean, and hygienic.[59] The group's immediate goal was to standardize materials and rationalize production methods, chains, and systems, but their ultimate aim was to change deep-set patterns of consumption. Indeed, near the end of the Popular Unity government we see state-sponsored attempts to promote the benefits of eating *merluza*, a fish that was a rich source of protein but carried the stigma of being "popular" and "unworthy," in contrast to the status and purported health benefits of eating beef.

A second proposal, the design of an "economical and practical china set for popular consumption as well as of a series of gadgets for domestic use," built on these principles of "standardization" and "categorization."[60] Here, the Design Group's objective was twofold: "On the one hand, it was a matter of *reducing the number of pieces* (and molds) in order to rationalize production, and, on the other, ... [of] *improv[ing] the ways these were used* (for example, to better use storage space by designing cups that may be stacked)."[61] The group again sacrificed flourishes of design in favor of efficiency. Each piece in this set was given a regular shape, the teacup's lines reflected exactly in the teapot and sugar container, achieving a "formal coherence" among the set's different components and allowing plates and cups to be neatly, efficiently stacked and sanitized.[62] INTEC members hoped that the china set's homogenized form and dimensions could serve as a foundation for a holistic reenvisioning of domestic design that would range from the shape of household implements like spoons and cups to the depth of kitchen cabinets and the shape of shipping containers. Their designs also point to their belief that rational and standard design could *also* establish modern, progressive standards of use that could encourage, among other things, hygiene and health in the modern home. INTEC members and group designers may have reinterpreted the concepts or goal of development, modernity, and progress, but they couched their vision of a particularly Chilean socialist modernity in developmentalist languages.[63]

The refashioning of seemingly innocuous objects—especially those associated with consumption and eating—toward practical and political rather than aesthetic ends became the Design Group's calling card.[64] One of the team's most representative designs was a complicated contraption for measuring and dispensing the required amount of powdered milk prescribed by the government's promise to provide a half liter of milk per day for every child in need. The device was a new technology by which the proper dose of milk powder could be mechanically, efficiently, and exactly dispensed. But the ambitious original design was frustrated both by the "cultural" preference for the simple metallic spoon and the "prohibitive" cost of producing such a machine. The team therefore returned to a more "traditional" design but carefully calculated the length of the handle, the shape of the cylinder, and the weight of the implement to maximize the amount of material utilized. Ultimately, they fashioned a set of two nested spoons whose shape ensured that they could efficiently and precisely measure powder and, more important, could be quickly, fully, and hygienically cleansed.[65]

To this end, the group was immediately charged with creating rational systems of production, investigating new "typologies" of industrial creation, and implementing the design and production of a variety of everyday, "socialist" objects "ranging from china to furniture, electronics and vehicles."[66] Trays and spoons were only two links in a larger chain that would connect "the distribution and consumption of foodstuffs," two pieces of a project that would replace "the noneconomical hodgepodge of the present." This new system would achieve the "standardization of the measurements of containers" and "better use of raw materials." The group had to "create step-by-step a new stock of goods for popular consumption." Trays and spoons soon gave way to foods themselves.[67]

The third issue of *INTEC Magazine* chronicled Alex Trier's efforts to apply the principles of rational industrial design to comestible goods. Aware of the growing difficulties Chileans had procuring and distributing many staple foods and cognizant of the group's frustrated attempts to transform working-class habits, Trier reengineered a staple of the working-class diet— the ubiquitous combination of noodles and beans known colloquially as *porotos con riendas*—by enriching the common noodle with bean protein. Trier posited his project as a "rationalization of traditional dishes like 'chickpeas with rice' or 'beans and noodles' that have nutritious value because cereals and legumes are consumed together."[68] Having studied the comparative nutritional value alongside the economic ramifications of cooking both dried noodles and dried beans, Trier concluded that an enhanced noodle would be the most efficient method in light of Chile's economic and political reality.[69] For him, "enriched noodles are [simply] a vehicle to make legumes available to the consumer at a lower price than that they would otherwise have to pay, at an economic advantage and in a form that is easy to cook," with the added advantage of resolving or circumventing the contradiction between "traditional" and "modern" or "habit" and "innovation," instead "rationalizing" already accepted and approved cuisines.[70]

Trier, in short, conceptualized his noodles within the same framework and in the same language of modernity, efficiency, and rationality as the other objects the team designed.[71] His was a nationalist solution, using domestic products to transform culinary traditions and establish modern, progressive standards of use that could effectively foment socialist culture and habitus. These seemingly humble commodities were especially signifi-cant to the success of modern Chilean socialism. The design of everyday objects was a way to piece together an extensive and practical infrastructure over the span of a very productive year and a half; it was also an effort to transform the everyday practice of consumption in the Popular Unity, a practice organized around the principles of rationality, productivity, and modernity.

The Industrial Design Group's "interdisciplinary" team of engineers, psychologists, and designers sought to efficiently produce furniture and other objects that would "meet the needs of popular consumption," espe-cially in relation to affordable housing and everyday life in these dwell-ings.[72] Each individual piece was part of a larger project and a global vision, a rational system of production meant to create standard, industrial forms.[73] Their first proposal was the design of a set of affordable wooden furniture that fulfilled a MINVU request for subsidized housing. This was an expan-sive vision for a diverse set of living room and bedroom furniture unified by common design concepts. Relying on industrially produced, standard, and interlocking parts, they were easily assembled and easily adaptable to a vari-ety of floor plans and layouts.[74] In INTEC's depictions of these furnishings the chairs and benches are presented as "multifunctional," standardized yet adaptable to existing conditions, uniform yet "dynamic . . . and richly muta-ble," a standard that would be replicated in the design of furnishings for the state's larger projects. These were chairs tailored to the specific conditions of the Chilean context and fitted, anthropometrically, to "the measurements of the Chilean man."[75] The "scientific" studies that tailored furniture to par-ticular bodies were the most important factor in establishing "natural" con-nections between body, citizenship, and nation. The clear, "natural" associa-tion that the Industrial Design Group drew between modernity, nation, and the body nicely encapsulates its "integral" view of architecture and indus-trial planning and its attempt to shape systems of production and also attend to individual bodies and patterns of habit and use, thereby informing the practice of socialist citizens and citizenship. INTEC was part of a larger Popular Unity project that placed political and social change alongside transformations in the fields of urban planning, affordable housing archi-tecture, and the design of everyday objects—a more global vision of political and social change through urban planning and design.

THE UNCTAD III AND THE DESIGN
OF SOCIALIST MODERNITY

The UNCTAD structure was at the heart of this project. The third UNCTAD meeting assembled representatives of countries from around the globe with the mission to foster discussion between "developed" and "developing" nations regarding possibilities for economic change, trade, and relationships. In his inaugural speech at the meeting, as in his addresses to Congress, Allende established Latin America's "underdevelopment" as a historical condition, a repercussion of political and economic imperialism inscribed in contemporary economic relationships between developed and underdeveloped nations, metropole and colonies. This was simultaneously a critique of modernity theory and its ahistorical understanding of poverty, which posited subaltern "underdevelopment" as "natural," "inevitable," or "culturally" determined; an appropriation of the developmentalist paradigm, within the frame of a deeper structural and historicist argument; and, paradoxically, an acceptance of the teleological narratives of development and progress that underwrote modernity and dependency theory alike.[76] It also offered a basis for solidarity among "underdeveloped" nations that could together struggle to break dependent bonds, overturn global economic structures, and build new networks, relationships, and political systems that would allow them to move toward a legitimate pinnacle of modernity, development, and "progress." These nations' representatives reimagined the category as a unifying one, a means of building a common front across the globe. Allende's interventions highlighted the revolutionary potential of this perspective.

This social and political paradox was, for Allende, built into the urban landscape. Latin American cities, including Santiago, were shaped by the central paradox of the subaltern condition, or what he called the "tragedy of underdevelopment and the tragedy of our countries." Untapped national wealth was coupled with crippling structural inequities and overwhelming poverty that defined everyday life for the majority who lived in precarious housing in the urban peripheries, where "nutrition and health standards are no higher than in Africa." "The much-admired great cities of Latin America," Allende said, "conceal the tragedy of hundreds of thousands of people living in shantytowns, the result of fearful unemployment and underemployment, hiding the gross inequalities between small privileged groups and the broad masses."[77]

A wide range of politicians, planners, and architects saw in the UNCTAD structure an opportunity to develop a global vision of architecture, design, layout, and furnishings as an integrated whole that would symbolize and concretize a new form of socialist modernity.[78] After much debate, a multi-disciplinary team that included the United Nations Technical Office in Geneva, state-backed groups with ties to INTEC, and private industries was assembled with the intention to use Chilean industry to build furniture and a structure that would fit seamlessly with the complex's overall design. The editors of *Revista AUCA* (Architecture, Urbanism, Construction, Art) made these ties between state-driven industrial design and the UNCTAD's furniture clear.[79]

Revista AUCA had aligned itself with the Popular Unity project in the editorial it published immediately following Allende's election. "For the first time in the ordered path of Chilean politics," its editors began, "unexpectedly and surprisingly, a presidential election offers the country the certainty of profound changes to the socioeconomic and cultural structure."[80] They applauded these changes, perceiving an intimate and reciprocal relationship between political, social, and cultural change and the transformation of the physical environment and urban landscape. They believed that this larger political campaign and the government's commitment to social equality would liberate planners, architects, and designers to work not for profit but for social ends; in turn, architecture and design, placed at the service of a greater "social ethic" and "national project," could revolutionize citizens' everyday lives.[81]

AUCA's editorial board promised to serve this radical political, social, and urban transformation. Its editorial concluded, "Urban planners' bold imagination and tendency toward great sacrifice for the good of the population as a whole will be needed, in addition to the myriad efforts that the plan suggests. . . . As of today, *AUCA* will join this national crusade in order to fulfill its role in this modest but significant political battle front."[82] Although its pages focused on local and small-scale designs (including housing developments, individual building projects, and educational buildings), its editorial focus was always on the need for an encompassing vision of urban and social planning. The editors wrote, "Examining this from a more specialized point of view offers an opportunity to direct our attention toward programming, design, and nationalistic architectural production, toward interdisciplinary work, and toward professional experiences of high technical significance and the highest social ethics";[83] in contrast, and "as successful as it may seem, any isolated architectural project is born already alienated from the possible contributions it may add to its surroundings."[84] It is not surprising, then, that the magazine devoted particular attention to the UNCTAD III project and took pains to examine it in relation to a citywide vision of urban planning.

The editors' introduction to the magazine issue devoted to the UNCTAD building extolled the virtues of steel construction and proposed a new decorative architectural style that used exposed metal to create an image that was "healthier" and more "technical."[85] This emphasis on the material would allow architects and designers to participate in the "new mentality" that characterized Popular Unity modernity—namely, the desire to utilize design to meet political and social challenges rather than produce sellable goods.[86] The UNCTAD's facade, which literally exposed the building's functionality and in so doing transformed it into an aesthetic feature, was the greatest contemporary symbol of the valorization of utility.[87] Yet the articles that followed the editors' introduction, which centered on different designs of furniture suitable for the "standard of living and cultural level" of those living in affordable housing, established an equivalence between state-driven design and the UNCTAD project. Furnishings, chairs in particular, were the nexus between the state's housing programs and the UNCTAD.[88] Echoing the state's language, UNCTAD furnishings were characterized by their "multifunctionality" and ability to "adapt to the existing conditions."[89] Designers envisioned the built environment as a "matrix" in which each piece gained meaning only in relation to the other objects in the room. Seen from here, from within this integrated whole, it was "possible to imagine a new mode of domestic life."[90] Modern, adaptable, and flexible, these chairs fit a particular national modernity exemplified by the complex as a whole.

AUCA prominently featured sketches and prototype photos of the Garreton furniture line as examples of its commitment to solutions that could be integrated into a variety of settings.[91] UNCTAD architects and designers drew on principles and ideas that buttressed the Garreton design reflected in the state's plan for over 100,000 units of affordable housing.[92] On the one hand, then, INTEC designers leaned heavily on anthropometric studies to create an original line of chairs that would be products of a complex and integrated system of production and design but crafted to the particularities of Chilean modernity and an imagined, universal Chilean body. On the other hand, this ostensibly natural relationship that INTEC members drew between nation, rationalized production, and the body was echoed and amplified throughout the UNCTAD, where architects and planners wove the furnishings into their conception of the complex as an "integrated system" or global whole, informing the design of both spectacular, monumental architecture and minor, everyday objects.[93] These chairs, and the bodies they were meant for, were simultaneously part of a global economy and representative of a new national image based on efficiency, rationality, and adaptability. They were the incarnation of a very particular, homegrown socialist modernity.

Many of the firms that contributed to the building of the UNCTAD took the opportunity offered by *AUCA*'s publication of the official UNCTAD informational pamphlet to highlight their contributions to this symbol of national pride in a series of ads written in the language of progress and efficiency. On two full pages, the construction company DESCO juxtaposed one photo of the building a month into the construction process to a second photo of the completed lower *placa*, a mere four months later. The accompanying text laid out the overwhelming scope of the project: 172.5 meters long and 40 meters wide, seating 2,300 people, and supported by 16 pillars, the structure's foundation and frame were completed "exactly as scheduled," in under three months.[94] As David Maulen writes, DESCO was very much part of the INTEC-led effort to incorporate cybernetic technology into the efficient organization of labor and construction, technology crucial to the production of the spectacle of socialist modernity.[95] *El Mercurio* concurred with DESCO's assessment of its own efficiency, publishing a "panoramic view of the modern and enormous building constructed by DESCO for the UNCTAD III."[96]

One hundred twenty Maestranza Cerrillos workers built the UNCTAD's 1,074-ton metallic frame, completing its work in one hundred days. Its advertisement recalled DESCO's in its use of photography as evidence of the project's modern, industrial nature. Each image highlighted the UNCTAD's characteristic interlocking metal beams and used simple mathematical prose to buttress the power of the image. Maestranza Cerrillos resorted to bullet points to boast that it had created and assembled "50 by 2.75 by 3.80 beams, each weighing from 15 to 30 tons." They were the result of a "technical effort by a Chilean company, with Chilean workers, technicians, and professionals," an illustration of Chilean technological advancement.[97]

A number of firms followed this pattern, although none more clearly than ERAMCO, whose advertisement suggested that the company had fashioned "100,000 bricks a day and more in their modern factory."[98] With modern technology and motivated workers, its ad boasted, the company would soon be able to "double its current output of bricks."[99] *Revista Ahora* also extolled the breakneck speed of production: "workers' and engineer's productivity eclipsed the heights reached during the Remodelación San Borja. The rhythm with which each floor was built outstripped the technical capabilities of the construction materials themselves, and workers had to take their feet off the gas pedal. They had reduced the previous national standard of 4.5 days to complete each floor to 46 hours, and then settled on 50 hours as the optimal interval."[100]

It is not surprising that someone like Felipe Herrera, leader of Chile's UNCTAD commission in this initial phase, articulated a complementary vision of the conference and the complex's significance.[101] Herrera saw the conference as a "conversation" between "developed" and "developing" countries and the complex itself as a physical "site of encounter" or "point of contact" between members of an interconnected global community fractured by deep economic inequities. Drawing on Allende's speech at the ground breaking, Herrera invoked metaphors of maturation and growth to describe the Chilean nation-state's potential place within a global order: "The construction of UNCTAD's headquarters is also the point of departure of what could be called Santiago's maturation into an international city." For Herrera, the UNCTAD complex, built in mere months by workers laboring in consecutive shifts, was more than simply a symbol of Chilean productive potential; it was a material "fulcrum" and "springboard" into the future.[102]

What is unexpected, however, is that Andrés Guzmán's article in the special insert that the opposition paper *El Mercurio* devoted to the UNCTAD III articulated similar sentiments and concepts, also invoking the language of modernity and nation. Guzmán's commentary was framed by a series of five photographs that charted the construction of the complex from June 1971 to April 1972, and by the belief in the importance the UNCTAD III would have for the countries of the Third World in general and Chile in particular. He began by noting the ties between the UNCTAD tower and the Frei- and Allende-era projects to "rebuild" the city's downtown core, epitomized by the San Borja buildings. He was clearly awed by the scope of the project, overwhelming readers with the sheer weight of numbers: "89,000 cubic meters of soil excavated, 12,500 cubic meters of concrete, 1,220,000 kilos of metal for steel rods and 1,700,000 kilos of metal for the structure itself, to the cost of 162,000,000 escudos," enough to construct five residential complexes like those of the San Borja project.

But even here the structure's monetary value was outstripped by its symbolic import. Guzmán wrote in exhaustive detail of the structure's most dramatic markers. Outside, the complex was equipped "with gardens, rugs, air-conditioning, and all the advancements that could be found in a modern world manual." Its interior melded architectural detail, works of art and careful craft, and technological advances, including "telephone booths, [a] document reproduction center, [an] instant interpretation system, [a] heliport, electronically controlled elevators, drapes, and even door knobs." He took pains to detail just how the complex met or surpassed the standards and symbols of a global modernity and revealed to the world that Chile belonged among the pantheon of modern nations. Guzmán himself seemed surprised by the "euphoric dance of numbers, details, and enumerations." Yet his piece was part of an emergent tradition that sought to connect urban planning and architectural design to teleological notions of development and progress that was shared, though interpreted differently, by divergent political camps.[103]

These diverse elements and furnishings became in the UNCTAD part of an alternative material culture of Chilean politics in which politicians, planners, and builders invoked and expanded on the very notions of modernity, development, and progress but reinterpreted these terms as part of a broader language of socialism and nationalism. The conference building's design and the structural and technological framework that enabled the international, multilingual nature of the conference, played a key role in securing Chile's place within a global modernity. For instance, an *El Mercurio* editorial penned on the eve of the conference's inauguration printed a monumental photograph of the main conference room and highlighted the chamber's outstanding features in both image and text. "The interpreters' booths behind and on both sides of the podium will be able to translate simultaneously in the five official languages," the editor marveled, "through a network of wireless headphones while closed-circuit television cameras will broadcast the image of the presenter to the cafeteria, lounges, press rooms, and building tower." This modern amphitheater connected Chile to the modern world. It positioned Santiago as the liminal point joining "First" and "Third Worlds." The newspaper's editors framed their piece with a monumental image of an orderly, gleaming amphitheater, awaiting the arrival of world dignitaries. The image caption spoke to the significance of the symbol as a single entity: "all the details of the great stage[,] . . . its lighting system, artificial climate, communications and accommodations[,] are ready"; together these elements spoke to the amphitheater as a metonym for a modern structure and modern nation.[104]

INTEC's design philosophy and methodology contextualized and complemented Felipe Herrera's vision of the complex as an entry into the "developed world" and Allende's portrayal of it as the concrete manifestation of socialist unity and the potential of Chilean labor to build this unity. They were overlapping, reinforcing languages and practices, different threads of a larger, integrated project through which Popular Unity hoped to create a particular form of socialist, national modernity. The political discourses by which these different projects legitimated their increasingly polarized positions were akin: they valued modernity, progress, and nation, even if they disagreed on the interpretation of these concepts. As Marcos Valencia writes, "Modernization implied a process of technical, but also social revolution," and the UNCTAD was a symbol and an engine of a simultaneous technical, urban, and social transformation.[105] This process was repeated throughout the building: facade, construction materials, chairs, and furnishings were all representative of modernity and nation.

This focus on a single physical site allows us to move beyond simple dichotomies of plan versus use, Left versus Right, state versus grassroots politics. It reveals instead how complicated political discourse was built and rebuilt in specific places and practices that involved politicians, architects, planners, marchers and protesters. Studying spoons and chairs expands our understanding of the scope of political discourse, the key ideas that underlie it, and the means by which it was built. In this context, the UNCTAD conference, furnishings, and design all emerge as part of a larger network of "political things," a network that included material culture, architectural form, and urban design. Yet the UNCTAD complex, like INTEC's designs, did not simply reflect or capture an extant state policy, but helped fashion an alternative socialist modernity. It was also a building meant to encourage, or at least change, the experience of an egalitarian Chilean state and city.

The UNCTAD complex, then, was ultimately more than a totem, more than the linchpin in an emergent symbolic and material language in which the shape of national politics could be legitimately and legibly imagined and debated. It was also a physical site, a "meccano," or mechanism designed to encourage and shape the practice of an unorthodox political practice and political citizenship. The UNCTAD was built to be, in the words of the architect Marcos Winograd, an *edificio-ciudad*, or city-building, the material manifestation of an ideal, unified public sphere in which a variety of people could circulate, meet, and debate politics and private concerns. Winograd's compelling dyad suggests that the complex was a remarkably singular entity—a synecdochic piece that modeled a new way in which to understand the city as a whole.[106]

The UNCTAD's structure, design, and style established a productive if tense relationship between a global vision of modernity, movement, and space, on the one hand, and the local, quiet particularities of place, on the other. It was a larger attempt to conceive of a "complete urban organization" that simultaneously interrupted and highlighted the paradoxical elements of the city's physical and social geography.[107] Its architectural design was unique, but the building's facade was directly connected to the San Borja project complexes throughout the city.[108] The relationship between the UNCTAD tower and the San Borja buildings on the north side of the Alameda connected the neighborhoods on either side of the thoroughfare and transformed the structure into a bridge, a shared space in a metropolis that was otherwise geographically divided along class lines.[109]

The UNCTAD's main facade was oriented to this changing, modernizing city, and its main entrances gave onto, and welcomed, pedestrian and automobile traffic from the Alameda. The monumental tower and low-rise conference center were connected by a pedestrian walkway that was accessible through the main entrance on the Alameda and gave onto a large, covered central plaza. At street level, "the building retreated from the sidewalk," creating a "covered pedestrian path that lead to the entrance of what [was going to be] a subway station."[110] Its side and back entrances reached through tunnels, walkways, and entrances into the Lastarria neighborhood, a quiet, cobble-stoned enclave of meandering streets, colonial buildings, and restaurants and cafés where the city's intellectuals and progressive politicians met. Below street level, an underground passage was to link the complex to the Forestal Park, the Plaza Italia, and the *barrio alto*. The metro station scheduled to open at the complex's base in the near future was a key element of the plan, as the subway would link the building to the rest of the city and to the metropolis's poorest neighborhoods, opening the downtown core and the building itself to those who lived at the peripheries, away from the site of political and economic power.[111]

These design features point to a building that was conceived as a nodal point and a site of transformation in the city's physical and social geography. The complex established a seamless, porous border between the global and local, the public and private, the street and interior and subtly broke down the strict distinction between exterior and interior and public and private.[112] Winograd, at the time, equated the principles of circulation and integration with "absolute . . . modernity," the building with urban and social change that stretched well beyond its walls.[113] In fact, the UNCTAD complex was meant to be integrated into the city around it and, by serving as a point of contact and passage for santiaguinos across class lines, transform the city's urban, political, and social landscape. The structure was a central piece in an incipient project to re-model the city center along the principles of open circulation, to transform the city center and UNCTAD itself into an integrated public space that would facilitate, among other things, open, egalitarian exchanges and political communication.

Lawner agues that the UNCTAD was the city's most significant public space, even though it was an enclosed structure. He writes that the complex's lower level was conceived "as an open Center, a bridge used by the public to move unrestricted from Alameda to the Parque Forestal, or from Lastarria

Street toward the inside courtyard."[114] The UNCTAD's self-service restaurant, or *casino*, which held 600 people and served between 1,500 and 5,000 lunches a day at its peak, was a significant example of the architects' mission to encourage physical and social movement and break down physical and social barriers. "The back patio, contiguous to Villavicencio Street, and the natural extension of the casino," Lawner recalls, "brought together informal musical groups or solo artists, aspiring mimes, orators, and minstrels, and groups of young people chatted freely in the gardens. . . . We can say without hesitation that the people made the building their own."[115]

Lawner envisions the building interiors, including the cafeteria, as sheltered public spaces and sites of unrestricted passage. The similarity of the approach to the interiors and café, or casino, is not mere coincidence; it points to his view of each facet of the structure as an expression of the parallel between open public space and democratic political citizenship. The casino came to symbolize the government's attempts to equalize everyday forms of class formation. Whereas most workplace restaurants segregated white- and blue-collar workers, offering separate facilities and foods according to class lines, the UNCTAD casino was expressly open to people from all social classes. Hence, one worker could place the casino at the center of his tale of upward mobility, consumption, family, and masculinity, hoping that "one day I will make my family very happy by taking them for dinner to the UNCTAD building."[116] Similarly, Juan "Chin Chin" Tralma, a founding member of the Brigada Ramona Parra, emotionally recounted what a significant change it had been during the Popular Unity government to be able to finally inhabit Santiago's liminal downtown spaces with dignity, without feeling the stigma or shame that so often went with transgressing class boundaries. Eating at the casino, where he and his friends could stop in, argue politics over lunch, and be "well regarded," was a key instance of egalitarian exchange.[117]

These are all examples of the symbolic power that the casino held as an inclusive area where people of different classes who lived in different areas of the city could mingle and engage in political debate. Food and eating were here highly politicized, part of a complex synesthetic experience of egalitarian modernity that UNCTAD architects were trying to build into the very fabric of the landscape. The magazine *Quinta Rueda* explored the contradictions and complexities of this construction. Workers were having trouble acclimatizing to "life in the style of the UNCTAD; amid the most modern American systems, where the client chooses, eats, and only pays afterward," despite the president's argument that they should take ownership of their building. "It seems that this life in the style of the UNCTAD, with little smell of Chile and much scent of the movies, still intimidates workers like those of the Metro who currently drill at the cement outside of the Tower." Taking ownership of such a luxurious building was difficult, one unidentified worker reported, when "one returns home to sleep in a shack in the *población*." In this way, smell, taste, and touch evince modernity and citizenship and build these into the very practice of eating; yet this is a partial modernity in *Quinta Rueda*'s telling, always running up against a long history of underdevelopment written into the senses.[118] Discourses of progress and modernity were unable to contain the instability of contradictory, synesthetic constructions when the experience of modernity became physical.[119] Rather, a story of potential democracy and inescapable inequity played out in all its complexities in the embodied experience of planned and lived public spaces. The UNCTAD complex, and the casino in particular, can therefore be read as an evocative example of the ways in which Popular Unity planners articulated a concrete version of socialist modernity defined by the democratization of public space and erosion of class boundaries in order to foment an inclusive public sphere of political debate.[120] It served, to paraphrase Diane Davis, as the physical precondition for the creation of multiple, fluid, and changing political public spheres that addressed and transformed the inequities of class and gender and that must be analyzed in place.[121]

The UNCTAD structure was a stage upon which was fashioned and displayed a visual construction of Chilean modernity. It projected this construct to the world and into the future while shaping everyday practices of socialist citizenship in the present. It was the cornerstone of a broader attempt to not only represent but fashion a socialist modernity and citizenship.

THE DESIGN OF SOCIALIST CITIZENSHIP IN THE CITY OF THE UNCTAD

An early example of design as creative simulacra, connected to the construction of the UNCTAD building, can be found in one of INTEC's most ambitious projects—an experiment in cybernetics called Project Cybersyn.[122] Cybersyn was a four-part project that consisted of a telex network connecting each nationalized industry (Cybernet), a suite of computer programs meant to "collect, process, and distribute data to and from each of the state enterprises" (Cyberstride), an effort to simulate and predict future economic patterns (Chilean Economy, or CHECO), and an Operating Room (Opsroom) where this information was collected and implemented.[123] The Opsroom drew from the leading cybernetics expert

Stanford Beer's training in the German ULM School of Design, as well as the "merging of engineering and design that had taken place at [Chile's] Catholic University."[124] Seven chairs would face each other in a circle, fringed by projection screens displaying the information gathered by Cyberstride and relayed by Cybernet. It would create "a new environment for decision making" in which all information would be assembled, standardized, and rewritten in language readily digestible by both technicians or managers and workers who would take control of the national economy. Although it was never operational, a prototype of the room built with projection equipment imported mainly from the United Kingdom was completed in 1972. This exemplar captured the imagination of Popular Unity supporters and detractors alike and soon came to epitomize either the potential of Chilean socialism or the dangers of an Orwellian state. Allende ordered a functional version of the Opsroom built in the Presidential Palace after the October national strike, but it was never completed.[125]

The Opsroom, Eden Medina reveals in her groundbreaking analysis of Chilean cybernetic technology, "offered a new image of Chilean modernity under socialism." It was, in her view, "a futuristic environment for control that meshed with other, simultaneous efforts to create a material culture that Chileans could call their own."[126] This design, and the invention and representation of socialist modernity embedded in it, encompassed a range of unquestioned classed and gendered assumptions. For example, simple, large operating room buttons were implemented to obviate the need for ostensibly female typist and to instead accommodate workers' presumably broad and calloused fingers. This simple choice wrote a story of gender and class assumptions onto the bodies of those they envisioned in those chairs— the workers who would eventually assume leadership positions as part of the promise of "popular power" or "power to the people." It wrote these assumptions onto the very layout and outline of the space. The Opsroom represented the assumptions and benefits of a "modern" cybernetic approach both visually and materially. Beer himself argued that people "would need to be convinced of the superiority of this cybernetic approach, and he hoped the modern-looking control room would offer an effective form of visual persuasion."[127]

Beyond simple representation, I argue, the Opsroom in many ways created a complicated construction of socialist modernity.[128] Its ultramodern design made spectacle of the potential of cybernetics and of Chilean innovativeness. The Opsroom featured a series of screens made of new materials like plastic and fiberglass that displayed data on industrial production that were collected nationally and relayed via telex. But these seemingly computerized displays were in actuality slides hand drawn by top designers, the result of a "tremendous amount of human labor" that made possible this futuristic image of Chilean economic cohesion.[129] This spectacle was a carefully constructed narrative of economic progress and a visual composition of an alternative form of Chilean modernity that featured imaginative economic structures and radical forms of worker participation. The Popular Unity experiment with cybernetics was ultimately a creative exercise that fashioned an image of socialist modernity, a style upon which modernity was actively produced and projected. In the Opsroom, this creative exercise would be made material, put into practice by the workers who would sit at the controls.

Although the room was never made fully operational, the technology was actually and productively deployed in the building of the UNCTAD.[130] *Revista Ahora* noted that the record-breaking speed of the UNCTAD's construction, in 275 days, was possible because of the unprecedented use of computing and cybernetics to organize the logistics of production and the efforts of labor.[131] State-of-the-art Pert computational software, used to design and build Apollo 11, was employed to gather, organize, and coordinate building efforts.[132] Computers helped "regulate the flow of materials to the gigantic work. Workers' availability and needs, ironworks, the mixture of cement, and so on, all decisions made aseptically through the daily perforation of 50 computer cards. All construction methods were revolutionized so that the structural work could be completed by the December 12 deadline."[133] Pert software helped analyze "all data and details at every scale of the project, from the bolts to the temperature and even the general mood of the workers—anything could be a variable—and produced a Pert chart or 'critical diagram' of hundreds of activities, as well as auxiliary charts with minor tasks." Moreover, data collection was participatory, as seventy-five workers continually fed data into the IBM software cards, reflecting Popular Unity's express commitment to incorporate workers into production at all levels.[134]

The type of technology INTEC designers valued in the Cybersyn was therefore crucial to the construction of the UNCTAD. It was also integral to the spectacle of socialist modernity represented by the UNCTAD's dizzying construction. The UNCTAD site became a spectacle of dedication and efficiency that took place daily in the city center, as workers labored in rotating shifts for the better part of a year. The UNCTAD building itself became both a totem of the productive potential of a politically engaged citizenry and a site in which this citizenry could be realized. The author of *Revista Ahora*'s article concluded that the "UNCTAD III construction effort has become a veritable pastime for santiaguinos. Nobody who passes before the colossal work can help but enjoy the placement of the great iron beams that form part of the conference room ceiling or the vertiginous ascension of the tower."[135] Participating in or passing before the site was a ritual of socialist citizenship. At a broad level, then, cybernetics and technology were at the heart of the practical and symbolic construction of an alternative modernity written in many forms, including in the very design of spoons, chairs, and noodles, the UNCTAD building, and the Opsroom.

A political history that carefully considers architecture, design, and place sheds light on the surprising places where these political debates took root, where politics became tangible and corporeal, and where it was hotly contested. In the chapters that follow, I study the many ways in which a range of residents claimed city spaces and in so doing redrew the city's political landscape and shaped themselves into political citizens.

2. Streets, Citizenship, and the Politics of Gender in Allende's Chile

On December 1, 1971, thousands of women marched in opposition to Allende's Popular Unity government, banging pots and pans and waving empty shopping bags to protest what they saw as a dire shortage of basic supplies and the regime's inability to provide for its citizens. Women's protest became an increasingly significant political reality under Allende, but the December 1 "march of the empty pots" was transformative. Political historians risk missing the significance of the march when they reduce it to a "sideline to the main struggles that were taking pace during the tumultuous years of 1970–1973." The protest was a creative act that "heralded the public appearance of a women's opposition movement, one that grew and played an increasingly important role during the next two years of the Allende government.... [It] mobilized previously unorganized women against the UP and helped create a climate that would encourage the military coup that overthrew the UP government on 11 September 1973."[1] The march played on traditional assumptions of proper gender roles and practices in politics. It suggested that a dire political and economic situation had forced women from the safety of the home and into contested public spaces. Women's presence on city streets was evidence of the purportedly anomalous nature of Chilean politics under Allende.

The empty pots protest was an attempt to reclaim city streets from Allende supporters, reimagine public space as a site of oppositional practice, and thereby redefine the terms and limits of urban politics. Anti-Allende women fashioned gendered political languages that drew on tropes of family, masculinity, and violence to demarcate the space of the street as one of fractious conflict rather than egalitarian intersection.[2] They claimed new political identities in a way that undermined the perception that public space could be a legitimate arena of political debate. The protest was a public performance of "proper" political citizenship.

43

Multiple publics came together throughout the Popular Unity on city streets for as little as an hour or a day to articulate potent political arguments in novel languages, using new political tactics.[3] Marchers sparked a public conversation about the boundaries of legitimate political behavior and the limits of rational communication. They created debate about who could participate in "rational" political dialogue and on what grounds they could be disqualified from membership in a public arena. In other words, the struggle over public space was an attempt to challenge the limits of political citizenship by means of an urban dispute that paradoxically defined the language of public debate in often-exclusionary ways.

The march of the empty pots therefore offers scholars a window into the formation and function of the public sphere and the nature of political citizenship in late twentieth-century Chile. It illustrates how overlapping publics were established in unexpected sites and took unexpected forms, creating new means and languages of debate and an expanded array of tactics or "repertoires" of contention that were often shared across traditional lines of party affiliation.[4] It tells us about the *mode* of politics and the function and formation of the public during this period. The march convened a public characteristic of the Popular Unity–era struggle for the street—a fleeting and evanescent public rooted in ongoing and fluid contests over urban public space and engaged in battle over the terms of inclusion and exclusion from public political debate.

GENDER, POLITICS, AND THE PUBLIC SPHERE IN ALLENDE'S CHILE

In her groundbreaking study of gender, labor, and politics, Heidi Tinsman recognizes an apparent paradox between the expansion in opportunities for political participation for workers and peasants in the late 1960s and 1970s and women's continued exclusion from spheres of political influence such as unions and parties. Of course, many women had concrete reasons for supporting parties and unions and often saw women's participation in these spaces as necessary for a workable solution to local and national problems. These were arenas where they could find a measure of protection and assert a wider range of rights. Moreover, women transformed these arenas into places where they could effect larger change and carve out new tactics of gendered mobilization.[5] They drew on previous activism on behalf of men's strikes and actions to build newly politicized roles that often exceeded the gendered limits to women's organization and spilled over the limits of "proper" femininity.

Day-to-day experiences in political spaces beyond parties and unions, in associational spaces like mother's centers, food queues, communal pots (*ollas comunes*), and political marches and manifestations also mattered. They served as an uneven counterweight to political institutions largely "reserved for men." Mother's Centers, for instance, created "a state-sponsored, nationally recognized structure that represented women's interests as housewives at public and political events." They "promoted the idea that a 'good' woman was involved in civic life; in exceptional cases . . . they provided vehicles for women to collectively defend women's honor and challenge men's behavior."[6] They also "provided an important 'space' for meeting and interaction among women which was essentially their own."[7] While they did not offer a radical alternative to gendered political identities that continued to emphasize motherhood, virtue, and traditional gendered roles, associational practices did prepare "fellow Chileans for a reinterpretation of women's citizenship rights" and transform "the gendered underpinnings of political participation."[8]

Communal pots filled a pressing need and served as a show of solidarity during land and factory occupations and labor strikes. Running an olla común could "provide a sense of inclusion in a community struggle that allowed [women] to have opinions distinct from those of men." Participation in communal pots did not necessarily equal a greater degree of politicization. But, 85 percent of registered members and elected leaders were women, whose concrete associational efforts had carved out these spaces and institutionalized rules and leadership structures. The olla común did not simply "support men's collective action"; rather, "it *was* . . . collective action, sometimes the only form" available to women.[9] It was a gendered public sphere rooted in public and semi-public spaces and one example of how sites and forms of gendered politics were shifting in the postwar period.

Pro- and anti-Allende women mobilized in a variety of spaces under the Popular Unity. But women in opposition to Allende were especially adept at formulating forms of political identity and practice that Jadwiga Pieper Mooney calls "militant motherhood," which were "strikingly different from the references to motherhood maternal activists had used early in the century" and which would also establish "a lasting presence of women on the political arena."[10] It was under Allende that these women fashioned new, gendered political identities and ever-changing tactics of mobilization that would challenge the limits of legitimate political citizenship in democracy and also in dictatorship.[11]

My analysis of associational space—and, in what follows, gendered public protest—draws on and reformulates public sphere theory as a window
onto political change over time. I build on archival and empirical research
into urban conflict in downtown Santiago during Allende's presidency to
shed light on how the public sphere was understood, defined, and fought
over in the 1970s. Studying urban practice reveals how and where politics
was "done." It allows us to explore how the public sphere is rooted and
formed on the street and through the strategies and tactics of urban protest.[12] To adapt Mary Ryan's felicitous phrase, taking the city as the "political jurisdiction of this study . . . admits into evidence" especially significant
forms of often untidy, unruly, and "exuberant public politics."[13]

The march of the empty pots and pans offers a unique opportunity to
trace how the tactics of urban politics intersected, interacted, and informed
dialogue in the press and ultimately in Congress. It connected food and bus
queues, factories, hair salons, homes, and (most saliently in this chapter)
city streets and squares, weaving them into a complicated network of political association and mobilization. It was a creative exercise that remade
everyday spaces into sites of political contention, transformed domestic
tropes into fruitful political languages, and helped women fashion new
political identities and novel tactics of political organization and association.

MAKING GENDERED PUBLICS: THE PRESS, PROTEST, AND PUBLIC SPHERES

Marchers portrayed the protest as a spontaneous gathering of independent
women. A close reading of oral histories, published memoirs, detailed press
reports, and participants' testimonies before a congressional investigation
committee suggests that the march itself was pieced together through a
broad network of associational culture and owed its success to innovative
forms of organization that took place behind the curtains of this public
stage. On November 30, one protest organizer, Raquel Sellan, argued that
the women's movement would fundamentally transform political organizing. Whereas state parties accepted funds, trafficked in well-worn
brands, and met in brick and mortar headquarters, her group occupied a
peripheral location vis-à-vis party politics and more traditional sites and
forms of political organization. "We are not being driven by political groups,
nor are we financed by other organizations," she said. The movement had
"neither name nor headquarters." Women "set up piggy banks at beauty
salons to pay for ads." Finally, and most significantly, march organizers
"[got] in touch with their members by phone, leaving messages in beauty

salons, grocery shops, or simply through common friends."[14] These tactics brought together a new political constituency. Women across political party lines and traditional class identities convened to discuss and make public their worry about the lack of staple goods and their inability to care for their families. In short, protest organizers imagined and constructed a network of publics that located political practice in traditionally "apolitical" places and in so doing created new possibilities for political association.

Sellan's piece traced a subtle political geography that politicized everyday and domestic spaces.[15] Similarly, protest organizers proposed a network of alternative spaces in which they could articulate an unbiased, uninfluenced language of political contest that centered on their universal roles as "Chileans and mothers."[16] They also sought to influence and inform notions of proper political practice and to create closer connections between these markedly different spheres of political participation.

Newspapers played a central role in this emergent network of arenas of political association. Press accounts of the protest did not only rely on the facts. They were crucial sites of debate where participants fashioned languages of contention and where public opinion could be formed, challenged, and reformulated. March organizers, for example, circulated opinion pieces and full-page advertisements that detailed the group's list of gendered concerns that could be read aloud or cut out and displayed in salons, shops, and other spaces. These documents helped transform these "domestic," or "private," spaces into sites of political communication.

A piece titled "A Call to Protest," which was published in opposition-friendly papers, is emblematic of this phenomenon. The "Call" outlined the terms and reasoning that structured the protest, acting as a manifesto whose circulation and display established the terms by which a new political public was being formed. It provided the time and location of the march; asked participants to bring empty bags, pots, and pans; and sketched a language of protest that drew on familiar if newly politicized tropes of consumption, family, and masculinity. Organizers were announcing their entry into a wider struggle for the streets but also disassociating themselves from the posters, paintbrushes, and protests of the Left. The following day's *El Mercurio* quoted the organizer Nina Donoso: "Women will carry an empty pot, an empty basket, [or] a Chilean flag instead of the traditional placard. There will not be any speeches. We will be content simply to bang an empty pot in front of La Moneda."[17] The circulation of print and other forms of communication helped delimit a new political public around newly politicized gendered languages and structured an unconventional network of political association.

The press acted as a classic public sphere of political debate, but it was one that was intimately connected to the abutting, overlapping, and often contradictory arenas of the street and Congress. Protest organizers used the press to stitch together an innovative gendered geography of political association within complex urban and social landscapes. Their "militant," gendered practice was developed at the intersection of the press, Congress, and protest. A synoptic analysis that engages these three related spheres is therefore important to a full and rich understanding of the changing and complex nature of women's political activism.[18]

There is, of course, a substantial body of work on Chilean politics that points to the significance of these multiplying political spaces and helps us trace a history of urban practice in an alternative public sphere. Margaret Power, for instance, illuminates organizers' recruitment of female marchers from textile factories, party headquarters, local Mothers' Centers, and homes. Drawn from her broad cache of interviews, this example suggests a variegated network of places of political association, ranging from factories and neighborhood centers to party headquarters and the press.[19]

Occupying city spaces became a political tactic through which protesters repoliticized motherhood and fashioned new forms of political citizenship and new geographies of political contest in Allende's Chile. The seizure of public space allowed urban residents to imagine themselves as political citizens, to redefine the terms of citizenship in intricate and often contradictory ways, and to develop political arguments on the streets, in the press, and in debates before Congress. As Pieper Mooney concludes, "Anti-Allende women's militant motherhood had long-term consequences, not desired by them: it further transformed the gendered underpinnings of political participation."[20] On the one hand, marchers created a new geography of political association and a gendered political public in unexpected places; on the other, they made protest into a creative political exercise in its own right. They experimented with new modes of political participation that included gendered public practice and created new languages of political dialogue that effectively shifted the terms of debate to domestic concerns and consumption.

PUBLIC PROTEST AS THE MAKING OF GENDERED POLITICS

Descriptions of the protest published in early December were firmly rooted in the tangible experience of the march and in the specific geography of the city. These accounts did more than simply place the protest in a broader urban context; they spoke to the political and social significance of place in Santiago. The geography of protest was significant to protesters and commentators alike, and narratives that focused on origin, trajectory, and place were very much part of the political meaning made in protest. Participants who narrated their memory of the march to journalists, congressmen and congresswomen, and oral historians did so in relation to the march's point of origin—the Plaza Baquedano. The plaza was the place that gave social and political significance to the march: it both brought together and drew a dividing line between the middle- and upper-class "barrio alto" and the city center. It was a space traversed daily by a cross section of society, from economic and political elites to white- and blue-collar workers and middle- and working-class residents and students. It is difficult to overstate the symbolic place the plaza occupied in the city's social and political landscape.[21] References to it pepper the historic record. Maligning "those who believe that there are different kinds of women, those who hail from the Plaza Baquedano and those who hail from below the Plaza Baquedano," Teresa Donoso Loero spoke to the plaza's symbolic charge even as she attempted to downplay class distinctions in favor of an imagined universality among women.[22] Place was a central point of contention around which interpretation of the protest and its significance turned, and it was in charged places like the Plaza Baquedano that protesters connected the political discourse to languages of gender and masculinity in complicated and often contradictory ways.

Protesters and their supporters depicted their first steps beyond the plaza in heady, triumphal terms. A couple of days after the march, Donoso Loero told her story in *El Mercurio*. In her account, spectators buoyed protesters from above, showering them with confetti from their balconies, and enveloping them in a dizzying whirl of visual and material support, waving Chilean flags and flicking apartment lights on and off.[23] Donoso Loero painted a picture of gendered solidarity that rendered class divisions invisible: "*Pobladoras,* housewives, professional women, blue- and white-collar workers, militants of political parties, and independent women spontaneously blended into one noisy group that moved toward Santiago's downtown banging on pots and improvising chants."[24]

The triumphal narrative took a significant turn when the march moved into the city center. As marchers ventured "deeper" into Santiago's contested downtown core, the "chaos" of the city's streets turned increasingly ominous. The city center was the site of seemingly pervasive violence.[25] Protesters clashed with Allende supporters in front of the prospective United Nations Congress building, just beyond the plaza. The empty pots protest was a direct challenge to the government's narrative of political citizenship rooted in urban space and planning (see chapter 1). It engaged the "ideal" city of the UNCTAD building and transformed it into a contested arena in which the terms of political citizenship were disputed on the streets. It established a contest between the protesters' claims of "militant motherhood" in support of those "dying of hunger," on the one hand, and UNCTAD's narrative of production, efficiency, and modernity, on the other.

Marchers reported that pro-Allende construction workers pelted them with materials, rocks, and sticks from their scaffolding atop the UNCTAD building.[26] They claimed that they were trapped in a bottleneck behind Santa Lucia Park as they ran past the complex and that members of the Communist Party, Socialist Party, and the Movement of the Radical Left's youth brigades "descended" on them.[27] The police intervened forcefully, throwing tear gas to disperse the crowd. Testifying before Congress days after the march, one protester, Doña Pilar Lagarrigue, reported that there "was a huge flock of teargas bombs, really powerful bombs, about 10 or 20 of them.... [T]hey closed in on us ... [and] when we tried to retreat and behave like patriots and citizens, lovers of the Constitution that we are, they didn't let us. Armed members of the extraparliamentary leftist group, the Movimiento de Izquierda Revolucionaria [MIR] came down Portugal Street, 'Ramona Parra' came down Diagonal Oriente, and behind the police were more members of MIR."[28] Public violence against women appears here as antithetical to legitimate political citizenship and political action, a narrative that would continue to shape and structure public debate and public opinion in the press.

Violence against women emerges in this narrative as the undoing of this national political movement and of a tradition of public opinion centuries in the making. "We couldn't believe it," Nina Donoso wrote. "Surely no man, no mother's son, would dare touch us? ... But we were wrong."[29] For Donoso, this violence was not only unmasculine and cowardly but also uncivilized and unpatriotic.[30] In a letter to the editor of *La Tribuna*, Marcia Vidal de López elaborated on this theme: "I witnessed the hordes who descended on us, brandishing pipes, rocks, potatoes dotted with razor blades.... It is no mystery that these bandits were from the MIR or from the Ramona Parra Brigade who were awaiting the women to satisfy their bestial instincts."[31] Others wrote class and race more clearly into this narrative of failed masculinity. A letter penned by Manuel Galleguillos R. attributed the "cowardly attack" to "that horde of vagrants, bums, thieves, and murders that make up the Brigada Ramona Parra and elements of the MIR." But, like *La Tribuna*, which wrote of "Cuban interlopers" who sparked violence,"[32] Galleguillos tellingly claimed that the attacks were led by Cuban "*marranos* [dirty pigs or false converts] who should not forget that the harsher the slavery, the larger the number of men who want to be free." Maria Eugenia Negrete O. also turned to xenophobic, racist tropes by invoking "the bullying attitudes of those foreign monkeys."[33] Allende supporters were figuratively "tainted" by this association with Cuban blackness, their unsuitability for peaceful political exchange written directly on the bodies of those "short and agile hoodlums" who threw "large rocks at the columns of marchers," the "bandits" and "beasts" who showed a classed and racialized propensity for violence.[34]

These arguments regarding the inherent violence of working-class, racialized Popular Unity protesters shone through when set against the vulnerability of women in public. For the opposition, the potential violence latent in street protest structured a clear dichotomy between proper and illegitimate public behavior in terms of gender. It pitted disciplined order against uncontrolled masculine violence, civic heroism against animalistic aggression, democratic patriotism against foreign subversion. Being on the streets, in contested spaces, and subject to violence paradoxically allowed these women to expose the corrupt nature of a political world where debate was rendered impossible by interlopers who "descended" from the peripheries to occupy the city center and whose presence and comportment fractured traditional political and social order.

In this, the violence of protest highlights a central contradiction in the function of the public. On the one hand, women were engaged in building broad political repertoires that created spaces and languages in which to act as political citizens in unexpected ways; on the other, the march and the discourse that developed around it paradoxically justified women's ultimate exclusion from this expanded political field, reestablishing the limits of the public. Ephemeral public practice opened up novel space and gendered language for women to participate in public politics; it also, and simultaneously, buttressed conservative or hegemonic ideas of politics and gender. Violence was a point of contention around which these debates about the public hinged and around which people determined their legitimacy as political actors.[35] The skirmishes "proved" that women should remain outside of politics and Allende supporters should be excluded from rational debate because of the inherent potential of "irrational" violence on city streets. Violence, then, was a key trope that participants used to define the limits of "proper" political action in ways that justified conservative women's mobilization (as necessary in "dire" times) and simultaneously buttressed an essentially conservative definition of the natural division between the public and private realms (and the related notion that women "belonged" in the home in "normal" times).[36]

The march may have been urban performances that led to the creation of gendered political publics forged on the streets, but they were also crucial to the process by which the terms and limits of the public sphere were policed and solidified. The idea and language of "the public" became in Allende's Chile not an abstract theoretical debate but a point of contention in a negotiation of power between politicized actors that were aware of the significance of "the public" and "proper" public behavior, a debate that crossed and connected streets, press, and Congress.[37] For anti-Allende activists, "making" militant motherhood on the streets "established a lasting presence of women in the political arena—and prepared fellow Chileans for a reinterpretation of women's rights." Marching was an attempt to create a gendered discourse of politics by which conservative women "more effectively made their voices heard."[38] In so doing, they also reestablished traditional divisions between the public and the private.

For Allende supporters, debates over women in public served to redefine women's role in revolutionary politics but also to rethink the terms and limits of public action and public order on the streets, in the press, and in Congress.[39] These were, of course, contested definitions and processes, but the ways in which gender, masculinity, and the public became entwined in the December march would continue to have significant and lasting consequences. As Pieper Mooney concludes, "Women's mobilization implied a break with the past. The militant mothers demonstrated that women could seize interpretive power and claim new citizenship rights despite the perspective of male public voices and their attempts to squash autonomous political decision on the part of women. . . . Leaving behind the role of *apolitical* mothers, women were on their way to become citizens with new rights and obligations."[40] To be sure, gender was a means by which to debate the terms and limits of politics and the public sphere in the wake of the march, even when women themselves were not at the heart of protest.

CONGRESS, THE STREET, AND THE PUBLIC SPHERE IN THE "AFTERLIFE" OF THE MARCH

In the hours after the march, Allende declared the city a "zone of emergency," limiting public transit and physical circulation in light of heightened tensions. Newly appointed to oversee the city emergency zone, then-chief of the Santiago garrison, Augusto Pinochet, ominously warned of the potential repercussions if the military were forced into the streets to impose "order": he proclaimed that "when the military leaves the barracks, they do so with the intent to kill." Pinochet censured *La Tribuna* for inciting violence; *La Tribuna* responded by emblazoning its front page with an image of an empty pot every day for the month after the protest, suggesting that the debates, symbols, and languages that came out of the march would frame or inform all topics taken up in the paper. And, indeed, the march was discussed in newspapers, magazines, and journals in the weeks that followed, where opinion pieces, letters to the editor, and heated articles fueled a lively discourse on public protest, gender, and politics. These debates were immediately taken up in Congress, speaking to the close relationship between the streets, the press, and the traditional arenas of political debate.

Days after the march, ten members of the increasingly radicalized Christian Democratic Party brought a motion to impeach José Tohá, Allende's minister of the interior and most trusted adviser, on the grounds that he had not only failed to safeguard female marchers, but actually placed them directly in harm's way and incited violence against the nation's mothers and wives. The impeachment immediately set off a heated debate in the halls of Congress organized around detailed testimony by participants. It created a fraught arena of dialogue and a rich resource for historians of political change.[41]

The impeachment document argued that the government was guilty of "having forbidden women from exercising their right to meet, and then allowing armed hordes to treacherously attack women."[42] It held that the Intendencia had altered the "projected and approved" route mere hours before the march and even authorized a parallel march by a pro-government group that would cross the path of the empty pots protesters. The document accused the minister of interior of recognizing the prevalent "climate of violence" but refusing to provide proper and safe conditions under which women could exercise their right to public meeting. It claimed that his decision to alter the requested trajectory (Plaza Baquedano through Parque Forestal, down Merced and Santa Lucia, turning on Huérfanos and Estado, proceeding to the Alameda and finishing on Avenida Bulnes) was made with the express "intention" of "allowing armed bands to attack the women."[43]

Testifying before Congress, protesters Teresa de la Maza and Pilar Lagarigue supported this contention, organizing their argument around their recollection of the clash in front of the UNCTAD building. De la Maza set the scene: "We were told not to pass because the Ramona Parra and Elmo Catalán Brigades were going to provoke us and would even mistreat us. We responded that we would fulfill our commitments and that we would not be fearful. But we couldn't contain the women because they said that it didn't matter if they hit us. No matter what happens, this will prove what women can accomplish in Chile."[44] Lagarigue completed her counterpart's argument: "This, again, is what I know of the UNCTAD: we warned the *pobladoras* with us on the way down from Providencia toward the Plaza Baquedano that they should not march in front of the UNCTAD. But when they boxed us in there[,] . . . trying to guide us like cattle toward the Alameda, forcing us to walk by the UNCTAD. And there, I was really laid low, as they threw ten bombs toward me. . .[Those] who marched in front of the UNCTAD were insulted, were stoned."[45]

Members of the opposition in Congress claimed that the president and his closest adviser were "morally responsible" for this invective. Their role in inciting gendered violence rendered Popular Unity rule illegitimate. Silvia Pinto's influential article in *El Mercurio* argued that the government's inability to protect the safety and public rights of women marchers was the "last drop" that fractured the relationship between the Popular Unity and the PDC and "left women with no alternative but to present a public face" in protest.[46] In turn, PDC representative Wilna Saavedra suggested an implicit irony in the government's support of the proposed Ministry of the Family when the representative of the family on the street "does not have the protection or attention of the government." She contrasted the order and respect with which women protesters marched to the violence they encountered from construction workers who were erecting the UNCTAD building, again making the implicit argument regarding the discipline necessary for reasoned political practice in the subtle language of class and gender propriety: "Women protested in an orderly and respectful manner. Yet they were met with the rocks hurled at them by the Ramona Parra and Elmo Catalán Brigades . . . who attempted to silence the protest using traditional Marxist methods."[47]

The head of the Senate and the PDC, Patricio Aylwin, placed the blame for the violence squarely on the shoulders of government officials who put the protesters directly in harm's way: "It is the government that is responsible for 'bottling up' these women between the Alameda, the Santa Lucia hill, and Mac-Iver Street, where they were attacked with rocks and tear gas. The women's outrage was provoked by the government prohibition that they march freely through public space. The Political Constitution recognizes that fundamental right, but armed groups did not allow this right to be protected."[48] Aylwin articulated a classic understanding of the public sphere as necessarily distinct from both the influence of the state and the violence latent in urban action and in this way effectively undermined the potential of public protest as a valid form of political practice.

The desire to police the boundaries that separated the streets, the public, and the state was written into the reason for impeaching Tohá. The document claimed that what is "incredible is that this has happened in downtown Santiago, a few blocks from La Moneda and with the full knowledge of the minister of the interior."[49] Reporters monitored the multitudes that massed around the Congress building during the monthlong deliberations of Tohá's impeachment. *La Tercera* reported that over two thousand workers attempted to "alter the [January 6] proceedings" in which the *diputados* (deputies) voted in favor of the impeachment, noting their alarm at the presence of armed police in the streets surrounding the building. The crowds clamored for a voice in national political debate, thereby connecting the state's political decision-making process to a complicated geography of partisan street protest. For the opposition, the possibility that the world of urban protest would impinge directly on the state was an ongoing concern, but its fear of the crowd on the street was never clearer than this moment, when the masses threatened to spill into the halls of power.

The empty pots protest performed "proper" public behavior, establishing the boundaries of acceptable practice in gendered, classed, and sometimes racialized terms. The Congress's debate over "public order" drew a line between "rational" and "respectful" politics and illegitimate strategies of public politics, a distinction that ultimately devalued the street as an inclusive space of debate and exchange. In turn, Tohá defended himself from impeachment before Congress by challenging the rhetoric of violence and the limits it placed on proper political action. He conceded that his "mandate . . . [was] to achieve public order and sanction public liberties." But he articulated an alternative definition of "order" that served as the centerpiece of the Popular Unity's platform for radical political and social change.

Tohá argued that the only way to address order and disorder was to pay attention to "real" material and economic causes. "No, for the Popular Government public order is not about restraint or repression," he proclaimed; rather, in a "revolutionary" society, "public order can be achieved by carrying forward the revolutionary and democratic process, framing it within the legal order."[50] Tohá cast effective government as one that encouraged rather than restricted public expression, even disorderly forms of expression. Whereas the traditional role of conservative governments was to *maintain* public order, the role of the revolutionary government was to *expand* the public and achieve a new type of social, economic, and political order. Only a politicized citizenry that could occupy, appropriate, and struggle over public space could play a necessary, "dynamic" role in national politics. Tohá used his defense to formulate an alternative definition of rule that was not threatened by but instead depended on the fluid forms of political participation that occurred in a truly democratic public.[51]

Tohá recognized that he was creating a confrontation "between two profoundly different theories of political action." Whereas the opposition collected testimony and accounts of authorities' culpability in enabling or facilitating violence against defenseless marchers, Tohá concentrated on the ideological differences and the discourses of class that underwrote the flawed impeachment document. In this way, he was able to protect the Popular Unity's institutional legitimacy and reposition the government as "guarantor of the Constitution."[52]

The definition of and debate about the "public" and "public order" was itself a field of contention in Allende's Chile. Tohá's impeachment became a dialogue about the terms of inclusion in and exclusion from the public sphere. This discourse generated around the figure of the public itself played an important political role, organizing novel forms of political association or, alternatively, rendering invalid certain forms of inhabiting space and imagining political practice. Tohá's writing gives us insight into an alternative vision of the public that highlighted equity, inclusion, and circulation rather than "proper" forms of public behavior as the things that should determine the shape and limits of urban citizenship.

Allende interceded on Tohá's behalf after the announcement of the Chamber of Deputies' decision to impeach, again couching his arguments in terms of the debate over violence, urban politics, and proper public action. "I opposed a demonstration of pro-government women that was to be held the day the ladies of the Barrio Alto held theirs," he told his supporters, "because nobody likes to see a clash between women." The government had the support of the masses, and therefore the capacity for uprising, but it was committed to the constitutional road precisely because it abhorred violence.[53]

Allende gave his on own analysis of urban politics in ways that developed this line of political thought. His treatment of the December 1 march was couched in geographic terms, based on the distinction between uptown (*barrio alto*) and downtown (*el centro*). He traced a clear divide between "ladies," or señoras, who live in the barrio alto, and real "women," or *mujeres*, who emerged as the true supporters of his government. Thus he effectively mapped traditional gendered and classed discourse onto the landscape of political protest and organization.

Later that month, Allende listed a series of violent incidents scattered throughout the city, later that month, letting them serve as a backdrop against which to understand a December 20 counterdemonstration that began in the Plaza Bulnes. The pauses he left between examples, transcribed here as semicolons, at once distinguished and connected these separate events, drew them together, plotting them onto a map of politicized aggression in a class-divided city: "[the] riot of Wednesday December 1st; the unscrupulous use by [Patria y Libertad] of the meeting of the wealthier women of Santiago; the heightening of class hatred hatched by the idleness that pervades the neighborhoods populated by the wealthy."[54] In his hands, the women who "descended" on the city center became interlopers in a democratic physical and symbolic space, an arena rightfully occupied by those who were versed not in the "idleness of the wealthy" but in the realities of labor and strategies of peaceful protest. He then referred in detail to politicized acts of physical aggression in the city: "the attack against the National Committee of the Radical Party and of the Central Committee of the Communist Youth headquarters[;] . . . the attack with truncheons and chains against popular leaders on the streets of Santiago; the riot in Avenida Providencia; the arson of the district office Las Condes; the machine-gun fire against the Socialist Party; the invasion of shock troops with helmets and baklavas." Referring to the destruction of pro–Popular Unity political party headquarters by name effectively grounded Allende's argument in an urban landscape with which his audience could identify, while his comments regarding assaults and aggression on the city streets alluded to a climate of violence instigated not by an unruly or bestial "pueblo" but by right-wing militias or "shock troops." Allende here established a geography of classed political violence that positioned aggression as a broader social phenomenon emanating in the segregated arenas of the city—the middle- and upper-class neighborhoods of Providencia and Las Condes—rather than in the city center or in the classed bodies of the "hordes" of his supporters.[55] All of these examples, he concluded, "show that the rise of sedition has the backing of unpatriotic people willing to plunge Chile into a bloodbath.[56] Below I examine two competing protests held in April 1972 to unravel the "afterlife" of the march and the effects it had on Chilean urban politics.[57]

COMPETING PROTESTS

These two marches, one in opposition to and one in support of the government, were parallel performances of political discourse held less than a week apart. They articulated radically different arguments based in surprisingly similar terms, languages, and suppositions. They shed light on the contested nature of public space and the ways that intricate connections between politics, gender, and public protest developed well beyond the December 1 march. The first of these protests gave participants and analysts an occasion and object around which to express their anti–Popular Unity outrage publicly and in new languages.[58] *El Mercurio*'s April 12, 1972, editorial predicted that the opposition's "March for Democracy," organized to protest the Popular Unity's "assault on the Constitution and the law," would be an unprecedented and "transcendental" gathering of Santiago's "democratic-minded citizens."[59] The piece positioned the language of democracy and freedom as the proper one with which to express disapproval of the state. The full range of opposition practices and the myriad arenas and discourses that they created can be seen in the advertisements that opposition parties published in the days surrounding the march.

The Partido Nacional (National Party), for example, published a half-page advertisement in the April 11 edition of *El Mercurio*. The top half of the advertisement was a photograph of a mass protest in Valparaíso; the bottom half was a simple caption that read, "Tomorrow Santiago will shout ENOUGH! Of incompetence; violence; corruption; abuses."[60] The PDC followed *El Mercurio*'s editorial line, calling all members of the opposition together across party or ideological divisions, to unite "in an act of mass mobilization that shows a categorical and undeniable faith in Democracy that fuels their willingness to defend our constitutional rights and guarantees."[61] Similarly, the Sociedad Nacional de Agricultura (SNA; National Agricultural Society) called "rural men and women" to protest the "abuses, affronts, and mistreatment" they were suffering.[62] On the morning of the rally *El Mercurio* published an unattributed, full-page advertisement that gave instructions.[63] The authors of this concise piece delineated the terms under which protesters could rally: "There will be only one march, which will begin at Avenida Matta and Arturo Prat at 6:00 P.M., and continue on the protests' end point."[64] Newspaper contributors argued that the protest could, if properly organized and attended, bring together "independents, militants, workers, professionals, men, and women [in order to] illustrate their repudiation of the sectarianism, injustice, violence, and the attempt to coerce the Chilean people economically into accepting Marxist mandates."[65] *El Mercurio*'s coverage complemented rally organizers' language, providing an image of a "pueblo" as a cohesive whole coming together "in order to protest the violation of freedom and fundamental rights consecrated in our Constitution."[66] The paper portrayed the march as a protest against the steady erosion of liberty and democracy. Santiago's *intendente* (mayor), Alfredo Joignant, barred marchers from passing in front of UNCTAD building, a decision the opposition saw as a familiar intrusion into and control of the public sphere, an attempt to gain a leg up in the race to claim these charged spaces.[67] The press was an arena in which to both outline and contour the narrative of protest after the December 1 march of the empty pots.

Place was as important a point of contention for those who reported on the march as it was for those who organized it. *El Mercurio* bracketed its front-page articles with a hand-drawn map of the intended protest route carefully outlining its anticipated trajectory. It also included detailed instructions on starting points and meeting places, cognizant of the intricate political and social geographies that marchers would traverse and transform. The paper argued that the "overwhelming" presence of women and men—blue- and white-collar workers, youth, peasants, and housewives—all united under a single flag on city streets, was proof enough of the opposition's strength. It contrasted empty thoroughfares and shuttered windows to the "sea of humanity" that spilled into the capital's thoroughfares during the march.[68] But it was orderly protest that was vital in this context. Organizers circulated detailed instructions, delineated proper conduct, and circumscribed acceptable iconography. They took pains to convey that "flags, pennants, bracelets, or any other indication of party membership is forbidden."[69] The national standard would be its lone unifying symbol.[70] The Frente Nacional de la Actividad Privada (FRENAP), an organization that portrayed itself as politically independent, published a full-page ad in *El Mercurio* that was dominated by a large flag and accompanied by text that exhorted marchers, "Cover the City with This Page as a Symbol of Your Patriotism."[71] This message may have originated as an advertisement in the newspaper, but it was meant to be pasted on city walls, designed as a public expression of political opposition wrapped in patriotic imagery. *El Mercurio* extended the model, encouraging participants to carry portable radios as they marched "in order to hear proper instructions," blurring the sharp distinctions that public sphere scholars draw between private concerns, public debate, and the state.[72]

Newspaper headlines proclaimed the marchers' success in the face of significant obstacles.[73] *El Mercurio*'s lead article quoted the only two speakers at the rally at length: Eliana Vásquez, a shantytown dweller with seventeen children, and Patricio Aylwin, PDC and Senate leader. The article gave special attention to Vásquez's speech, wrapping the text of her intervention around a photograph of protesting women whose caption read simply,

"Women were on the front lines of this historic confrontation. The government media's threats did not scare them, and instead, they finished their housework early in order to make this date with Democracy."[74]

Vásquez's contribution articulated a (gendered) narrative that coupled state building and everyday concerns: "I am here to speak in the name of Chilean women. We are here because our country has called on us. We have come, as we always do, to finish the task we have before us. Today, that task is to defend Chile's destiny, defend our children's future, defend Liberty, defend Democracy."[75] Carefully chosen as the representative of "the people," she offered an opposition discourse that because of its class and gender formulation transcended party politics: "An entire population, an entire nation is assembled here, hundreds of thousands of Chileans, men and women, white- and blue-collar workers, homemakers, youth, and peasants."[76] Appropriating and reinterpreting the Popular Unity slogan, "The people, united, shall never be defeated," she continued: "A people [have been] united beyond political parties and particular interests, and under one flag, the flag of our Motherland."[77] Referencing the nationalist language with which we have become familiar, she concluded, "We are here to tell the entire country, the entire world, and anyone who will listen, that we will not accept that our nationalism, our liberty, and our Democracy be destroyed."[78] Her speech provided an explicit counter to Allende's own nationalist discourse.[79] "Since he was sworn in," Vásquez contended, "the Honorable President of the Nation has not missed one occasion to tell us that his government is leading Chile to a Socialism that tastes of meat pies and red wine, a pluralist Socialism that is rooted in our national history of respect for institutions and justice. . . . However, reality has belied these words at every turn."[80] Vásquez's speech attributed street clashes and public violence to the Popular Unity's disregard for public and social order, to actions that were pulling apart the national family. In contrast, she proposed that a united opposition could "rebuild our patriotic brotherhood," prefiguring and laying the foundation for the military dictatorship's fascistic rhetoric of "national reconstruction."

El Mercurio made the gendered dimensions of the opposition's state-building projects explicit in issuing its "Call to Women": "The painful events we have witnessed in our Fatherland have sown the seeds of discontent in all the nation's homes, and we can feel fear palpably in the air, the by-product of the daily spectacle of the destruction of order, justice, liberty, and individual respect."[81] This call again drew on the familiar nation-family pairing: "Woman, your family has grown, its name is now MOTHERLAND, and proudly helps to raise the flag, with the red color of love, the blue color of the sky, and the white color of our conscience."[82] By April 1972, gender and the particular forms that militant gendered protest took had become key nodes through which to debate the terms, practices, and limits of political citizenship. Gender operated in relation to the common tropes of family and nation; in the bodily practice of public political performance; in urban mobilization; and in the weighty charge of ordered versus disorderly protest.

The march of the empty pots, Tohá's indictment, and the March for Democracy were all grounded in the confluence of public space and political expression. The opposition's protesters made a point of fulfilling the government's strictures. A constellation of editorials, articles, and advertisements positioned the March for Democracy as a disciplined challenge to the Popular Unity. By modeling legitimate political practice, these protesters simultaneously defined and discredited the street clashes that characterized Popular Unity politics.[83] Engaging in the struggle over streets and public spaces was an opportunity to establish the very terms and limits of legitimate public political practice; orderly action became an end in itself, the point and product of the opposition's public political performance.[84]

Popular Unity supporters answered with their own gathering less than a week after the March for Democracy. Allende supporters' rally was a direct response to the opposition's growing presence in public and in the print media and a refusal to surrender the "struggle for the streets."[85] *El Mercurio* recognized this gathering as the largest to date, drawing people from "various sectors" of Santiago to hear Allende, the only speaker of the evening.[86] The paper again carefully charted the movement of marchers through the city. It made special mention of the buses, trucks, and other means of mass transportation that brought marchers from around the metropolis and from the shantytowns that ringed the city. It reported that Popular Unity supporters gathered in unprecedented numbers along the edges of the city center, at the corner of Salvador and Grecia Avenues. But the UNCTAD building again formed a center point around which protesters cohered and the fulcrum around which the moral of the paper's story turned.[87]

The newspaper took issue with where and how Popular Unity supporters protested. Its conclusions were clear: the government had circumscribed the opposition marchers' movements, yet illegally opened spaces for its own supporters, who overreached. It described the unruly nature of the government's response in implicit contrast to the oppositon's discipline and order: "Everyone commented on the notorious difference in discipline between the two marches. . . . While last week's opposition march held itself to authorized areas, [yesterday's] pro-government protesters occupied all of the city's central arteries . . . It was a veritable celebration."[88] The paper pitted the pro-government forces' popular exuberance and informality, epitomized by its carnivalesque atmosphere, against the opposition marchers' "proper" and orderly behavior: "Popular enthusiasm went too far, not only in terms of Popular Unity–ordered slogans. There were also picturesque touches. For instance, there was an allegorical car made to look like a run-down truck ridden by a crowned child. . . . Posters pasted on the vehicle commented on the government's successful pint of milk per child program." The government's march was, then, a "veritable party," a "carnivalesque" gathering featuring color, song, and performance (including the traditional *cueca* and national anthems), that reached a crescendo when Allende strode to the stage to speak.[89]

Daniel James writes of the carnivalesque exuberance of public protest as a double-edged strategy. It could be a form of expressing class consciousness and claiming public and political presence; it could also be the basis for a critique leveled against workers "invading" elite spaces in order to transgress classed limits and form newly politicized identities.[90] *El Mercurio* spoke to this tension when it wrote that the march and its "show of flags was extraordinary, an unprecedented event in the history of our capital," but also when it painted marchers' exuberance as a sign not only of political might but also of an improper lack of discipline that threatened to turn the crowd dangerous.[91] The language of "publicness," and the terms of proper public behavior, became, and remained, points of conflict debated in the media.[92]

Allende's address to the protesters was itself a public performance that attempted to (re)frame the protest's meaning. He immediately positioned the march in the dual contexts of the UNCTAD meeting and the Popular Unity's history of street-level urban politics: "We have gathered. This long street has become too narrow [to hold us]. Hundreds and thousands and thousands have been unable to enter this avenue. The adjacent streets speak to the dense crowd that has come to reassert their rights and duties." He continued, broadening the scope of his vision: "We have gathered at an important international juncture. One hundred forty-one representatives of every continent have come to Santiago to a significant meeting of the third UNCTAD, which chose Chile because it is a developing country."[93] Allende argued that Popular Unity supporters had gathered before UNCTAD representatives and in the face of mounting opposition to evince the resilience of the political project. Street presence was again *proof* of the government's strength: "Never in our lives have we witnessed an act of this magnitude or transcendent nature. Men and women, young and old, have come here from all corners of the city, bringing with them their indomitable faith in the

Popular Unity. We have congregated here without fear, with the serene confidence of those who know their power."[94] The parallels with the opposition's rhetoric are clear and striking.

Allende verbally shaped his mass of supporters into a cohesive, national body politic, (re)defining the terms of legitimate national citizenship in broad, gendered, and classed terms: "Present is the man of the pueblo with his copper profile, with his iron will, with his . . . child's heart, with his tender female heart, with his strong male heart. Present is the man transformed into pueblo so as to defend the motherland of the working classes."[95] He then spoke of the UNCTAD meeting as an opportunity to enact crucial changes in political and economic policy: "We want economic freedom for Chile and Chileans. We want our own culture to bloom, to develop our technological capability and to shake off dependency. We, Chileans, will be truly free only once we eradicate unemployment, hunger, and moral and physiological suffering."[96] Allende ultimately intertwined the two threads of his argument. Because the Popular Unity program was centered on the pueblo, he concluded, it could only fulfill its promises by breaking the nation's dependence on foreign economic investment and technology.[97]

The relationship between street protest and its location around the UNCTAD structure thus becomes clear: local forms of street protest were folded into broader narratives regarding the state, dependency, and peaceful revolution through the public spectacle of political speeches and the ways in which these narratives were taken up again in print, radio, and television. The protests' symbolic success hinged on the fact that the Popular Unity had seized on the UNCTAD meeting as an opportunity to articulate its political and economic platform in concrete terms. They built on the public's awareness of the UNCTAD as a stage that was already charged with meaning and fashioned political discourses and gendered and classed bodily languages that santiaguinos would readily understand.

· · ·

What has this story of the march of the empty pots and subsequent protests told us about politics in the Allende period? Scholars have argued that the march was a turning point in Chilean politics because it allowed women unprecedented entry into national politics and created innovative avenues of political participation. In many senses, this is an apt point: it is not difficult to trace the ascendance of women as members of political parties, in Congress, or in increasingly active women's political groups. But, as Hilda Sabato warns us, political participation cannot be reduced only to party politics or voting patterns. Rather, she notes, it is more important "to comprehend the mechanisms in the formation of informal social webs interconnecting the diverse instances of power (the congress, the parties, the state) and . . . their relationship to the rest of society." In so doing, she sheds light on political practices beyond traditional sites of political negotiation.[98] The December 1 march can be fruitfully analyzed in relation to the public sphere and forms of political negotiation that cannot be reduced to the frame of Congress, parties, or the state. The march was a creative performance of political citizenship in public space that stitched together gendered and political languages that continued to develop in and influenced the overlapping spheres of the streets, the press, and Congress. It was a form of urban practice that created "new repertoires of contention," transforming conservative gendered identities and constructions of proper masculinity and femininity into bases for political organization.[99] In a word, the march was part of a significant transformation in how politics was fought and who could participate in this fight in late twentieth-century Chile.[100]

New questions regarding urban politics emerge when we allow for the existence of overlapping and contradictory public spheres and public practices. But we must not lose sight of how urban tactics structured political publics that might have formed only fleetingly but still influenced local and ultimately national politics. In Chile, fluid publics altered the fundamental mode of political conflict during Allende's government. Therefore, focusing on urban politics rather than only on party politics and the state prompts us to examine protests both in favor of and in opposition to the Popular Unity. It pushes us to pay close attention to the changing, gendered languages and tactics of political citizenship. And it suggests that political strategies took different forms including those I call "everyday urbanism."

Entwining urban, performance, and public sphere scholarship helps us to consider the ways in which we interpret gendered politics. This chapter has studied the material and visual culture of urban conflict, investigated how and where political languages were formed, and examined the relationship between the state, public debate, and the shape of gendered associational culture in the postwar era. It has scrutinized how gendered political citizenship and the public sphere were contested simultaneously on the streets, in the press, and in Congress. Chapter 3 analyzes changing forms of everyday political urbanism in relation to the opposition's October 1972 truckers' strike and Allende supporters' reaction to it.

3. *A ganar la calle*

The October Strike and the Struggle for the Streets

Spirited debates about food and scarcity continued into the second half of Allende's presidency. The march of the empty pots had effectively politicized consumption, created new, gendered landscapes and languages of debate, and turned the clashing of pots and pans into a ubiquitous symbol of political discontent.[1] By the second half of 1972, food and consumption formed the basis of powerful, gendered languages and practices of political conflict. *La Prensa*, for instance, framed a late August article with a mention of the already "traditional" clashing of empty pots, but the body of this piece was a detailed report of the public disturbances that spilled over the bounds of acceptable political behavior. Its journalists noted that "a horde of 60 or more subjects appeared at the corner of Fourth Street and South Salvador to stone houses, break windows, and cause further damage," fueling a narrative of increased political polarization and conflict in the press across political lines.[2] Violence was again a nodal point around which turned complicated discussions regarding the legitimacy of grassroots action, urban practice, and national politics. Yet the ways in which gender, violence, and urban action had been knit together in the December march were about to shift dramatically.

A national strike in October and November 1972, organized by the Transportation Owners' Association, built on and radically reinterpreted the gendered political languages of the women's march.[3] Truckers barricaded highways and entrances into the city, disrupting or impeding the circulation of commodities and the traffic of people and in so doing challenged the Popular Unity's ability to provide its citizens with staple goods and maintain relative economic stability. This chapter studies the October bosses' or truckers' strike (*paro camionero*), as it came to be known. It maps the trajectory of urban protest in opposition to Allende, identifying this as a fundamental shift in the terms and practice of Chilean politics. The march of the empty pots tied street protest directly to national politics. The bosses' strike also trafficked in gendered language of political dialogue and conflict, but the public debate surrounding the events of October 1972 reveals a fundamental change in how the government and the opposition mobilized, occupied, and understood public space as a site of political debate. The march of the empty pots had drawn on the symbolic power of the city center, building on the gendered significance of women's bodies inhabiting symbolically charged public spaces. The strike inverted this strategy, seeking to curtail or halt the movement of people, goods, and information through the city and the nation. It created a spectacle of stasis to complement the traditional means of mobilizing people in public spaces. And it proposed a mobile and active masculinity to complement fraught feminine political mobilizations.

The October strike transformed the relationship between urban practice, civil society, and the state and fashioned an expanded landscape of political debate—a geography of protest that spilled over the limits of a city center that had been the center stage of urban political performance.[4] It was part of a larger process by which new, politically significant spaces took root along the city's edges. Scholars have studied shantytown mobilization as a form of politicization, and pointed out that these "peripheral" areas were sites in which pobladores built significant political identities in the postwar period.[5] This chapter draws on their insights but shifts focus to the industrial arenas that ringed the city center, studying the local labor federations that arose along the industrial belt surrounding the city. These industrial sites, called *cordones industriales,* brought together workers from neighboring industries in support of the Popular Unity during the trucker's strike and to agitate for worker control and nationalization of industries.[6] The political scientist Frank Gaudichaud suggests that cordones privileged spatial ties and class consciousness over, but not necessarily to the exclusion of, traditional forms of political identity or association. This strategic shift allowed workers to exert pressure on the Popular Unity, exercising their right and ability to shape the Chilean road to socialism.[7] They were influenced by and reciprocally influenced national politics.

Cordón members pushed the cadence of change and influenced state policy "from below." But members did not always or only make claims on the state. They also proposed and produced "new forms of doing politics."[8] Members fashioned cordones into important public spheres of political association where workers, rural laborers, and pobladores—groups that did not necessarily have or hue to traditional party and union affiliations—created personal and political connections, experimented with new, democratic and participatory decision-making structures, and fashioned a wide range of legitimate political behaviors.[9]

The truckers' strike and the emergence of cordones had consequences that reverberated through congressional politics. The Popular Unity's reaction to the strike simultaneously shifted the relationship between the state and the military, aggravated the split between the government and the opposition, and intensified conflicts that were internal to the Left. Allende distanced himself from supporters who favored direct representation, or *poder popular*, to resolve the conflict. Trying to avoid the possibility of violent confrontation between the opposition and those who had mobilized in defense of the government at a grassroots level, Allende chose to strengthen his claim to institutional legitimacy by incorporating constitutionalist members of the military into his cabinet. Lost in this cabinet shuffle was the fact that both government supporters and the opposition had learned and adopted new ways of engaging, occupying, or controlling public space to advance their political program and in so doing challenged the terms and forms of politics.[10]

THE STIRRING OF PROTEST

Midway through Allende's second year as president, political tensions heightened in Congress and at the grassroots. The Christian Democratic and National Parties became increasingly close in the wake of the extraparliamentary armed group Vanguardia Organizada del Pueblo's assassination of Edmundo Pérez Zujovic, minister of the interior under Eduardo Frei. As the National Party (PN) threw itself behind the PDC's political moves, the latter grew increasingly antagonistic in Congress, especially in the face of the Popular Unity's plans to nationalize property into the Área de Propiedad Social (APS). Political conflicts coalesced around by-elections in O'Higgins-Colchagua for the Senate (lost to the PDC) and Linares for the Chamber of Deputies (lost to the PN). Simultaneously, the government's conclave at El Arrayán revealed internal divisions within the Popular Unity. Communists, Radicals, and Allende's followers in the Socialist Party agitated for moderation and continued negotiation with the PDC. A cadre of Socialist Party members led by Carlos Altamirano, members of the Movimiento de Acción Popular Unida (MAPU) and the MIR all pressured for the government to "accelerate the revolutionary process."[11] Then Allende vetoed a PDC-sponsored constitutional amendment that would prohibit expropriations until they had been authorized by the legislature. PDC members fought to override Allende, setting off a potential constitutional crisis. The opposition challenged the presidency's authority, raised the possibility of a plebiscite, and encumbered the government's attempts to enact change through legal channels.

This "growing conflict between government and opposition was . . . regularly taken into the streets."[12] Pedro Vuskovic, Allende's minister of the economy, helped pushed forward the rate of land and factory expropriations, creating even greater tension both in and outside the halls of Congress.[13] Rural and urban land seizures, factory expropriations, and street protest flourished. They also grew increasingly conflictive.[14] In the *comunas* of Cerillos and Maipú, for example, workers at Aluminio El Mono, Polycrom, and other industries located along Avenida Santa Rosa struck in an attempt to agitate for their incorporation into the APS. In June 1972, their requests unmet, they joined thirty others to make collective demands. Organized under the umbrella of a cooperative, the Comando Coordinador de Cerrillos Maipú, they pushed for nationalization. Workers barricaded streets and highways, organized congresses in factories, and confronted representatives of the state. A number of these industries were incorporated into the APS, and the Comando Coordinador became the Cordón Cerrillos-Maipú, which would play a key role during the October strike.[15] Allende reacted to increasing polarization and escalating tensions. He decreed a state of emergency in Santiago, Concepción, and Valparaíso in August 1972.

Local unrest began to turn into national conflict later that month. Truck owners in the southern province of Aysén mobilized to protest the death of a truck owners' *gremio* member, barricading local roads and threatening to shutter shops.[16] Truck owners and transportation workers were already unquiet. They saw in the government's promise of a national, public transport firm a general threat to private business interests and connected their grievances to a perceived attack on a conservative radio station and the national paper company, and therefore on free speech. A number of other "politically independent" interest groups, those that also presented themselves as unaffiliated with any political party, saw that the gremio movement might provide the foundations for an outright attack on the Popular Unity. In early October, National Party senator Francisco Bulnes seized on the tension between the state's economic policies and the business gremios' interests. He suggested to Congress that the state's actions were in conflict with the Constitution and that the government was therefore beyond the bounds of legitimate governance.[17]

Over the span of a few short weeks, the small, local, southern protest grew into an organized movement that stood outside of but was supported by opposition parties and funded, in part, by foreign interests, including the Central Intelligence Agency (CIA).[18] Transport workers, shopkeepers and other small business owners gradually banded together into independent gremios. Forming "an umbrella organization, the Frente Nacional (later Comando Nacional), they threw their weight behind the truckers." At its height, 600,000 to 700,000 employees and professionals, "including peasants, merchants sailors, doctors, lawyers and other professionals," joined the strike, successfully removing some 23,000 trucks from the road.[19] This was an unprecedented mobilization, in that it had national reach but was based on shared economic identities rather than the union and party structures that had traditionally shaped political association. It was quickly endorsed by the Christian Democratic and National Parties. But supporters were beginning to forge new avenues of political association and languages of political critique that stood at least partially outside traditional frameworks.[20]

Rafael Cumsille and Jorge Martínez, respective presidents of the Shopkeepers Confederation and the Central Chamber of Commerce, announced widespread business closures. Cumsille claimed that the movement enjoyed ample support from grassroots organizations throughout the nation, including the women's groups that had arranged the march of the empty pots.[21] He averred that the merchants' gremio understood and sympathized with the difficulties "that the country's consumers were living with" and had already received "many letters from women's organizations that represent mothers and housewives."[22] He tied himself to a tradition of legitimate political organization, even as he opened the possibility of extraparliamentary mobilization and violent urban conflict. For him, the movement could be the "base" of an "effective national unity" precisely because it stood outside the traditional realm of congressional politics and therefore offered an avenue of just protest.

The gremios opened a liminal space between the state and the grass-roots.[23] The contest over public space was crucial to their aims. They engaged the struggle for the streets and transformed them into an arena in which to challenge the limits of legitimate political practice. Like the march of the empty pots, the truckers' strike expanded on the traditional tactics of public political mobilization. Exactly *how* it reimagined the tension between national politics and urban space, however, was unprecedented.

THE OCTOBER STRIKE AND THE POLITICAL GEOGRAPHY OF PROTEST

The bosses' strike soon had national reach. This chapter examines its reverberations in and how it was played out on Santiago streets.[24] The gremio focused its energy on the battle for control of the city center in August 1972. *El Mercurio* reported on street clashes that disrupted access to Ahumada Street, downtown Santiago's most popular thoroughfare.[25] The more radically right-wing newspaper *La Tribuna* opened its coverage with a powerful image of an abandoned city center and a deserted Pasaje Matte (an important commercial walkway at that time). The photograph of the desolate commercial thoroughfare stood as evidence that "not one business" was open throughout the city.[26] Of these early clashes, perhaps the most spectacular was the burning of ETCE trolley car 814, set on fire at the intersection of Alameda and Estado Streets.[27] This action struck at what would become the symbolic target of the opposition's changing strategy of public protest—transportation and movement—and did so in the very heart of the city.

In response, the state threatened on national radio to invoke the state's Internal Security Law. The state agency Dirección de Industria y Comercio (DIRINCO) issued a resolution to forcibly open stores that refused to sell "basic necessities." Its representatives announced that this "closure of all commercial outlets will have grave consequences for the people, who will not be supplied with essential products as a result of the total paralysis of this very important system of distribution."[28] In a remarkable public performance, DIRINCO president Patricio Palma took the press on a tour of Ahumada Street, threatening to expropriate striking businesses as he walked. He made open spectacle of the government's ability to assure the circulation of goods, capitalizing on the symbolic importance of the city center.[29]

In the face of the state's attempts to control the street protests that grew stubbornly in both intensity and frequency, protesters moved away from the city center and charted an expanding geography of public political action and a new way of inhabiting the city. The target and tactic of the opposition's protest began to slowly change. The press responded by drawing a picture of an expanding local geography of protest that increasingly spilled out beyond Santiago's downtown core.[30] Perhaps more than any of its sister publications, *El Mercurio* contextualized all actions in the city center, including the trolley fire, within a wider spatial pattern: the "din of empty pots could be heard in the Villa Frei, in sectors of Providencia from Manuel Montt to Pintor Cicarelli to Mapocho [where young] people in Providencia set barricades aflame and threw stones at police vehicles and buses."[31]

By early September, a poignant *El Mercurio* article painted an image of urban anomie—of a city in smoke and ashes. Police were "fighting without pause to reestablish order, but ... protest violence doubled and large stores closed their doors."[32] Protests spilled over into neighboring areas, moving toward the Plaza Italia and Providencia as the police secured control of the city center. Small groups were soon "shouting slogans and blocking traffic" throughout the city.[33] These conflicts cleared the city of pedestrians. Only movie theaters, which served as a refuge from public disorder, remained open.

Downtown Santiago and surrounding middle- and working-class communities continued to occupy a central place in accounts of the political conflict written in the weeks leading to the strike. But articles such as these were beginning to explore the increasingly tight relationship between the city center and surrounding neighborhoods. The contours of the map of political participation were increasingly fluid, rendered unstable by a growing political conflict that transcended physical, social, and political boundaries and involved groups across the political spectrum.

In early October 1972, Senators Bulnes, Patricio Aylwin, Américo Acuña (Partido de Izquierda Radical, or PIR), and Julio Durán (Partido Demócrata Radical, or PDR) issued a joint challenge to Allende's rule in a special session of the Senate. This special session was convened to debate financial issues surrounding the nationalization of the National Paper Company, which supplied the Chilean newspapers with print. Opposition parties argued that Allende's government was illegally infringing on freedom of speech issues. It was therefore illegitimate.[34] These sentiments were echoed by "extrapolitical" groups. Jorge Fontaine, president of the Confederation of Production and Commerce, called for unity among political parties and extrapolitical organizations alike that could be "capable of confronting the totalitarian wave."[35] He couched his intervention in gendered language that aimed to move "virile" men into action. He directed his speech at those men who "are ashamed of having to hide behind the courage of women and the luminous idealism of youth."[36] *El Mercurio* added its weight to these challenges. The paper of record argued for the need for "solidarity" among parliamentary and extraparliamentary opposition and reserved a privileged place for members of its imagined coalition.[37] This rhetoric was largely successful, as the directors of a number of national gremios, including Fontaine, Cumsille, Benjamín Matte (president of the Sociedad Nacional de Agricultura), and Orlando Saenz (president of the Sociedad de Fomento Fabril), all expressed their interest in and allegiance to the movement.

Members of the Confederación Nacional de Dueños de Camiones (National Confederation of Truck Owners) called a national strike on October 9. The president of the national gremio of wheeled transport workers, Juan Marinakis, invoked nationalist rhetoric when he argued that it could not be that his "compatriots" in the south would be "treated badly as they labor patriotically to forge the nation" in the inhospitable areas of the nation.[38]

Speaking for truck owners, guild president and Patria y Libertad militant León Vilarín called for a "cessation of activities" that would affect up to twelve thousand cargo haulers.[39] Close to 400 trucks quickly ground to a halt in Talca, 134 in San Fernando, and another 577 in Rancagua.[40] *El Camionero* magazine, the organization's official publication, which represented the truckers' perspective in print, argued that stasis was a form of political expression: "We needed to paralyze the country in order to communicate our dissatisfaction with promises made and not kept to the country and the government. . . . When the truckers strike, Chile is paralyzed."[41]

Stasis provided an entry into a larger political debate. The "bosses' strike" was a vehicle through which the opposition could participate in the physical and symbolic battle over urban space and reveal the limits of government authority. Supporters of the strike gathered in downtown Santiago, where they articulated the terms and conditions of the protest. From the stage in front of the Universidad Católica, *La Tercera de la Hora* reported, "one could spot thousands and thousands of waving flags and lit flashlights, rising, even to the peak of Santa Lucia hill, illuminating Santiago as in a carnival night." "Santiago flooded the streets from Seminario to San Martín," ultimately "overrunning the Alameda."[42] The gathering provides a window onto the movement's complicated stance regarding urban politics.

Ernesto Vogel, a representative of the PDC in the nation's largest labor organization, the Central Única de Trabajadores (CUT), gave his account of the country's political and social state. "We have reached," he declared, "one of the worst moments in our history: of economic and constitutional crisis; of internal strife between class kin; of authority crushed by its own errors; of citizens' patience exhausted; and of a lack of social discipline leading to dangerous political polarization and upheaval."[43] He went on to connect economics, political instability, and class conflict to a vague conceptualization of anomie understood as the breakdown of social discipline and a concomitant increase in political polarization.

Patricia Guzmán then took the stage, also citing escalating political, economic, and social tension as the reason all opposition parties and extraparliamentary groups needed to move past peaceful means of confronting Allende, "no longer simply by marching, but rather in action."[44] She presented the relationship between Congress and the streets as a fluid and productive one in which public action could engender significant national political change. In strident words, she cast violence as an increasingly viable, even necessary option for claiming public space as a political tactic.

Patricio Aylwin took a slightly more ambivalent posture regarding the relationship between peaceful protest and more strenuous forms of civil unrest, yet he arrived at conclusions parallel to Guzmán regarding the "battle for the streets." "I think that the opposition's public shows of strength are very important," he argued. "Protests are significant in that they are an answer to the totalitarian threat posed by Marxist parties that have pledged to '*ganar la calle.*'"[45] He pointed to the political importance of public spaces and city streets and of a wider appreciation of the struggle to "win the streets." He was also aware, and not totally displeased, that extraparliamentary opposition groups were formulating new, more contentious means of engaging in the battle over city streets as a vehicle for political participation.[46]

By October 11, the National Confederation of Truck Owners had declared an indefinite work stoppage to protest the government's inability to supply them with spare parts. They escalated public confrontations on the nation's main highways. At six o'clock that morning, the gremios severed access to the highway into Rancagua in a violent confrontation that left one dead and one badly injured. Simultaneously, they erected a sixty-vehicle blockade on the roads that led into the city of La Serena, north of Santiago. Finally, they stalled trucks and burned tires along the Pan-American Highway on Santiago's immediate outskirts, impeding the circulation of goods and people in the city and along the nation's north-south axis.[47]

Then police arrested Vilarín along with the president, secretary general, and two other high-ranking members of the gremio, acting on the authority of a warrant issued by Santiago's intendente, Alfredo Joignant. *El Camionero* interpreted this as an attack on the gremios' movement as a whole,[48] insisting that relegating guild members to jail cells shared with "common criminals" was an indignity that its middle-class leaders should not have to endure.[49] The confederation responded to this transgression of political and social norms by quickly escalating its rhetorical strategy and confrontational tactics. It issued the first in a series of communiqués the following day. León Vilarín, the gremio's current sole spokesperson, called for the government to limit its nationalization of private businesses and guarantee freedom of expression to the right-wing Radio Nacional de Agricultura, located in the southern Chilean city, Los Ángeles.[50] The confederation's second communiqué declared that the truckers' movement was strictly "gremial" rather than political and was not supported by political parties. Finally, it issued a call for solidarity among transport workers and members of all gremios.[51]

The strike grew in scope and severity. A growing number of guilds adhered to the call for work stoppage in the days after its leaders were jailed. *La Estrella de Valparaíso* reported that a strike in support of the truckers in Valparaíso and Viña del Mar affected over 80 percent of retail and commercial establishments in the twin cities. The southern city of Concepción, it wrote, was nearly paralyzed.[52] By mid-October, the gremios formed an umbrella organization, the Frente Nacional, which became the Comando Nacional de Defensa in 1973. They had created a significant national movement that precipitated a moment of crisis for the Popular Unity.

Shopkeepers' and merchants' organizations decreed a national strike of indefinite duration on October 13. The National and Christian Democratic Parties threw their support behind the strikers. Allende responded with a midnight radio address accusing truckers of political machinations aimed at bringing down the government. The next day, the PDC convened a meeting of its "peasant, youth, women's, and professional wings to decide on a common strategy." They called on the state to free the jailed leaders and guarantee freedom of expression. On October 16 and 17, engineers, bank employees, gas workers, lawyers, architects, and transportation workers joined the strike, followed quickly by doctors and dentists. The state responded: it established a nighttime curfew, took control of radio stations, and requisitioned stores that refused to serve the public and factories that halted production. But, Paul Sigmund writes, "the observer walking around downtown Santiago felt he was in a ghost town."[53]

The image of a country paralyzed—economic activity stalled, commerce closed, and the flow of goods, staple foods, and people interrupted—became the enduring symbol of the strike's success and the government's failures. *Gremialistas* made a performance of their control of the streets, barricading streets with trucks, burning tires, and clanging pots and pans in neighborhoods throughout the country. Soup kitchens were established within barricaded spaces. Queues of peoples waiting for food became commonplace. Shuttered shops, deserted streets, and quieted avenues created powerful symbolism, a national spectacle of stasis. Whereas the march of the empty pots called women from their homes and into the streets to serve as a public expression of political discontent, the strike sent men and women off the streets and played on the image and experience of stillness and silence. The battle over public spaces had traditionally revolved around the presence of protesters in public spaces and their occupation of space physically, visually or aurally. The strike reimagined the relationship between presence and absence. It inaugurated new ways of engaging the politics of public space that built on but redefined the gendered language that was first articulated in the march of the empty pots.

Building on the spectacle of stasis, the gremio organized a daylong spectacle they called a Day of Silence (Día de Silencio). This protest further complicated and entangled the relationship between politics, place, and masculinity. It effectively closed the city down by calling on those men and women in opposition to Allende to remain in their homes and avoid commercial activity. The march of the empty pots politicized sound, the cadence of protest and the unmistakable clamor and clanging of empty pots reverberating throughout Santiago's neighborhoods. The Day instead found significance in stillness and quiet, turning an absence from public life into a "silent citizen's protest."[54] It was a partial return to the symbolism of the private realm.

El Mercurio framed its report on the protest with a suggestive series of photographs that spoke to this implicit contrast between public and private, sound and silence. The central image, an aerial view taken from the roof of one of the buildings adjacent to the Plaza de la Constitución, revealed a deserted central square. The absence of people and commerce signified for the paper of record "the discipline with which Chileans heeded the call for a 'Day of Silence.'" Another image showed San Diego Street abandoned, which, the paper claimed, was proof of the widespread discontent voiced silently by strikers and their supporters.[55] The article itself maintained that "commerce was almost completely paralyzed in almost all of the country's main cities." This was a unique form of confrontation that added a new dimension to the "enormous movement that censures the government's performance in every sphere of life in the country."[56]

Protestors, then, made a paradoxical public spectacle of their retreat into the home. The performance of silence drew its power from negation, creating a public world largely devoid of public political presence, in which the already politicized traffic of pedestrians, vehicles, and goods ground to a halt. It was part of a broader reenvisioning of the politics of movement and presence that stood in contrast both to the Popular Unity's massive urban mobilizations and the opposition's early entry into urban politics with the march of the empty pots.

THE SPATIAL POLITICS OF THE "TOMA DE PODER"

Popular Unity leaders responded swiftly to the strike. They correctly interpreted this form of protest as a new way of engaging in political conflict. *Las Noticias de Última Hora*, for instance, argued that the strike was an illegitmate affront to "mormalcy in our civic life."[57] It was the "putting into practice" of a "new phase of provocations against the Popular Government . . . which Partido Nacional leaders had belligerently promised and predicted."[58] Speaking on the radio, the president cast it as a political rather than a syndicalist movement, as a concerted attempt to cause disorder and unrest. But, he countered, "I must tell the country . . . Chile will not be paralyzed."[59] He called on laborers to maintain a state of alertness and to fulfill their obligation and express their adherence to the government by continuing to work and produce.[60] He also declared a state of emergency in twelve provinces, handing authority in these areas over to the armed forces to reestablish "the public order."

Popular Unity supporters reimagined the physical experience of political practice. The act of walking en masse across the city, to factories located in the industrial ring around the city, became a daily spectacle of resistance. The circulation or movement of people through city streets acquired even more potent political meaning because of the strike.[61]

The strike spurred a series of broader public debates about the politics and dangers inherent in inhabiting public space.[62] The street was politically charged. Reflecting on effects of the October strike, Winn finds that "more and more, the battle for Chile increasingly left the halls of congress and situated itself in the streets, markets and workplaces."[63] The street was also double edged. It could either secure or undermine the legitimacy of rule, safeguard or threaten a precarious political and public order. El Mercurio set the parameters and the language with which it would discuss the strike, its origins, and its significance. It argued that the Popular Unity did not respect legal traditions and that "even the government's own judges have long deemed that they had contravened the boundaries of justice."[64] And it articulated an increasingly common trope when it argued that the government had repeatedly violated the Constitution and therefore forsaken its claim to legitimate governance: the government overextended its authority, showed a penchant for nationalizing industry and commerce, and attempted to illegally control and curtail public expression, indiscriminately quashing public protest and the press.

The General Assembly of the Colegio de Abogados (College of Lawyers) weighed in, contending in a public report that the government strayed beyond the limits of the Constitution and broke its social and political contract with its constituents by repeatedly attempting to control public expression. Although the lawyers nominally supported the government's efforts to institute structural change in entrenched systems of economic and social relations, they suggested that the state's efforts to this end would lead to "social chaos." They argued that a just form of "social coexistence" was predicated on the institutional guarantee of individual rights; violating these rights, in turn, led to social chaos, everyday violence, and illegitimate government.[65]

Joan Garcés, adviser to Allende, offered a complex understanding of the relationship between public order, social inequality, and violence that ran counter to that of the opposition and the Colegio de Abogados. Responding to a Bolivian journalist's question regarding the nature of the Popular Unity's "vía pacífica," or peaceful road to socialism, Garcés advocated the use of a different term, "vía institucional," or institutional road.[66] For him, social inequality was a form of violence institutionalized in capitalist systems, "more cruel . . . [and more] efficient than the voice of the machine gun."[67] Parliamentary politics, the "via institutional," was a means of creating social change that had the potential to resolve forms of structural violence including class and social inequity.[68] Garcés proposed that Allende's subtle maneuvering, honed over the span of the president's forty years in the political system he was accused of undermining, could overturn the institutionalized, systemic violence that characterized capitalist political and economic realities. The Popular Unity would use the institutional road to build a radically "new society," run by "new men" with a "new conception of human existence, of social interaction."[69] Garcés proposed that Popular Unity political and institutional legitimacy was built on this radically different interpretation of "public violence."[70]

These ongoing debates over the terms of legitimate political practice, urban conflict, and violence were taken up in a series of congressional meetings. In mid-September 1972, Patricio Aylwin accused the Popular Unity of engendering political, social, and economic crisis, rampant inflation, and an increase in the cost of living. The government, he argued, contributed to the "collapse of legality" by protecting those involved in land seizures and supporting other "abuses by violent groups" who used "abusive means to silence radios and newspapers that oppose the government." It frequently failed "to acknowledge the right to assemble," facilitated the intervention and nationalization of industry, and habitually discriminated "between supporters and opposition when enforcing the law."[71] This created an "inferno raging in the people's households" which would be especially problematic "for housewives."[72]

The occupation of land and industry occupied a central place in Alwyn's rhetoric. He equated the struggle over public space with a drive for political power when he identified "tomas de terreno" (seizures of land) with "tomas de poder" (seizures of power). These were related political strategies to secure the "conditions for hegemony" in all levels of government and society. The Popular Unity was falling back on violence as a political tool in order to obtain "total power" and showing a "lack of moral stature to admit its failure": "physical violence, insults, threats, provocations, assaults, attacks, aggressions and murders" constituted part of a larger attempt "to replace reason with force."[73]

These discursive battles in public, the press, and Congress were part of a wider struggle over the "proper" use of public space, over how space, class, and violence would be politicized and over who could legitimately claim the public sphere as a political platform. The initial idea behind the strike—that paralysis, stillness, and silence could be political statements—was itself a radical reconceptualization of urban politics. But the paro—the strike—would gain even greater significance as a politically creative act in the second half of October. The very terms of this discussion would shift during its final phase.

PERIPHERAL PUBLIC SPHERES? CORDONES INDUSTRIALES AND THE SPACE OF POLITICAL ACTION

Hostilities erupted throughout the country. On October 16, violent clashes in downtown Santiago were met with police repression. Twenty meters of railway line in Quilpué and another twenty east of Valparaíso were dynamited. Private bus companies joined the strike in Valparaíso. The National Electrical Company's Engineers' Syndicate, the Taxi Drivers' Association, and the members of lawyers', doctors', and civil engineers' professional associations pledged their allegiance to the strike the next day. Leaders from an array of gremios established the Confederación de Defensa Gremial on October 19, signaling the group's newfound organization and its focused entry into the national political scene.

The government responded. Its tenth *bando*, or edict, declared a curfew and prohibited movement through the city between midnight and six in the morning for the entirety of the province of Santiago except for the port of San Antonio. Five hundred independent taxi drivers pledged to defy the strike and continue working. Eighteen of twenty-eight syndicates requested police protection to do so. A convoy of twenty-one trucks driven by two hundred workers broke through the National Gas Company's barricades in Melipilla and took their cargo fifty kilometers west to Santiago. Telephone company workers, Tierra Amarilla coal miners, and local neighborhood organization members all used newspapers to issue public calls for workers to organize against the wishes of "a minority."[74]

Speaking on national public television and radio on October 18, 1972, Allende first reiterated his promise to protect the flow of goods and peoples. "The truth is crystal clear," he stressed. "They wanted to paralyze this country." But, he continued, defiant, the "country was not paralyzed, and it will not be paralyzed."[75] He made specific mention of the metal spikes designed to shred automobile tires, the already familiar barricades and stalled trucks, and the interrupted distribution of gas, foods, and other essential articles. He argued that police had repressed those "provocateurs" that had created "difficulties" in downtown Santiago. His government, however, had not been drawn into these clashes: "We have tried to quell confrontations—and succeeded. We have told the workers—who with incredible abnegation have been working and manufacturing more in their factories and industries—to stay away from Santiago's downtown, to stay away from the downtown of provincial capitals."[76] Disciplined forms of resistance had stopped the strike.

Allende alluded to labor's mobilization along the city's peripheral industrial ring and to the specter of workers marching down from their factories into the city center but he emphasized his ability to focus this energy and protect the city center from the threat of escalation.[77] He proposed a sort of urban masculinity defined by the restraint with which his supporters fulfilled their roles in the Popular Unity's plan.[78] He also hinted at a changing landscape of political participation. On the surface, he acknowledged examples that pointed to a generalized increase in political conflict throughout the city and the nation. The intensity and significance of these clashes varied greatly depending on their individual location in the city.

However compelling, Allende's formulation both recognized and elided a fundamental shift in the city's political geography. Radicalized by the truckers' strike, workers in the peripheral ring organized politically and spatially, establishing dense networks among contiguous industries which came to be known as cordones industriales. Cordones were local organizations united more by geography, by their place in the city, than by party or union membership. The political scientist Franck Gaudichaud describes them as "unified and integrated" nodes located in the "main industrial areas and in working-class neighborhoods" and organized on "a territorial base that permits connections between unions of a particular industrial area and the other neighborhood organizations in the area."[79] Peter Winn defines cordones as "new forms of organization of a territorial character . . . which transcended the craft divides of Chilean labor unions to unite workers of the same industrial belt or geographic district."[80]

By October 1972, "perhaps 100,000 people were active in the Santiago cordones. They rejected party affiliations; they were not supported initially by nor were they fully responsive to the CUT; and they alarmed not just the opposition but also the Communist Party and the government."[81] Workers in these cordones aimed to participate in and even determine the nature of political debate and conflict. They transformed these industrial arenas into laboratories where they could experiment with qualitatively different forms of political participation oriented to local and national concerns. They forged new forms of political identity, citizenship, and practice.[82] Cordones may have been located at the periphery of the city and the fringes of traditional politics but they helped shape a crucial change in Popular Unity–era political mobilization.

These local forms of political organization emerged at a moment when the split between official and opposition groups was deepening and the schism within the Popular Unity regarding the viability of the peaceful and institutional road to socialism was widening. This crisis allowed members to engage the state in a complex debate over the cadence of political and social change, complicating the relationship between politics from above and from below. "It was the cordones industriales that organized the defense of their areas during the conflicts of 1972 and 1973," Winn writes. "The cordones, moreover, took advantage of these conflicts to advance their vision of revolution from below, pushing the seizure and socialization of factories well beyond the ninety-one enterprises on the government nationalization list."[83]

The strike, and cordones' response to it, had national scope, though the experience of each was local. As Winn points out, Santiago's workers were aware of, and responded to, events in other urban and industrial centers. When the former Yarur textile mill's sister factory in the south, Caupolicán Chiguayante, was burned down by arsonists, their counterparts in Santiago "armed" themselves with sharpened staves to "repel" aggressions from the Right in Santiago. They also mobilized to push back a violent attempt against a local CUP, extending, for the first time, their scope of action—and their resources—to those workers and residents in adjacent neighborhoods, "[taking on] a very important role in founding a local cordón industrial, the Cordón O'Higgins." In a word, events in other areas directly shaped political conflicts in and throughout Santiago, led to the formation of and experimentation with different forms of political practice, and informed both local and national politics. Workers in local cordones were ensconced in national political currents, but they also made these spaces into laboratories of potent political experimentation that propelled the cadence of change.[84]

In laying claim to sites throughout the city, and especially in the industrial ring around the city, workers, pobladores, and others were in effect creating spheres, practices, and languages in which they could put into practice new forms of political mobilization and identity. Cordones also provided a space in which members could organize around their day-to-day concerns and experiences. Many of these efforts referenced or sought to affect the state, especially to hold it to its promise to increase worker participation and control over industry. But many more were self-contained experiments in political association, experience, and citizenship that cannot be reduced to their effect on politics from above.

The Spanish translation of Winn's compelling history of the Yarur seizure, and the political significance of these actions, is especially interesting. Winn argues that workers here "enacted their own understanding of the Chilean Revolution—a model that other workers then followed."[85] This formulation, and the performative metaphor of enactment, speaks to the significance that Diana Taylor finds in the myriad "repertoires" that (political) actors used to produce and reproduce (political) meaning. Cordón members enacted a new political model through these urban strategies, through the embodied process of seizing public and private urban spaces as a creative act that brought into being new spaces, strategies, scenarios, and public spheres of political debate. Thus Winn's *Weavers of Revolution* lays the foundation for a study of how cordones were shaped into sites of political association and action.[86]

The early Cordón Cerrillos-Maipú offers the strongest example of the cordón as a laboratory of political citizenship. Cerrillos-Maipú was located in a particularly diverse area characterized by a mixture of rural land, variegated industry, and poor shantytowns.[87] The cordones, and Cerrillos-Maipú in particular, had a history that predated the October strike.[88] Workers , area campesinos, and neighboring pobladores had occupied some forty factories. They barricaded themselves in the streets when the Senate ordered them to abandon them in early July 1972.[89] They effectively cut the area off from the surrounding community.[90] They established "solidarity committees" tasked with connecting these different industries, later replaced by the more centralized Coordination Committee. This associational practice would lay the foundation for the assembly of "the largest concentration of workers in the manufacturing [sector] of Santiago." At its apex, Cerrillos-Maipú included some 250 industries and 146,000 workers who ably navigated their support for the state and their own demands on the Popular Unity regarding the immediate realization of "poder popular."[91]

Workers and pobladores throughout Santiago and the southern city of Concepción, including those of Cerillos-Maipú, responded to the opposition's strike by organizing broad networks based on spatial proximity and shared local concerns.[92] In October, they seized factories, kept them running, and acted as a symbolic counterpoint to the image and reality of a country paralyzed. They occupied streets, seized buses, and established distribution networks that circulated goods and fuel through informal channels. Oral histories attest to members' views of cordones as new forms of communal organization that took a more structured form in response to the truckers' mobilization. Fernando Quiroga, director of planning at the Chilean airline (LAN Chile), recounted, "The trucker's strike . . . [was] the largest gathering of forces that the right had been able to muster. . . . [H]owever, it was also the beginning of something else."[93] In the context of the trucker's strike, which intensified an already complex, multifaceted battle for city streets that radiated from the city center to the peripheries and back again, cordones carved out a space from which members could remake the political landscape into "something else," transform the city's political geography around vibrant, local forms of political organization.

It was precisely because they grew at the margins of, and in many senses in tension with, traditional political structures that cordones became spaces of radical political creativity. Sandra Castillo Soto suggests that while many cordón participants were "leftist militants and sympathizers, especially from the Socialist Party[,] . . . it is no less true that there was no organic support from Popular Unity party structures." Lack of direct state involvement gave members the opportunity to develop "ample spaces of popular sociability"[94] that members saw as a significant departure from traditional forms of political association based on party and union leadership.[95] In an interview with Castillo Soto, Hernán Ortega contended that cordones' innovative structure made possible widespread mobilization based on shared experience and a fluid distribution of available resources.[96] In other words, new lines of association went hand in hand with new political practices and identities. "While it is true that the *cordones* were formed in response to the strike," Castillo Soto writes, "they both built on preexisting forms of community organization and became an alternative to the state's inability to respond to *pobladores'* immediate needs."[97]

Drawing connections between industrial workers and pobladores based on spatial proximity and local concerns enabled changing forms of association and sociability, new ways of organizing politicized publics and changing tactics of debate or, in other words, "new 'alternative forms of sociability and democratic control' among the base."[98] Cordones "were transformed into spaces of encounter, popular sociability, and political debate" where participants could fashion innovative forms of "democratic" political organization.[99] Their members experimented with a range of forms of political association, authority, and administration. They established informal networks of exchange of materials that pooled different factories' resources. They created and maintained connections with neighborhood organizations outside of cordón or union networks. They established links with neighborhood groups, in an effort to secure the circulation of goods in the context of the truckers' strike. They organized soccer and volleyball games and other forms of play that cemented connections between industries and between industrial workers, campesinos, and pobladores.[100] Members, in short, shaped a "space of popular sociability" that encouraged a wide range of alternative practices and identities.

The strategies of occupation and association they created in response to the strike afforded them the platform from which to effect demands that addressed both immediate concerns and larger questions regarding their role in a socialist economy and state. Theirs were self-conscious efforts to reimagine the shape and structure of political representation that were most evident in the first days of the cordones and gained greater significance during the strike. The early forms of organization in the Cordón Cerrillos-Maipú, for example, culminated in the convocation of an open *cabildo*, or council, a political structure that emphasized direct representation and workers' fluid incorporation into decision-making processes. Although this experiment in direct political representation was short lived, it points to a willingness to play with innovative forms of political association and practice that were broader than the four hundred participants in the political council.

These efforts took a number of creative forms that were often oriented to the state and to encouraging the nationalization of individual factories, but they were also tied to cordones' local concerns and local practices. Hugo Cancino outlines a general structure that took shape after the truckers' strike and was loosely adopted in a range of cordones, even as he identifies significant variations among individual industries. Worker assemblies formed in each industry within the geographic scope of each cordón. Each factory would elect two or three representatives to the cordones' council of delegates. The council of delegates, in turn, elected the cordón's directorship from its members, including a president and organizing, action, defense, press, and cultural secretaries. Cancino highlights the ways in which this arrangement stood outside of regular party and union structures.[101] In fact, primary sources that shed light on individual cordones' organizations suggest a sustained interest in experimenting with self-reflexively "flexible" and "open" configurations. The magazine *Tarea Urgente*, for instance, detailed how the newest cordón, Santiago Centro, inverted hierarchical decision-making structures. The magazine urged workers to establish "popular assembly" as the "ultimate authority" in the cordón. These workers would be charged with the final say in outlining the cordón's program of action and electing the members of each individual committee.[102]

Cordón members' experiments with direct and flexible representation transformed individuals and institutions. Helia Henríquez claims that workers filled a dual productive and political role, coupling labor within factory walls to "presence outside of industry, in the street, in public space." The labor leader Hernán Ortega recounted that "leaders were made on the street . . . in the day-to-day," leading his interviewer to conclude that this "dynamic created a new form of political action" based on cordones' "own innovative physiognomy, with their own frameworks, each of which differed from other worker's institution's traditional organizational practices."[103] These innovations were "imagined and put into practice by its young leaders."[104] Cordones were, as a whole, independent of the CUT's political leadership. Their leaders were chosen in the workplace, not by the state, and could change very quickly as a result of decisions made in any individual factory workers' council. Ian Roxborough's investigation of cordones' decision-making structures and practices supports this reading: "*Cordón* meetings were totally open. Anyone could attend and participate, even though only the delegates could vote. . . . *Cordones* were centers in which to create a more flexible and malleable form of politics."[105]

Barricades, street clashes, and other forms of urban contestation on the city's periphery were creative, public performances of political action by which members controlled access to space and place and in so doing allowed cordón participants to engage state representatives. Workers addressed local concerns using innovative tactics tied to the control of space: "*Cordones'* spatial character . . . allowed them to use their geographic location strategically, especially as the majority of *cordones* were located in areas of highest circulation." Cutting off these entry and exit points with barricades gave workers control over their spaces, which placed more pressure on the authorities to respond to their demands.[106]

Faride Zerán, reporting for *Chile Hoy*, suggested that these tactics allowed workers to assert their presence in, and ultimately shape, national political struggles. Chronicling the rise of cordones over an extended period, she wrote that "thousands of men and women, Cordón Cerrillos-Maipú workers, took control of the community's roads."[107] The seizure of factories and the spaces surrounding them, the push for nationalization, and workers' insistence that they remain so in the face of Allende's recalcitrance were all examples of workers' role in national politics and evidence of their ability to negotiate effectively both with the opposition and with the state. Zerán affirmed that "workers claimed to use [barricades] not because they stood against the Allende's government but because it was the only efficient form of being heard immediately. Copihue Packers was expropriated after *cordón* actions, and Sylleros only after the area was barricaded."[108] In short, they recognized cordones as experiments with "new structures and ample spaces of popular sociability" where members could propose new definitions of fair labor practices, new types of association, and new languages of political debate.[109]

Scholars have dismissed these efforts and experiences for having limited repercussions in national politics. CIDU analysts, for example, saw the cabildo "as an initial experiment in political organization" that had indisputable "immediate and tangible effects." They nevertheless claimed that that the cabildo failed to consolidate direct "political results." Its "great potential" to form the basis for "a popular political movement was [therefore] never realized."[110] Interviews with cordón participants point to different types of "political results," less direct than the "tangible effects" on the state and on the cadence of political change that Winn finds for Yarur, yet equally significant in the long term.[111] Many cordón members recall their experiments with direct democracy as an opportunity to imagine a type of political citizenship in which the ability to weigh in on national politics was not workers' only goal, or even the ultimate raison d'être of their participation in cordones. Instead, as Pablo Muñoz suggests, cordones' greatest contribution was to offer workers a chance to participate in these experiments in governance and therefore fashion novel political identities: "I think it was a significant participatory experience. That is, for me, what *cordones* accomplished. A participatory popular movement, with real control over territory. . . . I think that it is a model for what a political movement should be."[112] Luis Ahumada, active in the Cordón Vicuña Mackenna, agreed: "For me, the *cordón* was the most advanced example of *poder popular* in practice. We decided when to seize the factories, we came up with solutions to union conflicts, we created solidarity between different syndicates. We also began a number of things that, in retrospect, we didn't accomplish."[113]

Winn writes that "over five hundred enterprises were nationalized under Allende—often after being seized by their workers—and most experimented with worker participation in their management."[114] Taking control of their factories during the strike gave these workers the opportunity to weigh in on how a worker-run factory would function without management or professionals, how to rethink the division of labor and workplace hierarchy, how to build connections with the Popular Unity's food distribution organizations (Juntas de Abastecimiento Popular, or JAPs), and how to form vigilance and defense committees overseeing seized factories. Mario Olivares recounts his experience as an active member of these organizations, his excitement palpable through the transcription, bracketed by exclamation marks: "We began to speak of real power for workers. . . . We might not have been clear in terms of ideology, but we demanded greater participation in all areas, not only in the production side!"[115]

Gaudichaud traces a broad "social geography" in the last year of Popular Unity rule that included cordones, "comandos campesinos," "comandos comunales," and "comités coordinadores."[116] Each of these cordones, comandos, and comités had different types of connection or reach into neighborhoods, communities, and community organizations—including those devoted to neighborhood health and distribution of goods at a local level. As Alan Angell writes, the cordones were "maximum expressions of *poder popular* . . . in the working-class belt surrounding Santiago that brought together local inhabitants and workers in a joint effort to run the enterprises and administer services in the area."[117] Delving into workers' experience founding, organizing, and participating in new governing structures, Gaudichaud ties the "occupation of factories, farms, [and] lands" to the "everyday democratization of interactions and address between workers and management, housekeepers and homeowners, peasants and landowners or administrators." The seizure of land and factories and the practice of poder popular in these spaces led to a "democratization" of everyday interaction, which recast poder popular into a veritable *fiesta popular,* or popular celebration. The effervescence of these performances spilled over the bounds of "proper" political behavior and had the potential to overturn and transform traditional social relations and structures of authority.[118] In other words, poder popular was a carnivalesque performance that had the potential to transform social geographies and social relations.[119]

Cordón members' references to affect, emotion, and dignity must be taken seriously. Winn lays out the connection between economic theory, labor, and self-image: "If their new spending power brought workers into the consumer market, their new power at their places of work altered their working conditions and self-image." The experience of "poder popular" was transformative: "Add to this the workers' own projection of their views, desire, and power beyond their factory gates and into the public spaces of streets, squares, and stadiums," Winn concludes, "and the surge in their self-image and status is clearly explicable."[120] Different forms of political participation allowed workers and pobladores to build new forms of political identity; they were part of a larger process of building political citizenship that was tied but not reducible to its effect on the state.[121] Workers' attempts to organize in this manner marked a crucial change in Popular Unity–era political mobilization: the formation of cordones was a decisive step that propelled both a radical rethinking of the site and form of political association and a significant spatialization, or "territorialization," of politics.[122]

The manifestos published by different cordones reveal significant changes in the model of politics and political citizenship in Allende's final year. They are political documents that express both an understanding of contemporary political realities and an "ideal" vision of a political future. *La Aurora de Chile* recognized these as both imagining a public sphere of association and debate and organizing a concrete political public around the expression of these ideals. The manifesto circulated by the Cordón Vicuña Mackenna during and immediately after the truckers' strike had the potential to "agitate" industrial workers and thereby transform the cordón into an incubator of power that could pull together "the entire *comuna*." The Cordón Cerrillos-Maipú quickly reimagined the cordones, "seeds of embryonic power," as fully formed "organic entities." Together, they proposed that cordones were to become nodal points in a dense network of local organizations and political associations.[123]

The Cordón Cerrillos-Maipú issued a second manifesto that reiterated the connection between territorial control and real political creativity. In a joint declaration penned by the cordones in response to the state's decision to turn back some factory nationalization in 1973, the signatories proposed an urban geography of political mobilization that was centered on the peripheries of the city: "These industries cannot be returned to their owners. This is a . . . decision . . . expressed in factories, on the streets, in the Presidential Palace, in their manifestos, in the *asambleas* and *cordones*. . . . They have essentially two tasks at hand: (1) establish *asambleas* where people work, section by section, factory by factory[;] . . . (2) . . . [r]emember that the street belongs to the Left and that we must win the struggle in factories and in the streets."[124]

Their articulation of cordones' creative potential was direct: by establishing territorial control over the city's outlying districts, they could become public spheres of political debate, association, and sociability that stood alongside La Moneda as a site of politics. They must also be recognized as incubators for new political practices and as catalysts for the democratization of political authority. A close reading of these diverse sources suggests not so much an ideal public sphere in which inequities are bracketed and violence eschewed as one in which the shape and limits of legitimate political practice, and the role of either peaceful or violent public acts, could be debated.[125] These were arenas in which workers, pobladores, and campesinos from neighboring rural areas could, and did, propose alternative modes of political association, practice, and identity that came out of a heated, sometimes aggressive struggle over streets, lands, and factories.

POLITICS IN THE AFTERMATH OF THE STRIKE

In challenging the structure of Chilean politics, cordones developed almost as much friction with the Popular Unity as the Popular Unity did with the opposition. The state responded tentatively to their claims.[126] Allende argued that workers should be careful in their efforts to force the nationalization of their industries and to push the cadence of national political change. The president of FENSA Industries' syndicate, a Communist Party militant, argued that "the Communist Party does not participate in alternative organizations, nor does it ally with 'bomberos locos,'" or violent extremists. Theirs were "disciplined militants," he argued, who should not use tactics like seizure of industries and government ministries, which "may be legitimate under a bourgeois government" but were not legitimate under the Popular Unity.[127] They juxtaposed disciplined action in support of the state to undisciplined, uncontrolled activities that broke ranks, challenged the "proper" cadence of political change, and threatened to redefine the city's political geography. Fearing unrestrained shows of "popular support," the Popular Unity's strategy was to assure disciplined movement through public space. The initial declarations of the head of the Zona de Santiago delineating the first set of rules or orders for the population under a state of emergency regulated the movement of goods and peoples through the city.[128] Similarly, for Allende, his authority over "la calle," the street, spoke to his ability to convene and control massive popular mobilization. He excoriated the opposition and dissident Popular Unity supporters alike for playing directly into the hands of the gremios by engaging in battles over city streets that involved barricades made of burning tires, thrown rocks, and broken bottles, all of which undermined the government's commitment to democracy and legality.[129]

Cordón participants stood in tense, critical support of Allende.[130] Workers voiced their displeasure at the government's political maneuvering to *La Aurora de Chile*, proposing a fundamental critique of their position in relation to the state: "We, the urban and rural poor, are only used for certain purposes. They tell us: there is an owner's strike, the gremios hid the buses, so march. . . . Hold back your *pliegos* [manifestos] and demands. . . . Participate in public protests to carry placards and chant in favor of the government. . . . Keep the economy running. . . . And take to the streets to defend the Popular Unity." They countered with a critical, alternative vision of urban mobilization as the basis for new forms of poder popular: "Allende should not fool himself," the article averred, for it was "the physical presence of millions of workers on the streets that kept the government in power."[131] In this articulation, political voice and politicized masculinity came together in the struggle for the street, here in defense of a form of poder popular that stood apart from both the opposition and the state. In a climate of escalating political schism and intensifying public clashes, political citizenship had much to do with citizens' ability to stake out their place in a changing political geography and articulate novel forms of political identity and practice.

The Popular Unity's attempts to finally end the strike failed to recognize or capitalize on worker's creative politicization. The government ended negotiations with the gremios after receiving their list of demands, their *Pliego de Chile*. However, Allende continued to navigate the tensions between an increasingly organized opposition and a fractured Left. He concluded that the only way to resolve the strike and reestablish order would be to radically restructure his cabinet and incorporate members of the military.[132] Supporting this decision, his entire cabinet resigned on October 31 in order to clear the way for the proposed changes. Two days later, even as the Senate stripped Intendente Joignant of his position by a vote of thirty-two to fourteen, Allende swore in a new cabinet that included General Prats as minister of interior, Air Force general Sepúlveda as minister of mines, and Rear Admiral Huerta as minister of public works. He also established three new committees to oversee distribution of essential foodstuffs, distribution to industry, and regulation of transportation.[133] Prats, an important ally and longtime proponent of constitutional rule, argued that the relationship between the government and the military was not a "political compromise" but a "patriotic collaboration in the interests of social peace."[134] Prats immediately became the government representative in dealings with the gremios. Pinochet replaced him as commander of the army after his promotion.

On November 3, 1972, members of the new cabinet met with the previously recalcitrant gremios. The strike was suspended two days later. Strike leaders claimed that their fundamental goal was to "to count on government authorities acceptable to the *gremios*."[135] The presence of the military in a cabinet headed by the commander in chief of the army fulfilled this goal and assured them that "in the future, there will be true respect of the letter and spirit of our laws and our Constitution."[136] Speaking on national television and radio, Prats stated that the government would no longer "allow stoppages or sudden walkouts that harm the economy or adversely affect people's lives or their health. If such an emergency were to arise, the government will use the full weight of the law against those responsible, whoever they are."[137]

But the political landscape had already been irrevocably altered. Conflicts on city streets continued, as different groups fought for material and symbolic possession of public space and the public sphere. On November 10, for instance, the youth section of the Far Right National Party vowed, using a common homophobic slur, to exact vengeance on those "maricones" who had attacked their leader, Sergio Onofre Jarpa. They promised to make their forceful presence felt "in every neighborhood in Santiago." In so doing, they made explicit once again the deep connections between political mobilization, masculinity, and violence.[138] They also pointed to the growing territorialization of political conflict and its extension into different urban spaces. Indeed, the months that followed would bring an escalation in the tensions between national politics and local experience, a fractured Left and an increasingly unified Right, government and grassroots organizations, and the city center and its periphery. By Allende's third and final year in power, urban residents had fashioned a growing political repertoire. Their actions had knit together a complex political geography and set the stage for an even more pronounced escalation of everyday, public conflict over the terms and limits of political practice.

. . .

The food queues that proliferated on the streets and garnered wide attention in the press in October and November became some of the most significant but overlooked sites of political association fomented by the strike. The long queues outside stores and supermarkets became patent symbols of political conflict and economic crisis. The state saw them as material consequences of political sabotage that exacerbated social inequality. For Allende, queues showed that the "ultimate challenge for the Popular Government is to be efficient in providing for the masses' needs. The enemy understands this and lies in wait. It is not surprising that they organized the 'marcha de las cacerolas' and that they systematically instruct their agents to infiltrate the lines for meat, lines of housewives who are unable to find certain products or groups of workers waiting buses that will never arrive."[139] Queues were a social space in which the opposition could foment political, economic, and social disorder, where concerns over food and sustenance could be shared and discussed in public.

The opposition, in turn, portrayed the queues as symbols of the breakdown of political and social order. Like Allende, Patricio Aylwin recognized that queues were social worlds and places where people argued and debated the current national situation.[140] Whereas the march of the empty pots had emphasized the symbolic importance of the city center, queues that grew out of the disrupted distribution of goods and food throughout the city were everyday spaces of debate located with greater frequency in the barrios than in downtown.[141] Queues occupied a distinct place between the public and private worlds, as they were social spaces in which people discussed political concerns with an eye toward the everyday domestic concerns of the home.[142]

The long lines were just one node in a new political landscape that was beginning to emerge from the truckers' strike. They were part of a remapping of the capital's political geography in which the city center was no longer the only or the most salient space of public political debate. Queues were part of the new way of understanding where and how politics could be done that this chapter has traced. By the end of October 1972, the street had been imagined and recognized as a place for political action and debate. "La calle" was a simultaneously physical and symbolic entity that held a number of sometimes contradictory, often conflicting politically and socially significant expressions together. This ability to embrace divergent meanings suggests the "multivocality" of the street as a symbol and a site. It was at once a space of concerted action, an arena to be occupied and defended, and a place of exultant but peaceful celebration. At the same time, peripheral neighborhoods, shantytowns, and, as this chapter suggests, the industrial ring around the city emerged as seats of political activity that were beginning to look dissimilar from traditional forms of mobilization in the traditional sites of political activity.

The truckers' strike marked a shift in how and where politics was fought out. The strike, and workers' responses, interpolated or fashioned a politicized public whose ties could escape the frame of national parties. Truckers halted the flow of people, goods, and industries and made a spectacle of barricaded streets, of soup kitchens erected to feed protesters, of queues of people lined up for increasingly rare goods, and of shuttered industries. In response, workers and pobladores marched, clashed openly with opponents, walked to work through empty streets, and seized stores and industries and demanded they be nationalized. The occupation of factories, in turn, provided the space and opportunity for discussion regarding the shape of legitimate political action, debates in which worker and poblador support for Allende's government was offered but offered from a critical vantage point, for cordón members did not as a rule agree with the rhythm of political change. Factories became "a space of popular sociability . . . in which popular subjects fashioned their own, politically radical perspective . . . and a new social praxis."[143]

The strike and the responses that it engendered were therefore creative acts that generated new sites and forms of political mobilization on factory floors and in factory yards, at street barricades, and in queues. Urban residents' public actions set the stage for an even more pronounced escalation of everyday, public conflict over the terms and limits of political practice. In late July 1973, truckers declared a new transportation strike, once again closing stores, halting work, and resisting the government's confiscation of striking vehicles. This time, however, these techniques went hand in hand with heightened "street clashes, which proceeded from fists to arms, terrorist attacks to key areas of the nation's infrastructure—oleoducts, bridges and high voltage electric cables (which caused large-scale blackouts)—as well as strikes against Leftist leaders' homes and families."[144] For the Far Right, this escalation aimed to establish the conditions for an immediate military coup; for Christian Democrats, the goal was to create such chaos that the opposition could control more than two-thirds of Congress in the March 1973 parliamentary elections and impeach Allende.[145] In turn, cordones had extended their sphere of influence and pushed "poder popular" forward as a viable goal, and industrial workers had been radicalized by the experience.[146] The military coup and its turn to state-sponsored violence attempted to silence debates over the shape and limits of Chilean politics. But early experiences of political mobilization and urban action proposed a radical shift in where and how public politics could be thought of and experienced and how urban residents came to see themselves as dignified political citizens. The next chapter examines this process in relation to ephemeral visual practices that include political posters, murals, and graffiti.

4. Political Palimpsests

Posters, Murals, and the Ephemeral
Practice of Urban Politics

Patricio Guzmán's 2004 documentary, *Salvador Allende*, begins with the filmmaker carefully handling "almost all that is left" of the deposed president—his wallet, monogrammed glasses case, Socialist Party membership card, and watch. The microphone picks up the amplified sounds of Guzmán looking through objects imbued with the weight of "a dislocated history."[1] The camera rests on shards of Allende's heavy-rimmed lenses, fractured in the coup but preserved under a fiberglass cover; on pencil sketches for a collaborative mural; and on the pockmarked pages of a family photo album, turned by weathered hands to reveal the stubborn images of a faded past.

But it is the architecture of city walls that shapes Guzmán's narrative. After the titles, Guzmán appears to the viewer before a wall bordering the highway that leads into Santiago's Pudahuel Airport. His hands hover in the foreground, peeling away the layers of paint and dirt that cover years of history painted on the partition. He continues to chip away at the palimpsest, hammering with a rock when his fingers can no longer free color and image from the gray coat that obscures it. The archaeology of the wall before him structures his presentation of memory and forgetting as imbricated processes that continually double back to define and redefine each other. In voice-over he explains, "The reappearance of memory is neither comfortable nor voluntary. It vibrates and moves with the turns of my own life. I am here, in the same place I left thirty years back, at a simple wall near the airport." Guzmán's greatest films return again and again to the problematic of remembrance. Here, the palimpsest offers a compelling way of seeing the relationship between persistence, silence, and erasure: "Power cultivates forgetting, but recollections emerge from under the layer of amnesia that blankets the country, and memory vibrates just under the skin."

Guzmán then interviews Alejandro "Mono" González, founder of the Brigada Ramona Parra muralist group, "the man who painted the city's walls and wrote Allende's name in every Chilean street." As he has done in published and personal interviews for years, González recounts his memory of public visual practice in democracy (and dictatorship) as the story of the flowering of political identity and political practice. The muralist exclaims on camera, "The walls had to be, and were, of the people. . . . We acquired power in the streets, and built a method of working. From there rose the . . . Street Art Brigades." Guzmán revisits these walls that staged a conflict between dialogue and silence, expression and erasure, disappearance and reappearance.[2] He presents the painting, erasure, and reappearance of public art as part of a complicated process by which political citizenship was formulated, fractured, and re-created on city streets in democracy and dictatorship.

This chapter takes ephemeral forms of public art as part of a broader struggle over the terms and limits of political citizenship in Allende's Chile.[3] It focuses on political posters, placards, and murals as important examples of political things and as significant sources for a history of political change over time.[4] It examines how urban residents, many of whom did not identify as artists, used public art as a means of shaping political debate.[5] They took to the streets and seized city walls to generate a rich, adaptable visual language that gave them entry into a wider political debate and a chance to fashion themselves into political citizens.

City streets and walls are sites "where politics becomes concrete, physical, [and] corporeal," where political debate becomes rooted in place.[6] Santiaguinos painted, tore down, and painted over murals and posters under Allende, making walls into arenas where political languages and identities were forged and the shape of the Chilean nation and the limits of Chilean citizenship reimagined. Yet, the political significance of street art and writing was paradoxically rooted in its very ephemerality. Painted at the busiest intersections of the city center or in the poorest shantytown squares, posters, murals, and graffiti, or rayado, were meant to last mere hours or a day. Many were quickly ripped down or painted over. New pieces were layered over older ones. Existing works were transformed, their meaning altered. In so doing, they helped constitute a public sphere of political debate rooted in new conversations taking place on city streets. Public art was both a vehicle of and a metaphor for the fluid, relentless political exchanges that characterized the three years of Allende's presidency. This chapter takes these materials seriously as sources for political history.

EPHEMERAL PRACTICE AND THE PRODUCTION OF
POLITICAL AND VISUAL LANDSCAPES

An innovative tradition of public political art emerged in Chile in the 1960s. The Communist and Socialist Parties were at the vanguard of this movement. Though the PC relied heavily on its national newspaper, *El Siglo,* and other groups published their own daily and weeklies, Popular Unity coalition members recognized the need for broader forms of communication with which to reach a broader base of support in working-class and progressive middle-class sectors. Public political art and propaganda, a familiar but informal practice among the Chilean Left through the postwar period, played an increasingly integral role in Chilean politics in and around Allende's final presidential campaign.[7] The PC and PS were especially adept at organizing young militants into disciplined groups charged with painting "every wall" in the city with Allende's insignia.[8]

The Communist Youth's muralist organization, the Brigada Ramona Parra, or BRP, quickly established new trends in urban politics and visual practice and began experimenting with innovative means of communication. Receiving loose instructions from a central committee, small groups of Communist youth took to the streets "to paint, to denounce."[9] They were brought together again to participate in a march from the coastal city of Valparaíso to Santiago to protest the Vietnam War in 1969. Their assignment was to create simple slogans along the nation's streets and highways.[10] What began with this iconic march from the coast to the capital soon turned into an organized, creative enterprise that played a crucial role in a wider contest over political representation.[11] Scholars estimate that that there were close to 130 organized BRP groups throughout Chile by the time of the coup, each boasting between eight and ten members.[12] The BRP central committee would determine the subject the brigadas were to address, and the heads of each chapter would scout and plan the location and debate their message. Their work was collective. They emphasized daily dialogue about all aspects of their works. Afterward, they organized discussion about the works they painted.[13] Local chapters and their members retained a significant measure of autonomy as to their final product.

Peter Winn argues that the "battle of the poster and the paintbrush" was critical in Allende's electoral campaign.

> Incorporating party members and independents, *allendistas* and the
> politically uncommitted who favored *los cambios*—"the changes"
> proposed in the Popular Unity program—the CUPs [Popular Unity
> Committees] saturated the working-class and lower-class

neighborhoods with their posters and propaganda, campaign speeches and cultural events. Gradually, their chants of "¡Unidad Popular! ¡Venceremos!"(Popular Unity! We Will Win!) became more powerful and more confident. It was the new politics in the service of an old politician, but all for a New Chile. . . . Pasted on crumbling walls and plastered over public buildings in working-class districts, painted on construction sites and along the river walls and park walks, the messages of the Allende campaign seemed to be everywhere that a worker turned, with their promises of populist benefits and visions of socialist transformations. By September, it was clear that Allende had won the battle of the poster and the paintbrush, while the election had become too close to call.[14]

Yet muralist groups and poster makers emerged from Allende's electoral victory as even more significant political players, engaged in a prolonged physical struggle over key walls throughout the city. The journalist Marc Cooper described the phenomenon as he saw it from his apartment in Santiago, where he witnessed the transformation of city walls into palimpsests of political debate.

> From the upper-story windows . . . splotches of political campaign posters left over from the 1970 presidential race could still be deciphered despite the tattering of wind and bleaching of the sun. . . . But now the street had been plastered with hundreds of new posters. It was like walking through a political rose garden in full bloom. Youth brigades of the Socialist and Communist Parties—the two major pillars of the Allende government—had spent the night covering up any blank wall in sight. And where blank space was scarce, they merely painted and pasted over the previous week's endeavors.[15]

Winn focuses on the relationship between politics from below and from above in the broader context of factory seizures and suggests that the poster and the paintbrush were representative of the success of party mobilization. We can see in Cooper's description of posters, murals, and rayados signs of their central role in the struggle to shape or define the practice of political citizenship. The poster and the paintbrush became significant tools in an ongoing attempt to claim city spaces, transform them into arenas of public political debate, and reshape the mode and limits of political citizenship and practice. By the end of the electoral campaign, brigadistas were so adept and experienced that they could complete their signature slogan (in which they combined the V of "vote," the X of "for,"[16] and the A of "Allende" in one compact image) in mere minutes. They mobilized in such great numbers that they covered city center walls with a reported fifteen thousand of these slogans the night before the election.[17]

BRP muralism offers a fascinating window into the complexity of Chilean urban politics. Until the elections, the brigadistas painted simple, direct slogans. They often called for unity, implicating the pedestrian in a larger, inclusive, and potentially powerful group of Popular Unity supporters. The slogan that they chose for the days before the election, "For Allende, We Will Triumph, Unidad Popular,"[18] imagined a single citizenry, a coherent "we" they could move to vote.[19] Other slogans sought to provide a glimpse of the potential future: "Children Are Born to Be Happy"[20] was invented by an eleven-year-old member of the BRP and reflected the promises of political revolution and social change at the center of the Popular Unity platform.[21]

The BRP's "Another Chile Is Possible" reveals the careful consideration the brigadistas gave to typography.[22] The multicolored letters grow in height and width as the slogan advances, moving from left to right. Intertwined with images of the Chilean flag, this rayado uses form and color to strengthen its textual message and the shape and dimensions of the standard public wall, typically two meters wide and twenty centimeters high, to its full potential. It is emblematic of the BRP's purpose and technique. Rayados like "Another Chile Is Possible" and "Let's Build a New Chile"[23] imagined a community of citizens who could participate in constructing an alternative vision of the state and nation. They did so in central, symbolic areas and in peripheral neighborhoods, making particularly good use of the standardized walls that ringed empty lots and private property throughout the country.

Yet another group of slogans, however, dealt mainly with the particularities of place, with the local concerns of the neighborhoods in which the BRP lived and worked.[24] They were created by and painted for members of impoverished, marginalized communities, adorning the walls that surrounded small local plazas, private homes, and housing projects. Here BRP members used handmade brushes with coarse bristles, the rudimentary materials used in house painting. They employed what they had at hand, including *tierra de color* (a crude pigment), *cal* (lime or whitewash), chalk, and burnt oil, "cheap materials . . . that we used to reach many people."[25] Their slogans were equally immediate and engaged social issues that concerned subaltern groups, ranging from housing to malnutrition to education, and proposed, again, the possibility of a different future for Chile's poorest families.[26] An image painted in the city of Temuco in the south of the country coupled a line from Pablo Neruda, "I Have a Pact with the , People Written in Blood," with an image of a spoon filled with powdered milk, using poetry to connect the immediate needs of local residents, the

BRP's commitment to work for social and political change, and the state's promise of milk for its youngest citizens. They cited the Popular Unity's promise of social and political change and imagined a nation built on new prospects of its children.

These rayados chart an alternative geography of political participation and engagement, one that has not been recorded or examined. They reveal an increasingly politicized urban community that inhabited spaces outside the centers of traditional politics, even if they traveled to and worked in the city center daily. Brigadas claimed or took possession of public space as a means of facilitating political expression and representation for people traditionally excluded from political debate. They proposed an alternative definition of the socialist state and nation and tied these to an inclusive vision of the city.

Allende's victory in turn sparked charged emotions that ranged from panic to elation. *El Mercurio*'s headlines portended economic turmoil, and its pages were replete with notices of auctions and estate sales as many elite families closed their houses and fled the country. Other papers reported hundreds of thousands celebrating on Santiago's streets throughout the night, working a full shift and then returning to celebrate the next evening. But the Popular Unity government would not be ratified until November 1970, and representatives of Chile's center and right-wing groups sought both parliamentary and extraparliamentary means of blocking Allende from being sworn in as president.[27]

The BRP responded with a simple but subtle slogan: "We Won" played off of their earlier "We Will Win," proclaimed success and called forth an image of unity, stability, and support at a time when "victory" was close but uncertain. In the months that followed, the brigadas continued with this public dialogue. Their rayados invoked and called on the Popular Unity to fulfill its campaign promises of political and social change. After Allende's victory, the BRP advocated for the nationalization of Chile's copper mines and supported Allende's commitment to provide every child with a half-liter of milk a day. They reflected on, interpreted, and contested what they saw in debates, speeches, newspapers, and pamphlets.

The BRP engaged in dialogue with the print media. The opposition's newspaper headline was the reference point against which the brigadistas conceived their place in the political process, as they scrawled their responses to newspaper headlines on city walls.[28] They also addressed the language of debates in Congress regarding Popular Unity political and social programs and engaged it in a range of posters, pamphlets, and other texts that circulated through the city's streets. *Puro Chile,* a left-wing newspaper sympa-

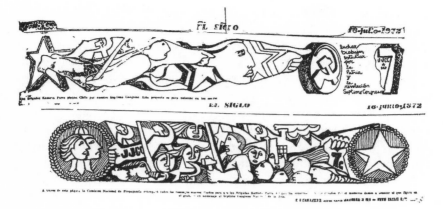

FIGURE 1. Drawing by Alejandro "Mono" González, Brigada Ramona Parra
cofounder. Originally published in *El Siglo*, July 18, 1972. Reproduced in Eduardo
Castillo, *Puño y letra: Movimiento social y comunicación gráfica en Chile*
(Santiago: Ocho Libro Editores, 2006), 107, from the personal archives of
Alejandro "Mono" Gonzalez.

thetic to MIR, published full-page spreads mixing image and text, usually
heavy on words, and asked its readers to cut and paste these on city walls,
bridging the space of the page and the concrete partition. *El Siglo* later published Mono González's sketches on their front pages, which brigade members throughout Chile would adapt and translate on the nation's walls (fig.
1). Similarly, Chilean photographic archives show a wide range of home-
made placards, caricatures, texts, and pictures drawn on cardboard or fabric
and carried in marches and demonstrations.[29] These examples suggest that
BRP rayados were part of a larger tradition, an urban world where people
participated in political debate using a range of public expression that
included text and image, visual practice, and public performance. It is not
surprising, then, that Mono González has called the city wall the "people's
blackboard" or the "public newspaper."[30]

Yet it was the BRP's mastery of technique that allowed them entry into
the broader and changing landscape of political debate. The rhythm and
cadence of their work reflected a highly specialized and flexible division of
labor, their visual production specialized, their assignments compartmen-
talized. Political change was again intertwined with innovation in aesthetic
and visual practice. The *trazador* outlined the text in black. The *fondeador*
followed, coloring the background. The *rellenador* filled in the words or
images with the BRP's characteristic primary colors, usually yellow and

red, even as the trazador continued his or her work. Finally, the *fileteador* retraced the design in a thicker line. The thick black outline was the key innovation that laid the foundation for the BRP's efficiency and aesthetic.

The trazador worked quickly, with rudimentary materials, roughly outlining the agreed-upon vision for the rayado and, later, the murals, on the wall. The *trazado,* or outline, played a role analogous to the design of a coloring book. Other brigadistas, university and high school students, workers, and other party members or members of the community would color in the letters or images. The trazado rendered experience unnecessary. Anyone who was willing to participate could take part in the process. The *filete,* the final pass in black over the initial outline, redefined the borders between the different elements of a rayado by washing over the inevitable splashes of color. Thus the thick black lines represented shadows, and thinner lines highlights. This simple technique lent a sense of perspective and movement to the piece.[31] The trazado was born out of the necessity for speed and communal practice, but it was a technical innovation that ultimately defined the brigade's aesthetic identity and potential role in political communication.[32]

Alessandro Portelli analyzes how people craft their life histories in relation to different narrative modes, constructing key events around which they structure larger plotlines and trajectories.[33] The March for Vietnam was one of these events for BRP founders Alejandro "Mono" González and Juan "Chin Chin" Tralma. Allende's victory was another. Scholars of public political art in Chile have highlighted this shift from graffiti and slogan to mural art as a definitive event that ushered in a new chapter in popular politics and political art.[34] It was after Allende's election that the BRP began to work in images and made the relationship between image and text a central aspect of their means of political communication. For González and Tralma, this shift to illustration amounted to an "explosion" of creativity, image, and color, and signified a political opening and opportunity accompanied by the "dignity" of full political citizenship.[35]

The primacy that the image has enjoyed over text has helped obscure the importance that slogans held in political contests. For example, Susan Sontag has argued that the poster differs from public notices and other textual interventions in public space precisely because the latter is a form of communication in which the image overshadows text. Posters rise above the plethora of words that define our life in cities, the words on walls and signs and bills and money and such.[36] Similarly, the narrative and chronology favored by González, Tralma, and others who periodize Chilean public art define a clear arc in which Allende's election becomes a hard break, a sharp transition from muralists' hand-drawn slogans, or consignas, and rayados supporting Popular Unity candidates to more elaborate murals and posters featuring aesthetic innovation. This rupture marks for them the "flowering" of a new form of political practice.

My research suggests that in 1970s Chile the poster and the mural were intimately entwined with and part of an urban world brimming with text and picture, one that only partially conforms to the clearly defined chronology that suggests a progressive transition from word to image. While there was a definite explosion of public art and image after September 1970, this escalation was tied to a longer tradition of political mobilization that predated the Popular Unity and, as we shall see, persisted after its fall. These influences and continuities between political periods have been obscured by rigid periodizations that take the election as a watershed event.[37]

The introduction of imagery did mark a fundamental change in BRP public political presence and identity, which grew exponentially during Allende's tenure. Their opponents discredited them as armed "thugs" defiling the city, but in so doing they acknowledged the brigadas' growing significance as actors in a widening political drama taking place on city streets and walls. Both the BRP and the Socialist Brigada Inti Paredo were invited to show examples of their work in Santiago's Museo de Arte Contemporáneo (Museum of Contemporary Art) (fig. 2). Mono González became an ever more public figure, giving talks on innovative BRP aesthetics. Internationally renowned artists Roberto da Matta, José Balmes, José Venturelli, and others painted with the BRP, in the streets, and often in the brigada's distinctive aesthetic style. A photograph taken by Fernando Orellana of the BRP working along the route international dignitaries would take to celebrate Allende's inauguration reveals the brigade's new place in the city's political iconography and their turn to image, especially ones that featured primary colors and basic symbols united by thick black lines. It shows, in short, the beginnings of what would become the characteristic BRP style.

BRP members perfected their approaches on the streets and applied to their murals the techniques they had used previously in their graffiti and slogans. The trazado continued to be the most important aspect of their muralism. Where the trazador had sketched letters, he or she began to trace symbols, figures, and bodies, giving the mural shape but not determining color or detail. The rellenador, fondeador, and fileteador followed, quickly completing their signature images. This strict division of labor, and the cadence of their shared labor, resulted in quick, simple, yet colorful and powerful murals that combined image and text into an immediately recognizable "BRP" style.[38]

FIGURE 2.   Poster by Alejandro "Mono" González, Brigada Ramona Parra, 1971.
86.5 cm by 59 cm. Silkscreen. Image reproduced courtesy Hoover Institution
Archives, Poster Collection, CL 82.

Brigada members were engaged in a constant battle over public spaces, a battle that often entailed violent encounters with other brigades and opposition paramilitary groups. They developed tactics to navigate their physical clashes with Patria y Libertad, posting a lookout to warn brigadistas of impending dangers at their back. While conflicts with Patria y Libertad were physically dangerous, brigadistas also competed with mural groups within the Popular Unity. The Communist and Socialist Parties' brigades fought over the walls surrounding the Socialist Party's headquarters adjoining the Plaza Italia, routinely erasing or painting over each other's tags, some of which would last only a matter of minutes or hours. Police would detain public artists and take the opportunity to discipline them. Mural and poster makers would add sugar to their paint and paste when working in especially important areas, aware that they could be forced to eat their own material as an act of punishment if detained and trying to make the experience a little more palatable.[39] They continued to work efficiently, out of necessity, but also out of a belief in the power of simple, direct messages.

The figures brigadistas drew reflected the dimensions, structure, and movement of their own bodies, the way in which they could move, stretching, bending, and reaching to create the mural's characteristic rhythm, the connections between its different elements. "Your body influences the rhythm that one gives to things," González explains. "When we are painting, we move. . . . If I have to trace a text, and I can reach only so far . . . This has to do only with the body."[40] The mural could only be as tall as the trazador could reach with an outstretched arm and brush, and the arch of a particular line could only be as long as the trazador could trace with the movement of his or her entire body. "Your body is in the wall," González continues. "The mural conforms to your proportions."[41] Brigadistas worked without scaffolding or ladders. They sometimes lashed their brushes to a short piece of wood to give them some added length, but this was the only technology they employed. "I, for instance, am small, but my reach extends to two meters and twenty centimeters with my brush," González states. "I even have an elongated brush, which I extended with a stick . . . and which allows me to trace big circles, to extend my body. . . . [That makes] my movements fluid and fast when I am tracing an image."[42] The relationship between human form and urban environment is crucial, for the body of the trazador as it enters into a corporeal relationship with different urban walls, each with its own architecture and its own place in the city, shapes the final image. And in literally placing himself in the act of visual production, González highlights the embodied practice of political citizenship through aesthetic production.[43]

But the murals were also oriented outward, meant to initiate a relationship with the street and the spectator, the driver or pedestrian, in motion.[44] Brigadistas studied the nature of the urban landscape in which the wall was embedded and analyzed the relationship between wall and street. They paid attention to the ways in which the public used space. They were aware of the city as it moved around the wall, and this interest shaped their aesthetic: "Scholars of . . . visibility . . . study all these things—the movement of the spectator, the width of the letters, the typography. . . . We talked about this a lot, we discussed it a lot . . . [and we have] learned all these things in the street."[45] A mural painted at an open-air market could be long and drawn out because it would be carefully engaged by pedestrians, a slow, synecdochic reading in pieces: "You'll have to walk with it, you may have to begin from the end[,] . . . but you'll always have to keep it in mind." But a mural painted at a lively intersection had to be simple, vibrant, and accessible.[46] Here, muralists' consignas had to be especially direct, the letters drawn out in the city center. González argues, "People have to read slogans written with small, stunted letters from up close. . . . As the campaign went on, we slowly began to extend the lines with which we drew our letters. We began to look for form[,] . . . to pay attention to the speed with which a vehicle encounters our design. We would begin with an *A* [drawing out the vowel] and end up with the 'Allende' or the 'Venceremos.' On bridges, or on particularly long walls, our letters had to be longer."[47]

Brigadistas applied the same criteria when they worked with images, displaying the same awareness of motion and mobility. Their figures were simple, direct, and featured no more than two or three symbols per mural. "There is no benefit to complicated images," González believes. "We have to work quickly. We are not artists. We could not be drawing human forms, telling complicated stories."[48] Rather, the murals they painted in these areas could be grasped at once. "There are only two or three ideas," he continues. "There is a hand and a face, a fist, which has to do with struggle, an open hand, which has to do with generosity and commitment. . . . There are only two or three elements. The flag . . . has to do with nation, with identity, with struggle, with human relations. . . . The themes are simple."[49] These murals came to define and embody the BRP style and were repeated in different forms throughout the city. The spectator-in-motion passed in front of these engaging but familiar symbols, glimpsing them quickly, just long enough to piece together a narrative from the relationship, repetition, and juxtaposition of simple images.

The BRP's relationship to and engagement with architecture and mobility was clearest along the Alameda and around the Plaza Baquedano, the

FIGURE 3.   Mural by the Brigada Ramona Parra. http://www.abacq.net
/imagineria/arte.htm. Photograph by Fernando Orellana.

city's most meaningful physical and symbolic intersection. It was the border between downtown and uptown. It was also the city's circulatory nodal point, the place where there was the most traffic and the starting or end point of most rallies. The walls here came to be the most highly disputed and prized walls in Santiago, not only for protesters, but also for muralists, precisely because a mural painted there could be seen by hundreds or thousands of people in a single day. One poignant mural reveals a fist, which clutches a star, which becomes a woman who cries out, proclaiming the connections between the Party and the Nation (fig. 3). The BRP presented similarly styled murals around the UNCTAD construction site. These murals tied the conference acronym to the ubiquitous BRP symbols—the fist, the flag, and the star—painted across the wall's partitions to accentuate the brigadas' support of the project. In each of these examples, the muralists relied on the motion of the passerby traveling at speed through the downtown core to knit together and underscore the connection between individual symbols.

These central murals reveal one of the BRP's organizing technical principles: careful attention to the relationship between city wall, muralist, and spectator. After the state regularized building codes in Chilean cities, urban plots were divided by a cement partition measuring two meters and twenty centimeters in height and divided, at regular intervals, by vertical support beams.[50] The architecture, the physical, material structure of the wall, literally gave shape to the final mural. Brigada members often transformed imperfections in the concrete into features of their murals. A fissure became the lines of a human hand; a notch gave form to the pupil of an eye. The vertical beam was a division that the trazador could either overcome with a cutting, diagonal line or use to lend the mural a narrative structure like that of a film. These murals appeared as individual frames that could be connected by a common theme or the recurrence of images and color that overcame internal tension. In film, an image repeats itself with slight variations as a string of negatives passes before the projector's lens and the spectator's eye, creating the illusion of movement and structuring a visual narrative; in the city, the spectator moves before the mural, which in the case of the BRP often featured simple images, repeated with slight variations. The movement of people in front of the mural gave the images their narrative power, creating meaning from repetition and juxtaposition.[51]

In one mural, painted along Marcoleta Street, the human form faces forward, hinting at an overarching story of movement and progress. Two fists, one clutching the sickle, the other a flower, face each other, fracturing linear narrative. A dove is the center point and the focus of the piece. A stark contrast in background color creates a radical narrative break, shaping a clear relationship between a humble yet resistant figure and an image of redemption and growth exemplified by the dove and the elongated face and neck, now facing forward across the wall's partition and toward a growing, flowering future. The piece's narrative rhythm is initially structured by the breaks in the wall, which lend an overarching sense of dissimilarity and opposition. The trazador could overcome this division with a flowing line that superimposes a sense of coherence, making cohesive meaning out of juxtaposition and cacophony. In each case, the architecture of the wall frames the narrative and lends a particular pace or cadence to the piece, which the muralist then engaged with different aesthetic tools. It is the way in which the trazador and muralista sculpt and reconfigure this architecture by their choice of orientation, flow, repetition, juxtaposition, and color that ultimately shape its message.[52]

BRP mural's aesthetics in slightly quieter areas could be more complicated, fractured, or jarring. A BRP mural painted along Santiago's periphery provides a gendered image of nation and community. Here the flag and the dove are linked, and the dove, in turn, blends into the image of a woman, which is later repeated at the opposite end of the mural. Between these two images, a trio of agricultural laborers huddles, at work. Framing the mural is the image of a woman cradling a bounty of fruit and vegetables. Repetition is a key element. The women, worried or peaceful, have similar shapes, and their flowing hair spans the length of the mural. The flag turns into a dove cupped in the hands of a woman; the dove runs into another female figure; this second woman becomes a field plowed by the men, its bounty held by the last, strongest, woman. The brigada here wove simple images into a complex narrative, proposing an image of powerful and hopeful nationhood built on the labor of the gendered family.

These different techniques ultimately transformed BRP production: what had begun in the late 1960s as furtive slogans were now powerful, hybrid visual creations that pieced together a distinct visual language from various influences and became part of a larger world of public political debate under Allende. The BRP's murals were complicated, contingent, and ephemeral. They were replaceable, erased or painted over as the political circumstances changed or as other groups took possession of a space or a wall. Ephemerality was an unavoidable by-product of art for the streets. It was also essential to the BRP's marriage of politics and aesthetics, and its fluid and ever-changing language of political communication. The BRP transformed necessity into strategy, ephemerality into a mechanism by which to create and participate in political debate. Theirs was a language dependent on the structure of the city that had the potential to transform the urban landscape into an arena of complicated political communication.

The BRP exhibitions at the Institute of Latin American Art and the Museum of Contemporary Art shed light on how the BRP mobilized this visual language as a potent means of political communication.[53] The BRP poster, which González designed to accompany these exhibitions, exemplifies the muralists' visual language and its place within urban politics. It synthesizes BRP iconography and serves as an emblematic object of study. The most striking aspect of this poster is its deployment of color. Reds and oranges, offset by thick black lines, dominate its aesthetic. In the first two levels of the poster's tripartite structure, the national imagery of the deep reds parallel those of the Communist Party; the oranges recall the draw of the copper industry and are repeated in the skin tone of the lone human figure. This play of color symbolically ties the human form, the nation, and industry into the harmony and peace represented by a single dove. At the apex of the image, the Chilean flag has been transformed into a hand whose thumb and forefinger form the shape of a wrench. Nation and industry are expressed as related constructs as they stretch to an open flower whose pistils form an upraised fist. Their interaction forms a narrative in which nation and industry are entwined with hope, determination, and resistance. Here, again, self-fulfillment is achieved in labor, which is intertwined with the transformation of nature. This process of self-realization is inextricably tied to the formation of the nation. Articulating a version of the Popular Unity discourse of nation and citizenship, the BRP simultaneously recalls and reminds the viewer of the central role the Popular Unity citizen can claim in state formation. In short, the BRP works within discourses of nation, modernity, and progress, but it transforms these discourses into a vehicle to make potent demands regarding the role of the state in its citizens' everyday realities.

The move from the streets to the museum was part of the Popular Unity's commitment to democratize art, but it was in the street that visual imagery was collected and coalesced into coherent narratives, where the iconography of modernity, nation, and class were brought together as constituent parts of a larger framework of meaning by pedestrians in motion. This was an overarching aesthetic structure fashioned out of the particular juxtaposition of each element but that adds significance to each isolated term. Murals expressed, defined, and fixed—if only for a moment—a political stance or idea in a way that text alone could not. It was this particularity of visual language that made BRP's public political art a potent means of political participation and expression. In González's words, "Because we painted in the streets, with little time[,] . . . we had to incorporate metaphor and poetry in our language. We had to be aesthetically original. We had to be creative. And our creativity reciprocally made us reach a synthesis, be quick, be efficient."[54]

González presents the battle over public space as politically and spatially marginalized groups' efforts to reclaim their right to participate in the political process, to simultaneously assert their place in both a city that historically pushed them outside of its planned and ordered center and a political system that historically silenced their political voice: "So, we are saying that the reclaiming of these spaces allows popular groups to participate, to fight for their rights, to fight for their rightful place."[55] In this sense, public art became revolutionary: it was a means through which subaltern groups created place, in space and in politics, and in so doing, were able to determine their own destiny. At stake was emotion and pride, opposed to the daily humiliations, the symbolic violence of class conflict. González remembers, "In that time we appropriated space. We were government. [We were] masters of owned our own destiny."[56]

Aesthetics, color, and form play a crucial role in this practice of political citizenship. "It is our own popular aesthetic," according to González. "How we beautify poor, abandoned spaces, how we make do in the spaces where we live."[57] Beauty, aesthetics, and style appear as eminently political and, as such, legitimate subjects of the study of political history.[58] Significantly, González defines this as a popular aesthetic, one that used the materials available in the everyday of the city's impoverished shantytowns. We have seen how this popular aesthetic reflected the concerns of the pobladores. It was an aesthetic language through which pobladores, workers, and students could interpret and articulate their political ideas, bring their interests into conversation with and make them part of national political debates and imaginaries.

After Allende's victory, the brigadas painted openly in a number of "marginal" areas, and the painting of a mural became a ritual, a performance in which people from these communities could participate, "a social event . . . for poor people" and an opportunity for popular expression.[59] González explains, "Rich people have their events, when they marry, etc. Here, we do it in shantytowns, on the street, where people participate, co-operate; one contributes a bit of coal, one contributes a piece of bread, paint, and everyone works, they identify with it."[60] González's assertion, "We were not artists," becomes particularly significant here: he emphasizes that these performances were not aesthetic experiments but political experiments; they were public performances that called into being new forms of political citizenship. Neighborhood residents were invited to participate in BRP paintings in an effort to fashion community. Many painted or colored inside the trazador's design; others acted as lookouts in contested areas. In emphasizing these distinctions, González locates political muralism in a larger social world defined by class and place. He roots it in a broader narrative of political change over time, and in the physical, grounded experience of political conflict located in the bustle of the streets. Muralism emerges from these oral histories as a new form of Chilean public political engagement that "collapsed the distinction between imagining community and participating in it."[61]

Historical records wrest posters, murals, and graffiti from the context in which they were made, shown, and experienced.[62] Ephemeral visual products gain their full significance only as part of a string of images, next to, pasted over, or juxtaposed to other words and images and available to drivers and pedestrians as they weave through public space. Oral histories allow us to establish a sense of context and place and of the process by which ephemeral forms of visual expression became integral parts of political discourse and debate. They hint at a complex geography in which posters were put to use. A number of my interviewees remember seeing these posters carried as placards in mass marches, pasted on the sides of buses that wound through the city, at farms and factories during volunteer labor campaigns, and in long series in the city center or on the stages upon which politicians spoke during protests.

Read through the lenses of political studies, visual culture, and oral history, posters and murals emerge not as isolated objects or as finished, fixed forms of visual and political expression but as part of a longer process of public political contest that created new political sites, spaces, and imaginaries. Indeed, a close, interdisciplinary analysis of the everyday use of political posters and murals furthers our understanding of the relationship between urban politics, visual culture, and what Mauricio Tenorio-Trillo and William E. French have called the visual "imaging" of nation and citizen. French argues that in Tenorio-Trillo's hands, "imagining" has become "imaging." Tenorio-Trillo has chosen this word to underscore the importance of form, style, and façade not *over* content but *as* the content of nations, nationalism, and modernity. At the same time, "image" captures the roles of elites in creating a vision of the modern Mexican nation through writing, architecture, painting, and science[,] . . . ingredients in the creation of the national image that do not yield a holistic model or ideal type of nationalism. Instead they sustain a multitude of voices within a conceptualization of nationalism and national image that is not neatly defined, but contradictory and always in the making.[63]

WALDO GONZÁLEZ HERVÉ AND THE SHAPE OF POLITICAL CITIZENSHIP IN CHILE

Waldo González Hervé's work was foundational in the history of Chilean design and sheds light on a complicated relationship between constructions of nation and the image of citizenship in the late 1960s and 1970s. González Hervé was the first to graduate from the Universidad de Chile's program in visual arts with a specialization in poster and propaganda. He worked as a professional graphic designer, poster maker, and ceramic sculptor and taught at the Escuela de Artes Aplicadas and the Universidad de Chile, counting the graphic designer Vicente Larrea among his students. He was prolific during the 1960s and early 1970s, designing and producing two posters a month between 1971 and 1973 when he worked for the Polla Chilena de Beneficiencia, a state-run lottery whose funds were earmarked for government charity and social programs.[64]

The posters González Hervé produced for this organization loomed large in the national imaginary. González Hervé recounts that his posters, whose message was aimed at the people (*el pueblo*), were displayed in public and private spaces alike: "The first poster I made disappeared immediately, as people took them home, and we had to triple production."[65] He drew from a variety of influences, ranging from the Mexican muralists, who used public art to pose social challenge to the Chilean painter and woodcutter Pedro Lobos, who depicted the Chilean working classes' everyday diversions. His works are visually and symbolically complex. He experimented with "unusual materials," including the thin paper used for kites, by then a symbol of childhood innocence threatened by the stark reality of poverty and a common referent in Victor Jara's "nueva canción." He elaborated a distinct methodology that gave equal weight to image, text, and color as three facets of his own "visual code," a style that lent weight to the combination of national symbolism and social concern that was characteristic of his work.[66] His distinctive style combined national symbols and pertinent social concerns. One poster, published in September 1971, advertised a lottery of five billion escudos, with proceeds going to a national Christmas charity. The image is a study in contrast of colors. At its center, a ribbon turns into a human hand as it embraces two children. The ribbon is the color of the Chilean flag, while the children are deep black, their lines, hair, and clothing traced in white, referencing the black clay pottery of the Chilean south. The national symbolism is twofold, as the flag is supported by the traditional, folkloric yet utilitarian ceramic production that stands in for an autochthonous "Chilean" people. The caption is telling: "For mom, for dad, and for me . . . health has become a right not a privilege." This poster mobilizes, then, intersecting narratives of nation, tradition juxtaposed and joined to a shifting story of citizenship rights.

A number of his most characteristic posters feature women and children's bodies. González Hervé drew his human shapes in thick lines, exaggerating the size of arms, legs, hands, and feet by favoring an ascending perspective, making a point to draw strong, broad bodies, often coloring them carefully in varying shades of brown.[67] González Hervé's February 11, 1973, Polla poster builds on this tendency, depicting families of dark-haired, broad women, children, and men waving flags and drinking milk (fig. 4). The caption reads, "With the People and the National Milk Plan, We Will Abolish Malnutrition." The message is readily evident: with milk, and in particular the half liter of milk the Popular Unity promised the nation's children, the national family and national body would grow strong. González Hervé's series, then, valorizes the national, traditional, and popular, linking aesthetic form, use of color, and textual content to create a linear connection between nation, politics, and social issues.

Too often, in the context of the political polarization that marked Allende's Chile, posters have been analyzed as direct manifestations of their authors' support or opposition to the government, or signs of immediate direction "from above." Yet González Hervé designed posters for the state-run lottery, which raised money to address issues of social inequality, as well as covers for the right-wing paramilitary group Patria y Libertad's magazine.[68] The disjuncture between the government-sponsored Polla and the Far Right journal is jarring in an era that, scholars of Chilean politics argue, was characterized by growing political polarization. González Hervé's explanation is clear: he himself was apolitical, interested only in communicating with "the people" and powerfully committed to exposing and ameliorating social, not political, problems.[69]

The ease with which he pulls apart his political ideology and social commitments does not by itself challenge the notion that there indeed existed

FIGURE 4. "Con el pueblo y el plan nacional de leche." Poster by Waldo González Hervé. 1973. 46 cm by 65 cm. Offset. Reproduced in Eduardo Castillo, *El cartel chileno, 1963–1973* (Santiago: Grupo B, 2004), 68.

an increasing, almost overwhelming polarization (although it does impel the historian to question the pervasiveness or nuance in this story); nor does it undermine the links between political programs and social questions on which the Popular Unity platform was built, a relationship that also structured much of the era's public art. But it does reveal the benefits of looking beyond neat dichotomies of Left and Right that structure many studies of Chilean politics and focusing instead on particular individuals and works and their place in a broader "landscape" of competing urban and visual practices and products.

González Hervé's retelling also hints at the importance of reading oral histories as complicated constructed texts. The narrative arc of his story is, overall, a tragic one—of an important and respected artist who was black-listed after the coup and found work as a teacher but not a producer of poster art.[70] This is the story of a calling unfulfilled. What makes this tragic, in his account, is that he was not politically active, merely socially conscious. This is an interesting formulation, but it is one that tacitly accepts the military's discourse that those who were politically active somehow deserve to be repressed or, at least, that it is understandable that they be marginalized. We can see how the military's official discourse shapes the memory and explanation of the past if we read the structure and form of González's narrative, even if against the grain. González Hervé's telling suggests the close relationship between past and present, filtered through decades of silence.

THE VISUAL PRODUCTION OF NATION AND CITIZEN: THE LARREA GRAPHIC DESIGN SHOP

The set of posters produced by Luis Albornoz, Vicente Larrea, and Antonio Larrea in the late 1960s and early 1970s drew from a range of potent images—symbols of nation, community, industry, childhood, and harmony—that carried weight in the Popular Unity platform and in the era's visual culture and put these symbols and signs together in creative and flexible forms. They were produced quickly, one day to the next, in response to or engaging with diverse sources, including posters, murals, and graffiti—even the informal placards on which protesters scrawled messages and carried through the city in public demonstrations.[71] Their work reveals a subtle and ever-shifting understanding of the role of visual culture in the construction of "nation," "community," and the terms of socialist citizenship.

The series of posters they produced to promote collective, volunteer labor provides insight into this complex process of imaging and imagining.

The Popular Unity recruited volunteers to work in the reconstruction of outlying areas of Santiago after a violent earthquake struck the central valley soon after Allende's election. The posters transformed natural disaster into a metaphor for the reconstruction of a nation brought together by acts of solidarity that cut across class and gender lines.[72] Form, color, and a playful, almost joyous tone unite this series. An initial poster, framed by a simple textual message, "Working for Chile: National Volunteer Efforts," places a jumbled world of agricultural, industrial, and urban labor slowly emerging from the devastation of the earthquake on the shoulders of a young child clothed in working-class garments featuring the Chilean flag (fig. 5). Another poster in this series, "Chile Rebuilds United," presents another stage in this process of reconstruction. An ordered public has risen out of initial confusion, one complete with housing, schooling, and various forms of labor but still under construction. A third, "Chile Works for Chile," portrays a smiling family in front of a tractor, surrounded by workers and the Chilean flag. These examples draw a clear relationship between volunteer labor, the family, and the construction of a *national* community.[73] This relationship is naturalized in paired images. One poster, "Life Is Reborn out of Reconstruction," features colorful flowers emerging from a fissure in the earth (fig. 6). Another, calling Chileans "To Work," uses the same color palette but portrays two birds building a nest, seamlessly tying natural imagery to symbols of family and communal labor (fig. 7).[74] As David Kunzle writes, the "earthquake is interpreted allegorically, not just as a natural disaster but as the spirit of the new Chile breaking through the barren rocks of the past."[75] This is, of course, not a linear sequence of posters but a complex series of images that presents a narrative of progress within a web of connections and equivalences.[76] This type of equivalence is evident throughout the era's visual culture: "The cog of the machine becomes the rising sun, the wrench is like a guitar, the pick is like a book."[77] In the Larrea and Albornoz volunteer labor posters, these relationships build an image world in which a cohesive, harmonious national community becomes an expected, teleological result of the gendered labor of individuals, a symbol of national solidarity that encompasses and subsumes rather than highlights class conflict.

These relationships continued beyond the singular "event" of the earthquake. A poster published to publicize the second day of volunteer labor in May 1972 is dominated by an outstretched fist holding a short shovel (fig. 8). The shovel, in turn, is transformed into a Chilean flag. Below, a pencil sketch recalls this imagery: young women and men wave flags and hoist shovels as they parade through city streets. Again, a community

¡ A TRABAJAR POR CHILE !
MOVIMIENTO VOLUNTARIOS DE LA PATRIA

FIGURE 5. "¡A trabajar por Chile!" Poster by Luis Albornoz,
Antonio Larrea, and Vicente Larrea, 1972. 54 cm by 74 cm. Offset.
Reproduced courtesy of Fondo Documental Larrea Albornoz,
Archivo de Originales, Facultad de Arquitectura, Diseño y
Estudios Urbanos (FADEU), Universidad Católica de Chile.

comes together around public gathering, volunteer efforts, and national
pride. The fist, the flag, and the spade are all drawn in a thick black line, a
technique that both lends weight to the image and recalls the visual lexicon
of the street brigades, making explicit the close connection and ongoing
dialogue between different forms of public art.

These arguments and relationships come through strongly in a series of
prints produced for the Popular Unity campaigns in support of the nationalization of copper. For decades, copper had been the main Chilean export

FIGURE 6. "Con la reconstrucción renace la vida." Poster by Luis Albornoz, Antonio Larrea, and Vicente Larrea, 1972. 75 cm by 109 cm. Offset. Reproduced courtesy of Fondo Documental Larrea Albornoz, Archivo de Originales, Facultad de Arquitectura, Diseño y Estudios Urbanos (FADEU), Universidad Católica de Chile.

FIGURE 7. "¡A trabajar!" Poster by Luis Albornoz, Antonio Larrea, and Vicente Larrea, 1972. 77 cm by 110 cm. Offset. Reproduced courtesy of Fondo Documental Larrea Albornoz, Archivo de Originales, Facultad de Arquitectura, Diseño y Estudios Urbanos (FADEU), Universidad Católica de Chile.

FIGURE 8.   "¡¡Chile trabaja por Chile!!" Poster by Luis
Albornoz, Antonio Larrea, and Vicente Larrea, 1972. 58 cm by 76
cm. Offset. Reproduced courtesy of Fondo Documental Larrea
Albornoz, Archivo de Originales, Facultad de Arquitectura,
Diseño y Estudios Urbanos (FADEU), Universidad Católica de
Chile.

and the almost sole source of foreign currency. Transnational corporations
may have owned copper mines, but miners played a pivotal role in national
politics and labor conflicts. State ownership of copper mines was an essential aspect of the Popular Unity's nationalist platform, and copper stood in
for independence from foreign influence. Celebrating the nationalization of
Chilean copper and drawing on a poem by Pablo Neruda, one of the Larreas'
emblematic posters provides a synthetic image of Chilean society (fig. 9).
It portrays a group of people, a series of ideal types ordered as a rough

FIGURE 9. "Cobre Chileno." Poster by Luis Albornoz, Antonio Larrea, and Vicente Larrea, 1972. 76.5 cm by 110 cm. Reproduced courtesy of Fondo Documental Larrea Albornoz, Archivo de Originales, Facultad de Arquitectura, Diseño y Estudios Urbanos (FADEU), Universidad Católica de Chile.

pyramid whose apex is a child holding a Chilean flag over his head and whose base is made up of copper bars that serve as a literal and metaphoric foundation for the national community. Arranged carefully, this pyramid effaces class hierarchy but maintains other differences. Peasant, doctor, miner, and teacher occupy parallel positions. Race and ethnicity remain potent means of preserving the presence of historical difference. Urban professionals look whiter, while rural working classes, including miners, fishermen, and *huasos* (cowboys), look darker.[78] This hierarchy is gendered as well: while male figures hold evident signs of professional identity, the dominant female image is that of the middle-class mother. Artists deployed these symbols of status, class, and gender in ways that revealed a complex understanding of the role that color, dress, mannerism, and bodily comportment played in creating and marking social distinctions.[79] Image and text together articulate a clear message: the Popular Unity is not simply a radical or revolutionary break with tradition, but instead proposes a new form of community that grapples with rather than elides historical inequalities. Where official Popular Unity discourse called for the abolition of class, race, and gender difference, the Larrea poster engaged this difference as constitutive of an egalitarian socialist national community.

This interpretation initiates an analysis of the ways in which the ordinary and everyday, and not only monumental or official spaces and symbols, provide a basic iconography and style for the construction of Popular Unity national imaginaries.[80] The poster accomplishes this task visually and textually. Neruda offers a network of interconnected terms drawn from the everyday that define the boundaries and terms of political discourse:

nation, plains and peoples
sand, gravel schools, homes
resurrection, fist, offensive
order, march, attack, wheat-fields
struggle, greatness, resistance.

Visually and textually, then, public art produced specific constellations of concepts and interpretations. It structured a "chain of equivalence" between potentially unrelated symbolisms and terms.[81] In this poster, nation and community are symbolized in the fist. The unification of people as a cohesive entity, resistant and strong, is tied to the need for order and sequence. A vertical analysis of Neruda's poem and the poster's imagery together uncovers implicit connections between nation, urban and rural land, resurrection, and political struggle. A horizontal reading of the poem's penultimate line integrates the military organization of ordered troops with the naturally tall, straight contours of wheat fields. As Foucault reveals in his analysis of Borges's classifications, establishing hierarchies and relationships between concepts and grammars is a process of suturing relationships of power and discourse.[82] This here becomes a visual process. Posters propose and communicate a visual language, grammar, and lexicon that knit together a densely articulated political discourse in which everyday objects can be understood as ciphers of larger social "truths." This is a visual system in which ordinary objects like helmets, shirts, and shoes take on potent political significance.

Gathering apparently disjointed, dissonant symbols into a cohesive portrait, the Larreas fashioned powerful meanings from juxtaposition. As in the cinematic montage or the photo-essay, the production of meaning, narrative, and truth lies in the interval, in the moment between fragments. The poster is a project of collection and re-collection, of remaking an existing historical and political narrative into a cogent, unified image. The Larrea poster "Chile Puts on Long Pants" similarly ties nation, skin color, and class to the transition from childhood, presenting nationalization as the liminal point between children's *pantalones cortos* (short pants) and the adult nation's and citizen's *pantalones largos* (long pants), between dependence and independence (fig. 10).

The Larreas' production forms part of a broader catalog of ephemeral public posters that engaged the campaign to nationalize copper and that connected a diverse network of institutions and organizations in support of nationalization.[83] A piece published by the Socialist Party's Vanguardia advertising agency illustrates the ways in which Chilean poster makers interpreted this theme of copper-as-nation or copper-as-sovereignty (fig. 11).[84] Divided into two semantic fields, its apex is a textual space.

CHILE
HAS DECIDED
ITS DESTINY.
THE ANACONDA COMPANY
WANTS TO TWIST IT!
LET'S DEFEND OUR COPPER, LET'S DEFEND CHILE!

This text establishes a juxtaposition between Chilean autonomy and the foreign-owned Anaconda Copper Company. It is a play on space and a play on words. The organization of the text and the emphasis on the verb *torcer* (to twist) recalls the serpentine contours of the anaconda. This stands in direct contrast to the linear order of the phrase below, which calls for Chilean autonomy. We have, then, a dichotomy between the insidious influence of

FIGURE 10. "Chile se pone pantalones largos." Poster by Luis Albornoz, Antonio Larrea, and Vicente Larrea, 1971. 51 cm by 75 cm. Reproduced courtesy of Fondo Documental Larrea Albornoz, Archivo de Originales, Facultad de Arquitectura, Diseño y Estudios Urbanos (FADEU), Universidad Católica de Chile.

FIGURE 11.   "Chile decidio su destino. ¡La Anaconda quiere torcerlo!" Poster, Editorial Vanguardia, n.d. Dimensions unknown. Reproduced courtesy of Hoover Institution Archives, Poster Collection, CL 78.

serpentine international capital and the well-defined sovereign nation whose autonomy is intimately, naturally tied to the linear shape of its physical form and national boundaries. This symbolism is echoed in the visual section of the work. The poster's central axis is a disembodied fist. The fist is an emblem of community, resistance, and determination. In this case, the Chilean flag emerges from the clenched hand and makes up its wrist, finally bleeding seamlessly into fingers grasping a copper bar. The fingers themselves are symmetrical, linear digits, simultaneously evoking the geography of the nation and the rigid lines of a brick of copper. The colors employed strengthen the continuity between national community and copper. The reds of the Chilean flag are mirrored in the auburn highlights of the copper bars' faded oranges; these oranges are themselves evoked by the skin color of Chilean faces and fists. In this way, copper becomes a metaphor for the nation and the nation becomes linked, naturally, to a self-realized miner and autonomous mining industry. This is the picture of a national community defined in terms of class and ethnicity and by geographic imagery, national symbols, and modern industry.[85]

As Sontag writes, "Posters and public notices address the person not as an individual, but as an unidentified member of the body politic."[86] Posters and murals paradoxically both presuppose and help produce the "modern . . . public—in which the members of a society are defined primarily as spectators and consumers."[87] They are, in short, simultaneously part of a broader visual landscape and productive of new geographies of political art and practice. Patricio Rodríguez-Plaza studies these visual landscapes or environments "without which the era is unrecognizable."[88] He finds that the "city supports the mechanical reproduction that characterizes the political poster, not only technically, but also in making possible the gaze of the passerby who lights his or her eye over and over on the singular or insistently serialized poster."[89] Public art also and reciprocally reshapes cities into arenas of political conflict.[90] Murals and posters emerge from and also create an urban world where people participate in a complicated political struggle on and from the streets.

The street also helps sustain a new way of seeing the city. Posters, murals, graffiti, and other forms of public art should be treated as the basis for "an entire mode of thinking about lived urban space," for thinking about how the experience of lived urban spaces came to be intensely political.[91] Francisco Brugnoli, a pioneer of conceptual art rooted in "found objects" and the city and an intermittent collaborator with muralist brigadas, has similarly argued that "the city is a space and a forge where we experienced and experimented with the world." Recalling his generation's perspective, he suggests, "Our work was not about murals, or about decorating walls. We were concerned with revealing the city's framework, mapping its interconnections, seeing what circulated through it and how. We saw the city as a web that could be analyzed [through art practice.] And by analyzing it, we exposed and revealed it."[92] In other words, public art is not only the object of analysis but also an "interpretive concept," an analytical prism through which to understand the complexities of urbanism.[93] Ephemeral objects and public practices are therefore important material for the study of political history.

. . .

Diana Taylor's definition of performance studies, situated between the archive and the repertoire, between text and performance, gives us a way into the relationship between history, memory, visual practice, and urban politics. For her, "What performance and performance studies allows us to *do* . . . is take seriously the repertoire of embodied practices as an important system of knowing and transmitting knowledge."[94] Taylor focuses not only on written sources but also on embodied acts, on texts but also repertoires, practices, performances and the scenarios in which they occur. "Instead of privileging *texts* and *narratives*," Taylor writes, "we could also look to scenarios as meaning-making paradigms that structure social environments, behaviors, and potential outcomes." The scenario forces scholars to pay attention to "features well theorized in literary analysis, such as narrative and plot," alongside physical or corporeal milieu and behavior "not reducible to language."[95] It forces Taylor to "draw from various modes that come from the archive [and] the repertoire" and to study the relationship between "writing, telling, reenactment, mime, *gestus*, dance, singing."[96] Taylor's scenario, and her emphasis on text and writing, motion, and practice, has the potential to broaden political historians' understanding of the sites and forms of political conflict. It is especially significant because it forces us "not to 'translate' from an embodied expression into a linguistic one . . . but to recognize the strengths and limitations of each system," to think about urban practices and performances as politically significant in and of themselves.[97] It is ultimately a theory of physicality, embodiment, and action as central to the production of citizenship. As such, it sheds new light on the study of public art and the production of urban publics and political debate.[98]

But Taylor's theorization of the scenario is equally essential to rethinking how visual practices and oral testimonies intersect as meaning-making practices. "Testimonial transfers and performance protests . . . are two forms of expressive social behavior that belong to the discursive workings of what I have called the repertoire," Taylor writes. "The embodied experience and transmission of traumatic memory—the interaction between people in the here and now, whether in giving testimony, in psychoanalysis, at a demonstration, or in a trial—make a difference in the way knowledge is transmitted and incorporated."[99] Taylor opens room for oral history as another system of knowledge and memory between the archive and repertoire, the permanent and ephemeral. Oral history emerges as an embodied practice of remembrance that is structured by and around visual traces, a creative exercise anchored in and organized around the record of past visual practice. In this light, oral histories are not only partial and open-ended; they also illuminate the apparent paradoxes inherent in the study of the Popular Unity.

My interviews of BRP members shed light on the problem and promise of oral history for this period. Especially contentious are the connections and contradictions between the muralist brigade members' narratives that emphasize independence, creativity, and masculinity in the fight for the streets and the "official" Communist Party rhetoric of disciplined and peaceful action that most often informs the members' recollections and retellings. Chin Chin Tralma, in particular, wrestled with these conflicting strands. After a number of formal interviews and informal conversations with the cofounder of the PC's muralist brigade, Tralma told me that while brigadistas were committed to and part of a revolutionary democratic project, the struggle for the streets "necessitated" an exertion of violence (and masculinity) in order to respond to threats and protect their claim to the streets. This is a controversial point in BRP narratives. The image of the brigades as paramilitary institutions, *brigadas de choque*, was widely disseminated in the opposition press. This became a particularly difficult subject after the coup, when the promise of an armed revolution came to be seen not only as a myth, but as a myth that legitimated the military coup. Brigade members have often denied their role in instigating or participating in violent confrontations. In the last of a series of interviews, Tralma related his group's violent clashes with other brigades on the Left and and the Right. His narrative was strongly gendered. Violence, for him, was not a measure of heightened polarization or increasingly uncontrolled conflict but a symbol of potent masculinity, an expression of political vigor and masculine aggression that secured rather than invalidated political citizenship.[100]

This is not a tale that undercuts BRP "official" narratives or points to the fallibility of memory as a historical source. Nor is it a moment of slippage, of authentic admission breaking through years of crafted narrative. Instead, the contradictions in this retelling enrich the broad sweep and connections between urban and political practice that come through so strongly in his telling. The "essential artfulness" of Tralma's oral history holds together or reconciles the apparent paradoxes and productive tensions that shape the history of this contentious period. Oral history organized around the traces of visual practice is itself an embodied performance of memory that complicates both individual and official narratives shaped by years of silence and repression. As an invaluable source for a political history that juxtaposes the study of visual and material culture to a critical analysis, oral histories like Tralma's allow us to consider complicated, even paradoxical perspectives on the past and shed light on the potent, overlapping, contradictory forms of political citizenship and identity played out on and produced in city streets and on walls.[101]

In the early scenes of *Salvador Allende*, Guzmán transforms the mural into precisely this sort of complex prism—an object of study, a methodological anchor, and an interpretive guide that, when followed carefully, leads the viewer to new connections and new interpretations. My own analysis of political posters, murals, urban practices, archives, and oral histories sheds light on how ephemeral forms transformed the city into an arena for political conflict and turned ephemeral practice into a vehicle for enacting new forms of political citizenship. It proposes a new way of seeing spaces, streets, and walls: as arenas of political conflict and citizenship. The next chapter examines these connections in an analysis of urban documentary film.

5.   The Politics of Place in the "Cinema of Allende"

The 1960s marked a turning point in Latin American film: it became a viable means of reflecting on and participating in the radical forms of political change that characterized postwar Latin American state formation. Until then, most Latin American film industries lacked the infrastructure necessary to produce more than a handful of commercial films. Only Brazil, Argentina, Cuba, and Mexico had developed significant national systems of cinematic production. The New Latin American filmmakers drew inspiration from French New Wave and Italian neorealists' tendency to film outside of the studio system. They experimented with new paradigms of cinematic production and representation to counterbalance technological and financial constraints. They used lightweight cameras to film on location. They turned to semi- and nonprofessional actors. They tackled immediate social concerns and articulated critiques of pressing social and political and issues.

Allende's tenure as president was studied closely by documentarians, who took to the streets with their cameras to record, analyze, and fashion their own narratives regarding the relationship between politics and the city. In this chapter, I turn from politically significant forms of cultural production created on city streets and walls to documentary films and documentarians' writings. I treat these not as transparent records of urban politics but as vehicles through which documentarians analyzed, engaged in, and commented on urban politics. Filmmakers articulated a radical new cinematic language or style based on representations of public political mobilization. They took advantage of technological changes that made cameras and sound recording equipment mobile. As they roamed city streets, their cameras examined the intimate connections between national political change and the everyday material worlds through which the

majority of Chileans engaged, understood, and expressed political sentiment and identity.

THE POLITICS OF THE NEW LATIN AMERICAN CINEMA

Latin American filmmakers subscribed to a common political commitment
and a belief in the adverse effects of underdevelopment. They did not, however, share a stylistic or aesthetic model. As Zuzana Pick argues, the incipient movement was characterized by "dynamic heterogeneity": filmmakers
brought with them an array of powerful yet dissimilar ways of conceptual-
izing and practicing their craft.[1] It is not surprising, then, that by the late
1960s these filmmakers sought to define a common ground and to find, in
Fernando Birri's words, "a unity in difference."[2]

The idea of Latin America was the key to this unity. The 1967 Viña del
Mar festival is hailed as the first festival of the so-called New Latin
American Cinema (NLAC). Politically committed, socially conscious, and
aesthetically innovative filmmakers from across the continent gathered to
show and discuss their movies in Viña. They pieced together a discourse of
Pan-American unity, a construction of "Latin America" that shaped their
conception of cinema and their filmmaking practice.[3] The "manifesto-doc-
uments" they produced were at once "theoretical statements made by the
filmmakers" and historical objects that "recover parts of Latin America's
past . . . that oftentimes go unnoticed."[4] Writers and filmmakers did more
than simply nourish themselves on the concept of Latin America and
related discourses of modernity and progress. They also reimagined Latin
America as a single body whose citizens shared an experience of what
Walter Mignolo has called the "darker side" of modernity.[5]

NLAC filmmakers refuted a "modernizationist conceptualization of
development" and offered "alternative models of social change" that could
reveal a "'new' Latin America."[6] They conceived of a continent-wide experience of underdevelopment. They also saw a shared need to break with the
economic, political, and cultural forms of (neo)colonialism that prevented
Latin American development and progress. The filmmaker Glauber Rocha's
celebrated, Fanon-inflected argument regarding the revolutionary potential
of hunger is a foundational, emblematic text. His writings on the "cinema
novo" and the aesthetics of hunger are a damning critique of underdevelopment but stay well within the discourses of development, progress, and
civilization.[7] Rocha couched his thesis regarding the detrimental effects of
economic dependency in the binary language of civilization and primitivism. Hunger was for him a "symptom of social poverty" and, ultimately,

"the essence of society." Herein lies the crux of his argument: "The normal behavior of the hungry is violent, but the violence of the hungry is not primitivism. . . . [T]he aesthetics of violence are revolutionary before they are primitive; it is the moment when the colonizer becomes aware of the existence of the colonized."[8] For Rocha, then, dependent capitalism produced the violence of hunger, which was in turn a vehicle for politicization, awareness, and analysis.[9] Similarly, Birri called for a cinema "which awakens consciousness[,] . . . which helps the passage from *sub-desarrollo* [underdevelopment] to *desarrollo* [development], from sub-stomach to stomach, from sub-culture to culture, from sub-happiness to happiness, from sub-life to life."[10]

NLAC filmmakers proposed a parallel transformation in cinematic and political structures.[11] They envisioned new systems of cinematic production and distribution as well as radically new visual and aesthetic languages. The lens, a traditional symbol of objectivity, scientific precision, and modernity, could be used to record, engage, and ultimately transform social realities that purely aesthetic filmmakers too often ignored. NLAC filmmakers "used documentary or the documentary style as both a witness to reality and a tool to analyze and, in principle, transform that reality."[12] Looking through their cameras, filmmakers could structure powerful arguments using a distinct visual language. Only then could film incite political action and be a tool for social change.[13]

Italian neorealism served as a model for a system of cinematic production in which it was "possible to make films on the streets . . . [with] average people . . . [and] imperfect technique" but which remained connected to and expressive of a "national culture."[14] NLAC filmmakers moved from the studio to the street, taking advantage of new, lightweight technologies for recording image and sound and focusing on nonprofessional actors or subaltern subjects in their fictional and documentary films. As the Chilean filmmaker Miguel Littín argued, this system could turn material disadvantage into aesthetic innovation: "We lack cameras, we lack film, we lack technical equipment, we lack everything, but we must never lack the desire to create a new and revolutionary cinema[,] . . . [to] search for a concrete way to be able to produce as our own country develops."[15]

While the NLAC was fed by a hemispheric project of political and aesthetic critique and innovation, its filmmakers recognized and developed national and local peculiarities. They turned to "authentic" national traditions as a basis for their political and aesthetic challenges. This "valorization of national culture" through film had roots and parallels in other cultural movements. In Chile, for example, members of the bourgeoning "nueva canción" movement sought to ground their politically charged songs in diverse national traditions of aural and popular memory. The folklorists Violeta Parra and Victor Jara embarked on ethnographic projects, traveling throughout the country in search of "lost" vocal and instrumental legacies from which to build their nationalist, politically inflected folklore.[16] Members of the NLAC worked from a similar premise. They sought to fashion a "decolonized culture" or "decolonized aesthetic" that "originated in the affirmation of living popular traditions" and, in many cases, was based on the direct participation of each nation's subaltern groups.[17] In a manifesto they published in support of the Popular Unity, Chilean filmmakers argued that an "authentic identity can only be founded upon national cultural roots after the abolition of foreign aesthetic models . . . and [a] return to the original sources of a national culture."[18]

The NLAC encouraged worker, student, and campesino participation in both production and representation. They screened versions of their unfinished films to their subjects and actors, sought to incorporate their suggestions in the final cut, and found alternative venues of exhibition, such as factory floors, schools, and public plazas, often the same spaces in which these films had been shot. In so doing, they challenged the division between film authorship or production and spectatorship or reception, which emerge in their work as active and interrelated processes. Maybe most significantly, they proposed that the subaltern subjects of their films could also act as authors of these works."[19] Fernando Solanas, for example, thought of his classic *La hora de los hornos* not as a finished product or spectacle but as a "film-act" whose purpose could not be achieved and whose trajectory was not complete until the spectator could participate in discussing, criticizing, and analyzing its intertwining "aesthetics and meaning." Birri, in turn, argued that film represented the "under-reality" that accompanied "underdevelopment" but that this representation demanded or required a response, an active "taking of consciousness" on the part of the spectator.[20] Projection for Solanas and Birri bridged performance and representation; for both, the spectator became a "social being," an energized and engaged participant in an ongoing process of discussion and debate around the experience of underdevelopment through watching and engaging film.[21] The act and the site of spectatorship became crucial to the purpose and interpretation of films.

In search of this type of "cinema of participation," NLAC filmmakers most often turned their gaze on local experiences, on the *subrealidad*, or subreality, of poverty and hunger, to understand the tangible, material experience of underdevelopment. Nondocumentary filmmakers eschewed trained actors and instead recorded "ordinary" people performing everyday realities.[22] Documentarians trained lenses on "marginal" people in situ, on the streets and in their homes. They lingered on bodies and gestures, clothing and objects, and understood these as important parts of local, political, and social geographies of everyday life. They revealed to their viewers the local landscapes that were enmeshed in but simultaneously transcended the particularities of place and that were always and inextricably tied to larger structural, national, and continental inequities. They portrayed "marginal" peoples, places, and practices as aesthetically and politically significant worlds.

For fiction and nonfiction filmmakers alike, the signs, symbols, and material culture of the local and the quotidian were the building blocks for the aesthetic language used to examine the relationship of the urban to the political. Their films were "hybrid forms," experiments in the "the breakup and renewal of symbolic representation and discourse through the constant interaction of the local with the national and the transnational."[23] Filmmakers could turn the urban and political margins into a platform on which rested a new type of historical thinking, a new set of political identities, and new aesthetic practices that reinserted "the peripheries" into a broader arena of political debate. Visual practice played a key role in the contest over legitimate public conflict and helped create new means and mechanisms of public debate.

Paul Schroeder Rodríguez suggests an alternative classification of the NLAC between the frame of national politics and the cadence of aesthetic innovation.[24] He finds that the NLAC "evolved out of neorealism" in two phases—the "militant" and the "neobaroque." The first, militant phase occurred in the early 1960s, when filmmakers were "part of a populist project of political, social, and cultural liberation." These filmmakers fashioned an aesthetic that "privileged documentary modes of representation" and rehearsed a transparent outline of social realities. The second, neobaroque period unfolded out of the militant phase. Participants "saw their work as part of a more complicated project of developing the cinematic equivalent to the emergent civil society's pluralist political discourse" and against the censure of authoritarian rule that characterized Southern Cone military regimes. The "uniting factor" in these two eras was a systematic critique of power structures and social relations achieved through experimentation with form and style. If the militant privileged realistic aesthetics, neobaroque filmmakers saw aesthetic innovation as the basis for political transformation. Schroeder Rodríguez proposes that there was an overall transformation in aesthetics, in which filmmakers' preference for neorealism gave way to a complicated critique of representation, objectivity, and realist aesthetics.[25] Ultimately, "by highlighting the rift between signifier and signified," the neobaroque films "call attention to the constructed nature not only of films, but, crucially, of social relations as well." They used techniques and tropes that subverted the illusion of transparency in order to challenge the truth claims of (authoritarian) states and their attempts to circumscribe debate into a monovocal narrative.[26] Chilean filmmakers played with political and aesthetic languages, combining documentary and neobaroque critiques in surprising ways and doing so under both democracy and dictatorship.

CHILEAN DOCUMENTARY FILM IN THE 1960S

The Chilean government founded Chile Films under the umbrella of the CORFO in the late 1950s.[27] Another important shift in national cinematic production occurred in the 1950s and 1960s, when Chilean film criticism and production took two parallel paths—the inauguration of "cine clubs," on the one hand, and of the Center for Experimental Cinema in the Universidad de Chile, on the other.[28] Established in 1958, the *cine club* of the Universidad de Chile held weekly screenings of foreign films, edited its own film journal, and sponsored a radio program. In turn, Aldo Francia's 1962 Viña del Mar cine club became a nodal point of the New Latin American Cinema outside of Cuba in 1967 when it hosted the touchstone Viña del Mar festival. The founding of the Film Institute at the Universidad Católica and the Universidad de Chile's Department of Communications and Center for Experimental Cinema, run by Sergio Bravo until 1967 and Pedro Chaskel thereafter, quickly followed. The Center sponsored and screened continental NLAC films like Solanas and Getino's *La hora de los hornos,* bringing influential images to emergent Chilean filmmakers. It quickly became the seat for the new style of production associated with Chilean documentary cinema in the 1960s and 1970s and the home of leading NLAC filmmakers in Chile.

Sergio Bravo, who directed the university's Center and influenced the generation of filmmakers I study in this chapter, spoke to the relationship between "Latin American film" and the particularities of the Chilean context. "We wanted to find a new language," he recounted, "to become totally independent from what we considered to be official Chilean cinema."[29] The quest for "a new language" is a recurring theme in the NLAC. Bravo credited Birri, especially his particular brand of "critical realism," as a key influence.[30] He also emphasized the importance of national and local circumstances in a foundational narrative of Chilean film and its unique grammar. "We were fairly mad," he recounted, "discovering the light, our southern light, which is a maritime light of great chromatic richness."[31] This pairing of traditional artisanal production and a particular "southern" light locates the Chilean iteration of the NLAC naturally in a wider national context of cultural production that sought to recover the value of the traditional and folkloric as the basis of an independent, nationalist cultural politics.[32] Bravo's own documentaries focused on "excavating and revealing local popular customs and practices." They were part of a larger project of reimagining the Chilean cultural landscape in relation to the value of the "traditional" and "popular."[33] Douglas Hübner suggests that Bravo created a "fundamental shift in experimental cinema and the new, let's say, new Chilean cinema."[34]

Five feature films were produced in Chile between 1968 and 1969, using scarce resources, and shared equipment. Raul Ruiz directed *Tres tristes tigres;* Aldo Francia, *Valparaíso mi amor;* Miguel Littín, *El chacal de Nahueltoro;* Helvio Soto, *Caliche sangriento;* and Carlos Elsesser, *Los testigos.* All five turned a critical eye on the politics of class in Chilean society, looking to highlight how the political and the social informed the everyday lives of the country's poor.[35] The films of Ruiz, Elsesser, Francia, and Littín were made consecutively and shot with the same camera.[36] The first four films are widely considered classics of Chilean cinema. Ruiz's film is dedicated to the Chilean poet Nicanor Parra and echoes Parra's ironic "antipoetry." Like Parra, he questioned traditional forms of literary and visual representation, placing the camera in a "realistic" position among the actors rather than in an "omniscient" position encompassing the action, highlighting the lens's limited perspective by allowing actors to wander in and out of frame and freely obstruct the camera.[37] Francia's *Valparaíso mi amor* paints an incisive portrait of the parallel physical and social geographies of the eponymous city, drawing out the interconnections and radical differences between the bustling port and the impoverished shantytowns that dotted Valparaíso's characteristic hills. Littín's *Chacal,* based on exhaustive ethnographic and archival research, charts the social dimensions of violence, gender, and poverty. Together, these directors challenged accepted modes of fictional film production (filming on location, on city streets, working from sociologically informed research, and encouraging community participation in all decisions) and representation (including an often critical engagement with neorealism and a search for a new language with which to examine national social realities). They showed a preoccupation with social questions and a willingness to organize political arguments around an analysis of individual lives and the everyday concerns of poverty, hunger, and inequality.

Chilean urban documentaries in turn focused on everyday realities to define a broad, contested image field in which to critique and represent the sites and strategies of politics.[38] The filmmaker Federico Salzman argues that in Santiago the street was "a territory in dispute, and a disputed territory that made everything possible, from combat and struggle . . . to artistic expression, creativity."[39] Yet, facing a significant shortage of film stock, filmmakers had to make quick decisions about just how to represent urban politics, and street protest in particular, in a variety of iterations: "miner's disputes, fisheries, *cordones industriales*, political protests, and land seizures."

> We had to think it through and carefully when the time came to make aesthetic decisions. . . . I remember that we were working on a documentary about informal coal miners in the area of Cabildo, Petorca, La Ligua . . . and we had the chance to protest with them, or follow them as in their march against Codelco. . . . I remember that we only had two small fifty-foot rolls [of film stock] and we had to follow them for quite a few kilometers, shit, we stood by the sidewalk and waited for the full parade to pass asking ourselves, Well, how are we going to film all of this? All the stock we have is, I mean, we can't miss. So, first, we made sure we had different scenes, that one noticed that there were changes in focus, in who supported the protest, and then the different groups and structures through which people supported the march, who came with their families[,] . . . but of course there were hundreds of types, so we had to give a lot of thought, a lot of time with pen and paper in hand.[40]

Exploring the creative relationship between politics, film, and the city, the filmmaker Francisco Gedda suggests a complex interplay between objective reality, the camera's subjective frame, and the historical context and cultural assumptions that permeate the aesthetic work. Fictional film and urban documentaries shared a "very strong testimonial character," as filmmakers "took to the streets . . . to give testimony."[41] It was in the act of editing, he argues, that filmmakers "deciphered" the "richness" embedded in this empirical information, to untangle the "codes" and "details within the image, the photograph, the frame."[42] His interpretation recalls Barthes's *punctum*, where the image contains the seeds and suggestion that escape even its creators' intentions. It also assumes an intricate relationship between the "transparency" of city streets and the argument or narrative fashioned from the engagement and analysis of this reality.[43]

The street is here a territory of political dispute. It is also, at once, a site of contention over the limits and potential of visual practice. Salzman recounts, "You saw all sorts of tricks . . . from where the photographer placed the camera, when he or she used traditional lenses, when he or she used wide angles in order to make everything look grander."[44] In short, filmmakers "had to come up with a strategy" to unravel the relationship between politics and the city. They were constantly considering and reconsidering the significance of protest, participants, composition, trajectory, and symbolism; what to capture and what to reject; how to piece together cogent visual and aural arguments in the editing room; and how to best represent these arguments visually. The struggle for the streets laid the foundation and provided the raw material for a narrative of political engagement in which the camera was an important tool. These works chart the dual formation of political and cinematic public spheres.[45]

Recalling his early work, the documentarian Carlos Flores highlights the effervescence in political protest as a defining characteristic of these overlapping publics. He remarks on the sheer numbers of people brought together: "Seeing that mass of people . . . so large . . . was the most impressive thing. Filming in those conditions was uncomfortable because of the size and fervor of the marches."[46] For him, protest was a "material manifestation" of successful political organizing and potent political conviction. His was a subtle recollection of the social significance of geography and body, of the small-scale spectacle of protest.

> You'd see a tall, blond person, with straight hair and light eyes, and you know beyond a doubt where they live, what car they drive, where they work, and where they're going to spend their vacation . . . and it was impressive to see, to see masses of these well-to-do folks march and chant. They had a chant that was . . . that was uncommon . . . "No meat *huevón*, no lard, *huevón*, what the hell is this, *huevón*?" But it was well crafted because the "huevón" gave it a certain circularity. . . . And it corresponded with the Right's claims, "No meat *huevón*, no lard, *huevón*, what the hell is this, *huevón*?" It echoed the landowner's exhortation [in an elite accent], "What's wrong with you, *huevón*," and they took it on, interesting that they would embody such a caricature. "What's wrong with you, *huevón*?"[47]

Flores interprets protest as a gendered, classed performance on which the camera played and engaged.[48]

Chilean documentary film must be understood as a means of engaging in a broad political dialogue written on the building blocks and aesthetics of gendered and classed performance. I focus on the documentary films produced during the Popular Unity, paying particular attention to Patricio Guzmán's *La batalla de Chile* and Pedro Chaskel and Héctor Ríos's *Venceremos*. These filmmakers experimented with new forms of visual representation, part of a broader process of reimagining the nature and limits of legitimate political engagement. Their films' visual language and analytical substance must be read as part of the wider tradition of cultural production *as* political engagement, of cinema as a means of entering into a broader debate about the nature and limits of politics and citizenship.

DOCUMENTARY FILM: PRODUCT, PROJECTION, AND EXILE

Carl Fischer proposes that we "can read the documentary" as a "chronicle" of "fleeting temporalities": the vibrant debate that characterized political conflicts on Santiago streets during the Popular Unity, the violence of the coup, and the historical perspective of exile. These temporalities are tied in turn to multiple political "performances" in film, including the recital of multiple masculinities, "which can help rethink the ways in which the history of the Popular Unity is written in film and literature."[49] Fischer's emphasis on plural temporalities is broadly important for an analysis of the apparent paradox or contradiction that animated the urban documentaries of the Popular Unity period. They are works filmed on local city streets but often completed in the international diaspora of exile. They are invaluable material and visual representations of a particular time and place, though many were destroyed precisely because they illustrated the particularities of political struggle, targeted by military officials censuring cultural production and by filmmakers looking to protect themselves or others who could be identified from the celluloid record. They are significant documents of Popular Unity politics, even though many were never shown in the era and others debuted in Chilean theaters only years or decades after their completion. My emphasis is on film not only as historical document but also as critical visual practice, a means of political analysis.

The coup's violence is certainly significant here, shaping documentary films's multiple temporalities first and foremost through repression and censorship. The military outlawed the projection and circulation of the era's films. The most famous example of this is Guzmán's *La batalla de Chile*. The director's uncle smuggled reels of footage out of the country; Guzmán and Pedro Chaskel edited the raw material into a three-part film while in exile in Cuba; the footage was first shown to high school students in Chile almost two decades later, a performance Guzmán made into a brilliant cinematic analysis of repression and memory, *La memoria obstinada*.

The story of erasure, exile, and completion, though crucial, intersects with a more complicated, difficult to trace local history of circulation or projection. Chilean documentarians attempted to replicate or experiment with a form of "direct cinema" in which filmed materials and early cuts of documentaries were shown to their subjects, often where they were shot, with portable projectors.[50] Cubans innovated this practice, incorporating rural poor people's reactions to, reading of, and suggestions regarding early cuts of unfinished films into their final products. Sergio Trabuco Ponce recounts his experience with Raúl Ruiz to a fellow colleague, Darío Pulgar: "We did the same with Raúl, in a documentary that I produced with him about the Juntas de Abastecimientos y Precios (JAP), when we interviewed Minster of the Economy Fernando Flores. We filmed it and then showed his responses in the *población* with a portable projection." Pulgar responds: "This element of direct cinema is clear in Raúl's [fictional] films. Rodrigo Maturana's dialogue in *Palomita blanca* could not have been done without direct cinema. . . . Direct cinema also helped us make the documentaries the Socialist Party commissioned."[51] Similarly, Trabuco speaks to the Peruvian filmmaker Jorge Reyes about his work with Nelson Villagra, star of the fictionalized film of violence and imprisonment, *El chacal de Nahueltoro*. Reyes compares the practice of showing material or film "on location" to the *tren de la salud* (health train), which carried physicians to "remote" areas, small towns and the countryside, without medical services. He recalls showing *El chacal* in the city's penitentiary, engaging the prisoners themselves in conversations about social issues explored in the film ranging from incarceration and sentencing to the death penalty. These are examples, for Trabuco and his interviewees, of the ways in which "direct cinema" could help filmmakers participate in the production of public spheres of political debate and concretize the types of publics they saw as crucial to a participatory politics. I pay close attention to contexts of circulation, projections, and reception where possible because, even when destroyed by military violence or completed in exile, many of these films were made on and shown in Santiago city streets, shantytowns, and factories.

Though Guzmán's *La batalla* was completed in exile, parts of the trilogy that makes up the film, including its final chapter, had originated in an earlier short, *La respuesta de octubre*, which presented the cordones in which it was filmed as spaces of political debate and experimentation. Guzmán recently recounted his first contact with Jorge Müller when filming in the factories of Cordón Cerrillos and Vicuña Mackenna: "[The film's] purpose was to show other workers how self-management was possible. . . . Jorge and I had a clear preference for 'planos secuencia,' long takes that would not fragment the action. . . . Our work was based on these two factors—a camera on the shoulder and improvisation. . . . *La respuesta de octubre* won the Circuitos Mobiles prize, sponsored by Chile Films, at the end of 1972. . . .

Five years later, I broke down the negatives and included it in the third part of *La batalla* (which I called 'El Poder Popular')."[52] In other words, films like *La respuesta* and *La batalla* were meant to create the type of democratic dialogue valued by proponents of "poder popular" to interpolate a public through the act of filming but also through projection and debate— different facets of what I call "film practice." *La respuesta* was shown in Chile before the coup.

Venceremos was also part of this tradition drawn from direct cinema. Shut out of commercial venues, this film and others were projected in poblaciones, in factories, and in rural areas in an attempt to garner support for the Popular Unity. Hübner recalls that they "would show our films for free in shantytowns, and began knitting a countercultural web . . . among socially conscious filmmakers." This began in the late 1960s and continued as a significant movement deep into the dictatorship. The projection of these films, and the debates they engendered, sponsored an alternative geography of political spectatorship that went hand in hand with the films' revalorization of the city's "invisible" spaces and people. Hübner argues that there occurred in this era a "qualitative change in the spectator," as viewers became both increasingly politicized and trained in the reception and analysis of visual material.[53] "Peripheral" spaces became spheres of political debate in these screenings and debates.[54] The multiple temporalities of cinematic production and overlapping geographies of projection, reception and debate are significant. I keep them in mind even as my emphasis in what follows is the study of documentary film itself as a means of political engagement, expression, and, ultimately, analysis.

PATRICIO GUZMÁN AND *LA BATALLA DE CHILE*

Guzmán's work proposes a familiar if tense relationship between place, politics, and documentary visual practice. After returning to Chile from Spain soon after Allende's election, Guzmán began to search for a cinematic language and corresponding system of production that would allow him to adequately film and analyze the political situation.[55] However, he struggled with the influences of NLAC's diverse approaches to "committed" documentary filmmaking and with the political and cinematic languages available to him in the national context. As Lopez argues, "Guzmán's search for an appropriate mode of cinematic representation for Chile under the UP [Popular Unity] parallels the increasingly blatant contradictions of the UP conjuncture."[56] By the time he and his five-person group (the Equipo Tercer Año, or Third-Year Team) began work on *La batalla de Chile*, Guzmán had experimented with a journalistic chronicle of events in *El primer año* and the dense, argumentative piece that relied heavily on interviews and giving voice to workers in *La respuesta de octubre*.[57] *La batalla* began as an analysis of the "complex, multifaceted social and political condition of Chile during the Unidad Popular" and was structured around an equally complex system of production and representation, which the filmmakers thought necessary to appropriately examine this political and social reality.[58]

The Equipo proposed a dialectical "nucleus" method that relied on concerted political analysis and rigorous planning to pinpoint "the key areas" or "battlegrounds" where political change and social struggle were enacted. Working from a close study of the press, the Equipo identified fifteen to twenty of these nodal points in the city.[59] They then divided these points into three central categories or sections, forming a physical and conceptual political map or landscape that gave shape to their film schedule. They settled on three key sections (Economics, Ideology, and Politics and Law) associated with particular locales or places (factories, universities, Congress, and the Supreme Court); these sections were then split into smaller units that corresponded to political and social problems that fit under these three encompassing conceptual umbrellas ("the rural question," "movement of goods," "wages and prices," etc.) In short, they determined the *spaces* of political debate in Santiago—the city's factories, universities, and canonic spaces of governmental politics—and related these to particular political practices. But the Equipo's purpose, and its particular talent, was to find the overlooked *places* where political debate became linked to the everyday experience—where economic crises were felt at the dinner table or at the market; where quotidian discussions and debates occurred over coffee, in the home, outside the factory gates, and in the streets; where the political became inseparable from economic inequities; where these were forced together by people engaged in complex everyday struggles.[60]

Even this short discussion of the Equipo's methodology begins to reveal the importance that Guzmán's crew gave to the city's political geography and to the significance of symbolic and everyday places within this landscape. They pinned up a map where they traced an ever-changing network of central and peripheral sites of political struggle. They guided themselves by this script-map, literally writing their understanding of political struggle onto the urban landscape and transforming the conceptual and practical frames into a loose structure that would guide their shooting and narrative.

The group, in short, imagined an intimate relationship between politics, the city, and the documentary. Guzmán described his early films as great murals on which the city's dynamic political debate was painted day to day, echoing the importance of the city's walls as sites on which a visual form of political participation was continually articulated, erased, and redrawn. *La batalla*'s script-map allowed the group to further explore this relationship between politics and place. They created an innovative production system, a radical methodology through which to understand and analyze the city's dynamic, quickly changing political geography; this methodology, in turn, led them to fashion a creative aesthetic language and narrative techniques based on the valorization of the local and everyday.[61]

La batalla focused on, and revealed, the myriad local and everyday sites where the macro, political, and socially significant intersected with, became inextricable from, and were expressed through personal and bodily concerns and realities. The Equipo believed that they could properly understand and analyze larger political and social realities that too often went unexamined by recording and engaging the visible and apparent manifestations of political struggle, the "counterpoint" created by a "dialogue between [political] opposites" and their respective "public actions."[62] The filmmakers took to the city's public spaces and its hidden, private places, focusing on quotidian symbols, on what protesters scrawled on their poster boards, on how marchers were dressed and on their outward political discourse. They kept an eye on those things that were so ubiquitous as to be overlooked. They attempted to make apparent and knowable that which is often taken for granted in the everyday and, in so doing, to reveal the everyday as politically and socially significant.

In her groundbreaking treatment of Guzmán's work, Ana Lopez claims that his oeuvre is defined by "a central representational characteristic," a critical understanding of and an innovative attempt to redefine the ways in which "documentary and fictional modes of filmmaking were combined and transformed" in order to revolutionize the political and social function of cinema.[63] The film's earliest sequence illustrates how the Equipo grappled with the tension between documentary and fiction. The film begins with a long sequence in which the sound of air force jets cut through the darkness of the screen before finally giving way to the striking image of the presidential palace, shattered by the jets' missiles. This image of La Moneda in flames became one of the emblematic images of the military coup. But the filmmakers return to it only at the very end of the film's Part II. The majority of the documentary is an exploration of politics in the period that met its end with the coup. The disjuncture between the film's opening, with the sounds and sights of radical military violence, and its jarring "return" to the dynamism of political conflict lends the film a distinct and complicated temporality. It sets the "present" of the coup apart from, and in opposition to, the "past" of Allende's Chile. It also gives the viewer the power of hindsight, the objectivity that comes with distance from the event, of an outcome foretold. This objectivity is supported by the recourse to a seemingly omniscient narrator who contextualizes the images on the screen.

However, the rest of the film retreats to explore the minutiae of the Allende period, and the relationship between present and past, and between objectivity and artifice, is rendered more problematic. We soon see that the crew is not interested in "explaining" the relationship between past and present, or between objective lenses and subjective narratives, transparently. Scene after scene in this section is structured similarly. The camera slowly pans along the length of a crowd that is itself slowly moving along the city's main thoroughfare. Protesters' rhythmic chanting gently drifts up to the filmmakers' microphone. But then the film cuts sharply to street level, initiating a series of frantic sequences in which the camera follows Guzmán as he weaves his way through the crowd, holding before him a microphone that captures the overwhelming din of people's chants, slogans, and arguments. The camera charges through the multitude, moving frantically among protesters so that the viewer struggles to decipher where the filmmakers are traveling, to whom they are speaking, and what political arguments are being made. The tension between the two perspectives is tangible: the filmmakers highlight the dissimilarity between the immobile camera that orders a massive crowd by filming it from a safe remove and the handheld sequences taken in the midst of a group of loud, disorderly, passionate marchers weaving their way through the streets and around the camera. These juxtapositions rupture the illusion of narrative coherence, undermine the authority of the narrator's present-tense story, and make visible the choices the filmmakers made as they pieced together their study.

The film's aesthetic creativity amounts to a formal challenge to the illusion of the lens's ability to simply record an objective reality, and this challenge develops formally throughout the film. Its most charged scenes are those in which the filmmakers immerse themselves in the crowd, swiveling and panning to follow marchers as they drift in and out of frame, adjusting to the crowd and to the changing urban terrain on the fly. Each of these shots begins with Guzmán clapping his hand over his microphone to allow the postproduction team to synchronize sound during editing. He can be heard shouting instructions to the crew, directing Jorge Müller, the camera operator, throughout the scene, his voice drifting in over the sound of the crowd. As Guzmán reacts to the action, Müller pans the camera dramatically, adjusting focus as quickly as he can. They allow the viewer to see and hear the technical scaffolding on which the film is built. This has a paradoxical effect: it simultaneously highlights the objectivity of the lens (as it gives the idea that the camera records events "as they were") and reveals just how the Equipo constructed its narrative (as it hints at all that the camera misses as it struggles to take in this complicated reality and exposes the Equipo's role in determining both what the lens records and what the film chooses to portray). The Equipo's reliance on sequence shots and frantic pans that reveal the limits of their gaze, along with their tendency to immerse themselves in chaotic street scenes that challenge and complicate any idea of order or context, undermines any claim to objectivity and undercuts the absolute authority of the omniscient narrator's present-tense narrative. Amid the instability created by these contradictions, the viewer is left with the responsibility of piecing together a coherent narrative from the visual and aural "evidence" collected on the streets, culled from interviews and footage on the streets.

The product is a film that appears to capture a knotty present in which politics is always changing and challenged, in which the smallest hint, the subtlest gesture carries and reveals political intent and becomes political practice. The film's street scenes, its analysis of public politics, are "written" in this particular visual style. They illustrate the everyday embodied process through which political debate is enacted. Its sequences call attention to the political importance of the body, of gesture, and of the material culture of political language. It stands as an example of the filmmaker Jorge Sanjines's argument that "every action, every word, every gesture takes on an unequivocally political tone, made more radical every day by the growing conflict due to the internal contradictions of this time of change."[64] Yet this is a film whose visual language simultaneously calls attention to the filmmaker's particular preoccupations, to the possibility that another structure, form, or focus would reveal a political reality very different from theirs, from the imbrications of the political in the personal. The sequence shots in particular "simultaneously [invite] and [obstruct] direct identification with the events recorded," creating "an epic work poised between direct and dramatized, immediate and mediated modes of apprehending historical facts."[65]

Guzmán's Equipo continues to explore the relationship between form and content, the visible and invisible, and the "personal" and "political" in a crucial scene in which they move from the streets into an enclosed, private apartment.[66] The Equipo pose as a camera crew from the opposition's Canal 13 television station sent to interview a family about their voting patterns in the municipal election in order to gain access to the right-wing family's home. Here, again, the entire scene is shot as one long sequence, and again the filmmakers establish meaningful contrasts, this time calling attention to the relationship between the visual and the aural in film. As Guzmán interviews different family members regarding their political beliefs and choice, Müller's lens wanders around the house, focusing on the minutiae of their everyday life, calling attention to trinkets and knickknacks, rhetorically linking what the apartment's location, view, and decorations reveal about the family's class status to the political sentiments expressed through words, gestures, clothing, and pins in the apartment and on the streets. The scene is a treatise on the way in which politics and class intertwine, how material landscapes and fabrics are suggestive of this relationship, expressed artfully through the tension between image and sound that builds throughout the scene. Here, *La batalla* closely examines the relationship between body, clothing, gesture, and accent as the material reality by which class is articulated and reinforced.[67] Nelly Richard writes that fashion codes "are one of the languages through which cultural identities are expressed in a dialogue of voices (canonical or parodic) with the already-constructed discourse of social class and sexual representations."[68] *La batalla* delves into the mutually constitutive relationship between class, place, and political participation, as well as that between political discourse and material realities that include geographic location, symbolic objects, and meaningful if often unintended aspects of bodily movements.[69]

Moreover, by allowing the camera to wander around the apartment, eschewing cuts in favor of a meandering path from face to face and object to object, the filmmakers slowly build a sense of place as the scene develops. Guzmán and his editor, Pedro Chaskel, use cinematic techniques commonly associated with fiction films, including complex sequence shots and the juxtaposition of sound and image, to build a sense of narrative.[70] Significantly, the story the film tells is one written in the language of politics, place, material worlds, and telltale bodily reactions while simultaneously and self-reflexively playing with and commenting on the paradoxical coexistence of the objectivity of the lens and the artificial nature of the way in which this narrative is assembled. In this way, *La batalla* proposes a cinematic language with which to understand a changing political landscape. And this cinematic language forms part of a new, changing vocabulary santiaguinos were using to debate political change as inextricably linked to, among other things, class and the material and visual environment within which class gains its meaning.

The filmmakers echo the tactics they had used to great effect in public and domestic places in the documentary's second part, which narrates the days and months before the coup. Filming the funeral of the murdered constitutionalist naval officer, Captain Arturo Araya, Müller's camera plays upon the armed forces' dress uniforms, contrasting the dark fabrics, which he overexposes to a degree that all detail is lost in inky blackness, and the pristine white of the immaculate gloves and the shine of official metals. The stark division between black and white, alongside a very limited range of grays, seems carefully chosen in this point of the film, reflecting the film-makers' belief, expressed by the omniscient narrator, that this is the particular place in which the coup begins to appear as a viable reality. The use of documentary and fictional techniques to build a sense of narrative out of colors, objects, bodies, places, and sounds is complicated, and can be read in both the structure of particular scenes and in the context of the documentary as a whole.

In the film's second act, the crew began to move away from street level more often, extracting the camera from the crowd to take advantage of the distance afforded by second- and third-story perspectives. This pattern of increased distance and growing preference for bird's-eye views becomes particularly striking in the scenes that frame the film's analysis of the failed coup attempt—the *tancazo*—with which Part I closes and Part II begins. This sequence begins at a large pro–Popular Unity rally. The crew films Popular Unity supporters marching on downtown streets, piled atop excavators and horse-drawn carts, forming a caravan of trucks belonging to different nationalized industries. From high atop a building, Müller's films a sea of people completely filling the frame, jumping up and down in waves, chanting, "Whoever doesn't jump is a *momio*."[71] From this perspective, we see that the plaza outside of La Moneda is filled, spilling into side streets, as Allende speaks. The next cut transports the viewer a few blocks north, revealing the Universidad Católica's downtown campus. The crowd's chants from outside La Moneda are audible, giving a sense of the relative proximity to the previous scene and highlighting the contrast between streets replete with marchers and the jarring emptiness of the avenues around the university, where only the silhouettes of students guarding thoroughfares littered with refuse from clashes break the monotony of deserted space.

Cutting back to the central square, the film lingers on the president's speech. Allende orates, his voice echoing from the loudspeakers, while the camera pans slowly over but not among the crowds. Whereas earlier scenes had played with contrasts between oral and visual narratives, the filmmakers limit themselves to supporting Allende's words, to strengthen his claims with their visuals. He speaks about the historic nature of the gathering, or *concentración*. He highlights its size, which overflows the limits of the plaza and fills downtown Santiago: "Never before in our History has there been an act of the magnitude and importance of this one." As Allende speaks, Müller fills the frame with images of Popular Unity supporters. A group wearing miners' helmets is shown from above and then again from street level; without cutting, the camera then pans slowly toward the surrounding buildings, where children hang from all the windows and balconies, their joyous waving contrasting perfectly with the solemn, disciplined crowd below.

In a subtle but crucial departure from the aural structure that marked the film's earlier vignettes, the filmmakers now eschew street and crowd noise, laying Allende's speech over pure silence and allowing his words to pace the editing. "We have had to create new methods in order to obtain part of the extraordinary, enormous crowd that fills these streets," he intones. And, as he continues, drawing an aural map of the city's central streets occupied by his supporters, Guzmán and his editor, Chaskel, follow his pace in the editing room, providing the images that presumably correspond to these same thoroughfares. "Moneda, Agustinas, Amunategui, Ahumada, Morandé, Huérfanos, Teatinos, most of the Alameda," Allende avers, his voice beginning to rise.

The accompanying images are striking. A multitude of flag-waving members of the MIR is followed by a line of tractors rolling down Amunategui and through the frame. People crowd every conceivable open space on Ahumada. Placards, posters, and banners provide a visual break, leavening what is otherwise an overwhelming, homogenous sea of bodies. "Never before in the history of Chile have the people been as present or more combative," Allende concludes stridently, and the filmmakers allow the noise of a cheering crowd to rise along with his voice, overwhelming the hitherto controlled and pristine soundscape. "Here, we can feel that History, to which we have entrusted our right to create a future defined by justice and freedom, and to open for ourselves a path to socialism." As Allende's words die down, the narrator articulates the cost of a copper miners' strike that ended shortly after this massive demonstration. Polarization, the omniscient voice informs us, is something that might allow the opposition to overthrow the presidency. "They have only one recourse left to them," he continues, before the camera returns to street level among people running frightened as six tanks and a regiment of soldiers fire upon the presidential palace during the "tancazo." The narrator's words are no longer playfully challenged by the film's cinematic form; rather, the film's aesthetics are increasingly traditional, preoccupied with the need to record and report the apparently overwhelming and ever-changing present, marked by the threat of impending violence. These subtle formal shifts reveal the crew's increasing distance from the cinematic language that they established in the early part of the film, a language that no longer seems adequate in the face of growing political and physical conflict.

This transition becomes even clearer in the following sequence. The film's first part ends at this point, with one of its most shocking scenes. In one of the few instances in which they incorporate material filmed by someone other than their cinematographer, Chaskel and Guzmán include the infamous images shot by an Argentine camera operator, Hendrickson, who recorded his own killing, his camera remaining fixed on the army official who fires on and wounds him mortally. The chilling image of the shouldered camera clattering to the ground alongside the cinematographer's crumpling body stands in for the inadequacy of the personal point of view and of the insufficiency of the camera's narration from street level. *La batalla*'s Part II begins with the same unsettling footage. But this time, Guzmán contrasts the Argentine camera operator's heartrending point of view with his team's own footage, taken from behind the shooter. Incorporating this change in camera placement reveals the privilege of distance. It is the team's position, slightly removed, outside of and apart from the action, that allows them to fully represent this new phase of increasingly violent struggle, while the dangers of having feet on the ground is only too clear. Part II of *La batalla* goes on to explore the problematic and privileged role of distance in cinematic representation.

The effects of political repression, and the first inklings of how visual practices would shift in its wake, is illustrated in the final images of the film's second part, shot by Chaskel in his living room. These scenes record the Chilean Air Force's Hawker Hunter fighter planes cutting through the late morning sky, the sights and sounds that open the movie, before cutting to the junta's initial televised address.[72] *La batalla* here shifts away from the movement of the streets and into the private spaces of apartments and families. Part II concludes privately and furtively, forced inward by the threats levied against public expression in Chile for years and decades after the military takeover. This unsettling shift neatly marks (and symbolizes) the end of Allende's experiment and the success of the coup, which the filmmakers call the "insurrection of the bourgeoisie." The ending of the film's second part, then, prefigures the military's control of public space, its ability to use the threat and reality of political violence to quell public protest and force citizens from the streets.

But, again, the bombing of the presidential palace is the singular event that structures the documentary. The sound of fighter planes skimming over Santiago's rooftops frames Guzmán's film. Slowly insinuating itself into the viewer's consciousness, building to a menacing rumble as credits roll over a black background, the sound marks the documentary well before the first shocking image of La Moneda in flames erupts on the screen at its opening, the repeated impact of the missiles loosed from these planes raising smoke and flames from the neoclassical building. As we have seen, the film-makers then cut away from these emblematic images of the day of the coup to the protests surrounding the 1973 municipal elections just over six months earlier, the camera and its kinetic gaze wandering frantically through the sea of marchers on city streets, building a story of political polarization and public conflict that, we now see at the conclusion of Part II, leads inexorably to the film's apex in the military takeover of the government. Though the documentary spends the majority of its time focused on the politics of the Popular Unity, the initial sequence of the bombing of La Moneda has already shaped the tale. Part II merely closes the circle. The denouement anticipated is the shadow that gives shape to the film, lending tension to the juxtaposition that the filmmakers establish between the different sites and forms of public protest.[73] The narrator and the title cards that introduce different political figures with information about the position they would later hold in the military government only add to this feeling of the documentary as a chronicle of a coup foretold.[74]

Thomas Klubock notes the stark difference between Guzmán's two connected films, *La batalla* and *La memoria obstinada*, in precisely these terms. Whereas *La batalla* takes place almost entirely in public space, *La memoria* is filmed in living rooms and schools. Whereas the Popular Unity–era documentary restlessly contextualizes the events and people it films, seeking out clues about the surroundings and place in the city, *La memoria* provides a sense of universality to the intimate and personal narratives the camera records by failing to establish place. We know something about the students who watch *La batalla* and discuss the documentary in response to Guzmán's probing questions, but we know less about how to place these protagonists and sites in historical context.[75] Klubock's answer is compelling. The ways in which *La memoria obstinada* re-creates this schism between public and private reveal the success of the junta's project over its almost seventeen-year rule.

> A number of writers have argued that collective memory is rooted in space, tied to markers, icons, memorials, and places. In *La batalla de Chile*, the camera focuses on rural estates occupied by peasants, worker-run factories, the presidential palace, the congress, the streets, plazas, the squatter settlements of Santiago, in short, the public sites of the revolution. In contrast, the spaces of *Memoria obstinada* are the interiors of homes or high schools, places with no social context or location in the city. What neighborhoods are they in? Which high

schools are they? What social classes do those interviewed belong to? Does social class influence the way they remember the Allende years? Do men and women remember differently? Perhaps one of the major successes of the Pinochet dictatorship was to fragment the collective identities and movements of the 1960s and early 1970s by imposing a combination of state terror and neoliberal "shock therapy." In this context, memory and mourning, like most of social life, were driven indoors and out of public sight. The kinds of remembering portrayed in *Memoria obstinada* are personal, taking place in closed spaces. The film produces a sense of places of public memory—the political party, the union hall, the factory, the plaza and street—closed down in 1990s Chile. . . . *Memoria obstinada* represents the difficulty of keeping memory obstinate in neoliberal Chile.[76]

Indeed, the final scenes that frame *La batalla*'s main narrative—the furtive images of public events stolen surreptitiously from the tenuous safety of private homes—are evidence of the military's attack on sites of public expression. Targeting symbolic centers of public protest (and extending their reach to peripheral areas and private homes in the days and years that followed the coup), the military government sought to engender precisely this reaction, to use the threat and reality of state-sponsored violence to fracture public space and end public forms of political expression. I develop a parallel argument in this chapter and the next—that an awareness of visual practice in democracy and dictatorship allows us to find significant continuities alongside this shift in "scopic regime," to see how visual practices of political debate and contest may have been transformed in contexts of repression but nevertheless served as the basis for significant traditions of resistance to the military.[77]

But it would be a mistake to ignore *La batalla*'s Part III, in which the crew engages the rise (and fall) of "poder popular." Considering the film in full allows us to further explore the ties between political narrative and aesthetic language. Part III studies the cordones industriales that workers formed along the city's periphery in response to the October 1972 truckers' strike. As we saw in chapter 3, the strike spurred a series of discussions about presence and absence in public space and a number of tactical moves on the part of the opposition and the government that were intended to secure physical and discursive hold over public space and its political and symbolic significance. Popular Unity filmmakers proposed their own interpretation of the political and economic realities that sustained tropes. Guzmán's Equipo entered the cordones in October 1972 to film *La respuesta de octubre*, the documentary short that Guzmán and Chaskel later broke apart and incorporated into the third part of *La batalla de Chile*. *La respuesta de octubre* reveals the growing and changing importance of the cordones in the city's political and symbolic landscape.

Guzmán explores the political importance of movement and sound in his work with potent effect. Responding to the discourse of stasis or paralysis, he highlights mobility and energy to argue for an alternative reading of the strike. He focuses on a group of workers, conducting his impromptu interviews on the factory floor. A handheld camera records disciplined, uninterrupted movement. Workers' words struggle against and are almost drowned out by the noise of heavy machinery. The camera remains constant and steady, while long takes and sparse cuts highlight the jarring effect of metallic sounds that constantly threaten to overwhelm the film and the viewer. In one especially poignant scene, the camera follows a worker who is transporting heavy bars of metal from a smelter into a cooling container. The worker puts his entire body weight against a metallic arm and uses this leverage to rotate the arm into position. He appears to float over the floor, defying gravity. The camera follows his surreal, languid movements as he retraces the same trajectory, exerting tremendous physical strength but gliding across the floor with seemingly effortless skill. Against this visual backdrop, the cacophony of the factory floor is transformed into a protagonist and permeates the viewer's experience of the scene. John Urry has argued that while the visual occupies a dominant place in "Western" thought and practice, the senses of sound, taste, smell, and touch also play key roles in the consumption and experience of urban places—which he calls their "sensuous geographies."[78] Image and sound join powerfully in the film to knit together a narrative of skilled and persistent action.

Indeed, sound is pregnant with political meaning throughout *La respuesta* and *La batalla*. The ambient din, the weight of city and factory noise, threatens to overwhelm the filmmakers' attempts to interview workers. They pose questions to laborers in or on their way to their places of work, allowing the sights and sounds of the city and factory to permeate the visual and aural fabric of the scene. The act of filming in and around these factories convenes a public and instantiates a heated debate about politics and popular power. But, at the same time, the sounds of industry intermingle with and often overpower the visual cadence in the cordón, and they subdue the texture of the voices of both interviewer and interviewee in this part of the film.

The aural plays an inescapable role in this scene and throughout the documentary. The crew interviews members of the opposition to Allende in their cars, obvious markers of class, and utilizes the sound of honking horns and the looks of passing pedestrians and bus riders to emphasize the difference between the worlds of the streets and the sidewalk. Throughout, the filmmakers create and mobilize a language made up of visual and aural cues through which they highlight the different ways in which automobilized citizens inhabit the public sphere and the street and hint at the political significance of this social or class difference. In the marcha de las ollas vacías, banging pots signified gendered claims on the state. In the Día del Silencio, opposition groups used silence and inactivity as a counterpoint to protests and marches. In the film, sound supports an image of the cordones as sites of continued movement and action. These examples capture the power of vision and sound as ephemeral crucial building blocks of an urban, public, political language. They reveal how visual and sound markers help to define political and social place in an urban setting and suggest the political importance of place even as they hint at how place is defined by the myriad, often subtle ways in which people move through and occupy space, materially and physically but also visually and aurally.

Throughout the film, Guzmán's narrator has engaged one of the central paradoxes of Popular Unity politics: its belief in grassroots mobilization coupled with its inability to incorporate the "power of the people," or poder popular, into the institutional structure of government. His decision to include a separate third section that engages popular power, especially the grassroots mobilization and territorial organization of the cordones industriales, is odd at first glance. In *La batalla*, the story of the rise of grassroots mobilizations that favored neighborhood organization in the event of armed conflict, a story to which the crew had paid close attention and which, chronologically, would fit in Part II with the October strike and the rise of worker-run industries before the tancazo, falls out of the narrative. That story is relegated to a third part released years after the first two. By omitting this important section from the film's main narrative, *La batalla* becomes instead a tale of the inevitability of a bloody coup perpetrated against "a people without arms." The potential and limits of popular power does not form part of but instead stands apart from the narrative of state politics that is coupled with, informs, and is shaped by the fervent participation of a range of actors in a constitutionally sanctioned political process. *La batalla*'s narrative ultimately, progressively fractures under the pressure of encompassing, containing, and expressing the tensions and contradictions of the Popular Unity and its strident opposition. The Equipo's careful consideration of the complexities of the political conflict, of the ebbs and flows within their larger declension narrative, breaks down as the story turns from one of aesthetic and narrative ambiguity to one of stark and inexorable progress toward a violent denouement. In a sense, this structure reveals the tensions inherent in the film's argument regarding Popular Unity politics.

It points too to the failure of a representational mode that leans on the language of modernity—articulated in relation to tropes of progress, teleological development, and, in Allende's gripping last words, an unshakable belief in History and its ability resolve internal, dialectical conflict.[79] These tensions are not resolved through the internal dynamics of history; they are dissolved in the violent denouement whose aim it was to eradicate the type of public politics that marked the Popular Unity, that was driven by constant, everyday conflicts and interactions, and that went hand in hand with shifting and contentious means of representing the form of political conflict that *La batalla* records, charts, and engages.

VENCEREMOS

Venceremos was conceived against the backdrop of the Popular Unity electoral campaign but quickly became an important part of a larger movement that sought to use film as an "instrument of analysis of contemporary Chilean social problems."[80] I interpret *Venceremos* as a search for an appropriate visual language by which to analyze and represent what Chaskel and his filmmaking partner, Héctor Ríos, saw as the social consequences of economic underdevelopment and to piece together an open-ended narrative, an argument regarding the political role available to filmmakers and spectators. These documentarians proposed a self-reflexive and complex understanding of their political and social worlds and of cinematic form. They saw themselves as fashioning a documentary aesthetic that could be at once "objective" (recording an incontrovertible "reality") and "creative" (structuring a partial narrative and argument out of the building blocks of the "real"). As Lopez writes of their NLAC counterparts:

> The cinematic analysis of the real was meant to serve as an enabling mechanism for the transformation of that real. As a re-presentation or restructuring of the "real" conditions of life in Latin America, it sought to bring to light that which was kept in darkness and silence by the socio-political and economic mechanisms of underdevelopment. And this light would also be shined onto the process of representation itself, questioning the filmmakers' own position in the filmmaking process, their engagement with their subjects, their position as social actors in the universe being recorded.[81]

Chaskel and Ríos attempt to record and depict a "hidden" social reality while going beyond this understanding of documentary as "memory" or "witness" to create an analytical historical "document."[82] They express in microcosm the trajectory of Popular Unity documentaries, which moved increasingly to analyze the relationship between political change and social reality, leaving the task of recording the political process to the newsreels of Chile Films. Like Solanas and Getino's foundational treatment of Argentine Peronism, *La hora de los hornos*, Chaskel and Ríos made *Venceremos* in explicit support of a political program—in this case, Allende's final presidential campaign. Following *La hora*, the filmmakers combined original and found material, image, and sound into a powerful collage through which they documented the deep social inequalities that defined Chilean society under Eduardo Frei Montalva's government.

Yet the film does more than simply "make visible" the "marginal" or "invisible." Avoiding the difficulties associated with live, synchronized sound, Chaskel and Ríos alternate between a dynamic musical score and ambient street noises, which they lay over simple yet powerful images of people collected exclusively in public spaces—highways, dog parks, city streets, and garbage dumps. They structure their film around jarring visual and aural juxtapositions that highlight stark spatial divisions and are always infused with class significance, thus articulating a complex narrative of the relationship between politics, place, and class in Chile as played out in everyday, quotidian interactions.[83]

Chaskel and Ríos well understood the social function of documentary film, and they brought to the screen people and places rendered socially and spatially "marginal" to national politics and society. The film begins quietly. It follows clusters of men dressed in makeshift suits and well-worn sweaters, solitary figures trudging through the dusty streets of a sleepy población, moving silently through the rich haze of the early morning light. The rumbling engines of makeshift buses suddenly break this resolute tranquility. These men, and they are mostly men, file into buses from the La Granja and Catedral lines, ready for the long, winding journey into the city center for work. These early images expose inequalities that shape the material world of the población, even as they establish the basis of the film's exploration of the physical, social, and economic geography of the city.

Venceremos begins in the población, but it is ultimately about the simultaneous social and physical distance that separates the inhabitants of these marginal spaces from Santiago's barrios altos and the ways in which these subaltern groups work in and pass through the areas that "belong" to the middle and upper classes but are built on the work of those they exclude. We can read the importance of this relationship in the documentary's early sequences. The relative peace of the film's first scene is quickly and force-fully brought to an end in the vignettes that follow. After a stark cut, the imposing fences and well-manicured lawns of the barrio alto replace the rough, well-trod streets of the población, and the fragile silence of a city still asleep replaces the sound of growling engines. This is a jarring transi-tion from periphery to center, from a población already awake to a city center that waits quietly for its workers to arrive. The filmmakers highlight the physical and social distance that separates the two areas by overlaying the former with songs from the nueva canción and the latter with European opera. Then ambient sound pours forth, but this time the sound is of cars crashing through the *costanera*, the highway that borders the river and serves as one of the boundaries between downtown (centro) and uptown (barrio alto). A man pulling a cart moves slowly amid the rush of automo-biles flowing blurrily past him. Then, as the nueva canción begins anew, we are presented with more men pulling carts amid the sea of automobiles. The cadence of their labored strides sets the tone for a final transition to a slow montage of photographs of children racked by hunger. This first set of vignettes encapsulates the film's central motif—radical social difference— yet also depicts the multiple ways in which these people experience their travel through the city, tying inequity to spatial distance. The vignettes suggest a particular argument and narrative about the relationship between politics, economic inequality, social distance, and the city fashioned from their manipulation, joining, and juxtaposition of image and sound.

Here, and throughout the documentary, the filmmakers use a mixture of "original" and "found" material—filmed sequences, photographic images, newspaper clippings, cartoons—to piece image and sound together in dis-crete episodes. They then juxtapose these scenes, creating significant ten-sion both within and between the self-contained units.[84] This technique produces a cacophony of clashing, sometimes-contradictory scenes, a diso-rienting rupture or disjuncture between them. The dissonance is heavy with political meaning. Chaskel and Ríos play on this tension, utilizing abrupt cuts and simple contrast to re-create in the spaces between images and sound the coexistence and juxtaposition of the "modern" Chile and the "underside" of this "modern" landscape. The modern Chile that they record is characterized by leisure, automobiles and races, dog shows and picnics. It is also a world of well-dressed, tall blond bodies at rest, a world defined by race and class. In the film, modernity comes at the expense of, and cannot exist without, its "dark" or "underside."[85]

The filmmakers begin their exploration of underdevelopment in the shantytowns that ring the city and contrast these with the modern city center. The starkness of the contrast mounts until, at the film's apex, elite leisure is juxtaposed to poverty-stricken children dying of hunger. In the film's most powerful sequence, Chaskel and Ríos initially train their cameras on a series of commodities in store windows to create a montage of modern, clean appliances and fashionable clothes and accessories set to a pop song whose chorus is, "I would like to be a winner, in life and in love." Abruptly the pop rhythms end. Initial silence accompanies a close-up of a child, dressed in a ragged sweater, sifting through a sea of garbage. The next scene reveals that this is literally a mountain of refuse. As a children's song begins to play, the camera pulls back to reveal entire families and groups of children working their way through the garbage, the detritus of the modern material world, collecting valuable scraps of wood, paper, and other materials. The camera lingers on the children's faces, eyes, and bodies and eventually completes its argument by taking the viewer into clinics where malnourished babies show the effects of dire poverty. The song concludes among images of malnourished children, bellies distended, lying in hospital beds. Opera once again accompanies the images of the city's elite, now at a dog show. Then the scene is interrupted. A malnourished baby's large eyes stare silently, questioningly, into the camera. The filmmakers' critique of the intimate connection between modernity, development, and underdevelopment is clear: the city's poor are situated between Santiago's barrio alto and its landfills, between the architects of modern Chile and what the modern generates and discards. Simultaneously they are defined by, live in, and sift through the refuse of the modern world against which their realities are set. In focusing on the intimate relationship between a "modern" Chile and a Chile racked by poverty and hunger, Chaskel and Ríos give voice and visual manifestation to Rocha's proposed "aesthetics of hunger."

Focused on the everyday material realities and embodied gestures that mark and segregate each of these spheres, Chaskel and Ríos's film challenges its viewers' expectations, denaturalizing the everyday and taken-for-granted by calling attention to the social context and political meaning of clothing, gesture, hair, skin color, and material culture.[86] The filmmakers focus on the local geography and material culture of politics and class, as their roaming handheld camera captures their subjects in their specific urban contexts and quickly moves into tight focus on faces and eyes, skin and clothes. They slowly, methodically, begin to situate their subjects in an overly rich "symbolic universe," a material world against which they are defined and understood, building an almost baroque form, an "excess of signification" where the material world takes on distinct political meaning.[87] Their focus on the everyday is the foundation for a political and aesthetic model: they are able to uncover and unravel the meaning within the symbols of modernity and its refuse, to find significance in what Nelly Richard terms the "ruined fragments of discarded totality."[88] This is a cinematic language based on the observation and analysis of the structures of political and economic dependence and inequality. It reveals rather than elides the jarring violence that is the product of hunger and creates the possibility that this violence can be politically productive.

Here *Venceremos* also draws from the Brazilian Undergrundi's "aesthetics of garbage," which understood waste both as the product of the violence of social inequality and poverty and as the metaphoric material for a cinema that "redeems the low" and "offers a history based on disjunctive scraps and fragments[,] ... [a] collage[,] ... a place of violent, surprising juxtapositions[,] ... a database of material culture from which one can read social customs or values."[89] I interpret *Venceremos* in these terms. It is a complex film, a hybrid form that, because of its temporary reconciliation of "disjunctive scraps," acts as a vehicle for critiquing the very modernity of which it is a product. The filmmakers piece together a visual language from these mixtures and scraps, aesthetic choices, cinematic techniques, and social analyses that is able to express and contain the tension between the modern and the unmodern. This language is apt for a critical exploration of the relationship between modernity and hunger, the city and the individual, and politics and the body. The film is founded on images of hungry bodies not as cinematic aberrations, unpleasant and unaesthetic intrusions in what is usually a medium devoted to beauty, but as part of an easily intelligible "political idiom" that finds crucial significance in everyday "corporeal dramas."[90] In this way, *Venceremos* reveals the existence, and revalorizes the place, of those rendered spatially and socially marginal, peripheral, or other, reasserting their place in the imagined community of the nation.

While *Venceremos* begins with an analysis that parallels social reality and the particularities of place, its narrative arc creates a sense of temporal change, charting a progression from an initial hardship, followed by crisis, and culminating in an explosive victory and the metaphoric dawn of a new day. This sense of change over time is expressed cinematically in the structure of the film and symbolically in ephemeral urban graffiti. The film culminates with images of protesters in the Plaza Italia battling police across the bridges that straddle the Mapocho River. After a jarring cut to silence over black, the first image we see is a simple BRP rayado, "Enough." Then revelers fill the streets in explosive celebration that lasts through the night. People embrace, wave flags and placards, and jump up and down in a chaotic, energetic, syncopated rhythm. Cutting to daylight, the camera lingers on another set of pro–Popular Unity rayados: "Pueblo: The road is open," "Toward the birth of the New Man," and, finally, "Venceremos" (We Shall Overcome). The study of graffiti provides a rhythmic sense of political practice rooted in the struggle over public space and of public debate founded in the ongoing conflict over these spaces. It allows Chaskel and Ríos to propose a historical trajectory that begins with hardship and repression, struggle and resistance, and culminates in a transformative Popular Unity victory, a narrative in which Allende's victory emerges as the chronological fulcrum. The film is, among other things, an attempt to articulate the intricate relationship by which public art and other forms of urban and visual practice did not simply support but also engaged and even reframed traditional political narratives; it is an exquisite example of how visual practice and visual production can serve as a prism through which to reimagine the traditional periodizations that characterize Chilean political histories. At a more fundamental level, it is also an exploration of the role that public art played in structuring not only national narratives but also local, individual political identities.

Venceremos, then, is an archive of evanescent visual forms and actions; an analysis of visual practices as a means of formulating political citizenship; and an argument, assertion, or visual essay that presents the *physical* landscape as a key player in everyday forms of political mobilization and debate. *Venceremos*, like *La batalla*, creates and explores the relationship between political commentary and the social realities that structure everyday life, bridging the gap and breaking down the distinction between the political, social, and everyday. Both films do so by creating an innovative cinematic form out of an amalgam of original footage, photography, animation, music, and synchronous sound—a collage of visual and aural information that can encompass the simultaneous tensions and kinship between the political and the everyday and between the filmmakers' diverse influences and preoccupations. And both films engage the ongoing contest for the streets, including a sophisticated look at urban politics and street art. The era's documentary shorts further develop these themes.

FILM, STREET ART, AND THE PRODUCTION OF POLITICAL CITIZENSHIP

Three short documentary films produced under Allende propose this form of ephemeral urban practice as critical to the formation of new kinds of political communication and new concepts of political citizenship. Luis Alberto Sanz's *Unos pocos caracoles* takes place mostly in the población

Caracoles. It charts the process by which the community becomes politicized and organized in the context of a history of hardship and marginalization and a present-day reality structured by the possibilities of mobilization provided by the Popular Unity. The landscape of the población is not merely background, but a crucial part of political mobilizations. The film begins with images of celebration on the occasion of Allende's election and explores what it might mean for the pobladores. In a voice-over layered upon images of Allende assuming the presidency, an interviewee speaks of a history of repression and a lack of political representation. He claims, "We are no longer used to living in a constant state of terror. . . . Before, when we used complain about an injustice, they would simply unleash the police, who would arrest anyone who spoke out." In this context, Allende's election emerges as a watershed moment after which pobladores lost their fear of the state and gained a political voice and the "dignity" that goes with the possibility of political citizenship and participation. The interviewees point to the Popular Unity's shortcomings, but they remark on the opportunity they now have to organize, express their displeasure, and make demands on government officials. "We now have a government that is ours," begins another interlocutor, speaking over images of Allende and Luis Corvalán, head of the Communist Party. "Allende himself has told us that if the authorities do not yet listen to us we organize, we go out and we make public the problems that we have known." These documentary films, in short, follow a narrative parallel to BRP life histories and their defining events. They also explore how the production of posters (and graffiti and murals) acts as a vehicle for the formation of innovative political identities and practices of citizenship.

Another work by Sanz, the didactic short *El sueldo de Chile*, incorporates original footage, photographs, and newspaper headlines to piece together a similar narrative, a story of the nationalization of copper as a crucial step in the country's economic development and political independence made possible by Allende's victory. The film's formal creativity and modernist use of collage, found material, and reliance on juxtaposition and dissonance encompass a familiar narrative arc. After setting a concrete time line centered on Allende's victory, Sanz moves on to explore the process by which community members organized politically in the población. He interviews a number of pobladores, editing their stories together to provide a sense of the place and the process. One woman tells the story of the founding of the población, how individuals worked with what they had to slowly build their houses out of found materials; Sanz supports her words with images of structures cobbled together from makeshift materials and juxtaposes this to the cement buildings and metal frame of incipient constructions closer to the city center. Again, scraps and refuse are transformed into the literal building material for a new city and a new citizen. This collage flows into another interviewee's comments: "Here everything is focused on the city center. All the benefits—electricity, sewage, sidewalks— were downtown. The barrios are completely abandoned." Later, a female interlocutor supports this claim, speaking of the lack of medical attention for children in the población, which is sustained visually by contrasting images of the modern, clean, well-appointed facilities available to middle-class children, their families, and their nannies.

After outlining this spatial and social division, the next vignette focuses on female community members, paying especially close attention to the material conditions of everyday life. Families eat basic foods, usually *pantrucas* (pieces of fried dough) and tea with sugar. Here the filmmakers are commenting on the intimate connection between food, distribution, and politics. Indeed, food, and in particular access to basic foodstuffs at fair prices, plays a central role in the film. Mobilized by their desire to demand a fair price for meat, pobladores begin to organize politically. The key image is that of a rayado painted on the side of a central building that reads, "Mobilized We Shall Overcome." In fact, rayados appear throughout the film. Initially, they form the backdrop of the march demanding fair prices and of children playing and are featured in an animated skit about a housewife learning of the possibility of a grassroots neighborhood organization from a rayado that proclaims, "The People Fight for You." Ultimately, rayados are more than simply part of the background. They play a key role in grassroots mobilization.

Miguel Ángel Aguilera, presente, Álvaro Ramírez's ten-minute short, shot and edited in six days in 1970 and screened in Santiago's poblaciones, articulates a similar contention regarding the importance of wall drawings. Set to the music of Violeta Parra, the film collects testimonials from Aguilera's family and neighbors after he is shot and killed in the course of a strike the day before filming. Against this aural landscape, the film's striking visuals present his fellow Communist Party members' outrage in the form of rayados scrawled throughout the city. Again, the city's walls become a sort of public newspaper that records changing forms of political discourse and debate and in doing so inscribe the city's public spaces into the political process.

Both these films focus squarely on the communal act and ritual of making, displaying, and organizing around posters and murals. At their most effective, the posters and murals are central vehicles for the politicization of residents. For instance, they lead to and culminate in a march in which poster makers move through the población, past the mural we saw residents making, and to city hall to protest food costs. On the one hand, the act of producing these ephemeral visual materials is one of building or expressing political identity and association; on the other, the posters and murals themselves face outward, calling out to interpolate the passerby and transforming him or her from pedestrian into political subject. These films present the physical landscape as a key player in everyday forms of political mobilization and debate. They create and explore the relationship between political commentary and the social realities that structure everyday life, bridging the gap and breaking down the distinction between the political, social, and everyday. They highlight the tensions between and the kinship of city, visual production, and practices of political citizenship rooted in public space. The city lies at the intersection of broader, international narratives about modernity, development, and national and personal maturation and the local, everyday tactics that give unique shape and structure to political and personal narratives and structures of political feeling. In this way, it grounds a public sphere of political association and new languages of debate rooted in urban practice. The practice of documentary film, even when its projection was impossible, created the space in which democratic, open conversation could take place and in which a participatory politics, no matter how ephemeral, could take root.[91]

.   .   .

Scholars of the New Latin American Cinema pay close attention to the relationship between the idea of a Latin America held together by the shared experience of underdevelopment and the particularities of the different national contexts in which its committed filmmakers worked. But they do not often examine the third level, the level of place, of the local and everyday, where the transnational and the national are experienced and understood, engaged and reenvisioned. The filmmakers I have examined all mobilize their understanding of place; of the importance of visual and aural cues, and the location of political debate; and of the physical gestures and material objects against and through which people understand and articulate political belief. The scenes I have chosen from the documentaries *La batalla* and *Venceremos* seek to reveal the central importance of this local political, social, and physical geography.

These documentaries can be read as arguments for and about a unique mode of political participation that was developing in Allende's Chile. They propose, explore, and record a public sphere of political debate rooted in public space and everyday material realities, a public sphere in which urban strategies give shape to radical new political identities. The city here is a backdrop, field of play, and scaffolding for a broader process of political effervescence, space claimed, acted upon, and remade by these urban tactics of political conflict. Urban space and practice supports a public sphere of political association and new languages of debate. These films shed light on this complex process.

Guzmán's films are not only records of the past, sources for political history, or visual narratives to read and decipher. They are part of a larger process of experimentation with the form and limits of political debate. Documentary film (and photography) played a key role in structuring this experiment and in reshaping the city into a palimpsestic confluence of structure, practice, and representation, both product and productive of a cosmopolitan socialist modernity. They effectively transformed the city by looking, recording, shaping, and projecting their narratives. They also played a key role in a broader process that transformed the diverse population of santiaguinos into political citizens. These films are therefore crucial for an analysis of political and visual practice in the Popular Unity—as visual documents and as part of a broader "repertoire" by which a range of groups seized or claimed public spaces. The production, projection, and discussion of these films created arenas in which these groups could engage in a broad political dialogue. The act of filming on city streets and in factories established vibrant spaces of discussion. Showing early cuts of films in the places they were filmed grounded them in broader arenas of debate. These diverse practices made the films into registers of, and provided Santiaguinos direct experience with, visual languages and forums of political analysis. They were part of a larger political landscape that included the tactics of urban protest, street art, and visual practices, including documentary film and street photography.

Conclusion

The Image of a Coup Foretold: Violence, Visual Regimes, and Clandestine Public Spheres

At the height of the Cold War, military regimes throughout South America reacted similarly to the social and political mobilization of the 1960s and 1970s. They utilized violence as a means to reestablish "order" in a social and political body "in crisis," thereby creating a radically new political, social, and economic reality.[1] These regimes' "national security doctrines" were founded on the image of a national "body" under attack by dangerous "internal enemies," disorderly political subversives that the juntas imagined as cancerous elements in need of surgical extirpation. To this end, the September 11, 1973, military coup in Chile inaugurated close to two decades of dictatorship and political terror. Under the military, "Chile would become a byword for human rights violations." The perpetrators of this violence paradoxically and teleologically "justified" it as a means of calming a specter of their own making, the potential of a "Marxist" takeover that could plunge the nation into chaos. Many of the victims of repression were "labor leaders and worker activists, whom [junta leader Augusto] Pinochet regarded as prime targets of his 'internal war' of 1973–1978."[2] Steve Stern has condensed decades of research on Chile's befogged history of military violence and repression and produced a magisterial overview that yields (conservative) estimates of the number of victims: around 4,500 dead and disappeared, 150,000 to 200,000 detained and/or tortured, and some 400,000 political exiles.[3]

State-sponsored violence was the mechanism by which the nascent regime consolidated power, destroyed the world of public political debate that had characterized the Popular Unity, and established a new political, social, and aesthetic order.[4] "As military regimes displaced civilian ones," Stern writes, "they defined a mission more ambitious than transitory relief from an untenable administration. They would create a new order. The new military regimes would conduct a 'dirty war' to root out subversives and their sympathizers once and for all, to frighten and depoliticize society at large, to lay the foundation for a technocratic public life."[5] Similarly, Mary Louise Pratt suggests that "Pinochet had, as Giselle Munizaga calls it, a 'foundational project.' People tend to think that military dictatorships aim simply to impose order, suppress opposition, and uphold established hierarchies, rather than to advance elaborate social and institutional agendas. But Pinochet had no problem at all with 'the vision thing,' and devastating the militant Left was only one small part of it (accomplished as in all these dictatorships, in a matter of weeks). When he spoke, as he did all the time, of 'the new institutionality' (*la nueva institucionalidad*), he meant a wholesale transformation of state and civil society, no fooling."[6] State violence and its reliance on order and hygiene was, in this macabre sense, politically creative.

A piece published in *El Mercurio* days after the coup spoke to the power of this language and the disciplining process it underwrote. It reported the junta's "decision to carry out a program to restore the capital city's lost history of cleanliness and order. This initiative should not only receive the people's support, but should also incentivize their voluntary collaboration."[7] Another article, written to mark the first anniversary of the coup, drew on similar language to propose that the Popular Unity's "populism was an excuse for a general lack of preoccupation with grooming and cleanliness, which transformed our cities into extreme examples of dirtiness and contamination."[8] This "contamination" could only be addressed by the "purge" or "purification of undesirable elements" in an attempt to "reconquer" ground lost in the political and social chaos of the previous regime.[9] The languages of order and disorder, and the ubiquitous metaphors of cancer and surgical removal, were common to the Southern Cone's multiple "bureaucratic-authoritarian regimes." Gustavo Leigh, one of the four leaders of the coup, established the language of and justification for the coup's violence in a public *bando*: to "extirpate the Marxist cancer that threatens the nation's organic life, by applying extreme measures, no matter the consequence."[10] The number of dead, detained, and disappeared speaks to the regime's willingness to use violence to remove those they defined as potentially "subversive."

Public and semipublic shows of force became part of the daily spectacle and experience of terror. The junta quelled land and factory seizures; quieted protest, mass marches, and street clashes; and ended "caustic public, rhetorical debates."[11] Military and police forces barricaded streets and imposed a strict curfew, fracturing the cityscape and separating family members and friends for days and weeks. They raided neighborhoods and homes, targeting shantytowns as "'dangerous' and 'subversive zones[,]' . . .

'centers of delinquency[,]' and, to a lesser extent, 'centers of disease.'" The National Commission for Truth and Reconciliation reported in 1991 that many of those bodies "dumped in the Mapocho River washed ashore in the [*poblaciónes* in the] western part of Santiago, where many of the land seizures had been concentrated." In the immediate aftermath of the coup, soldiers and police left the "disfigured and mutilated bodies . . . in the streets of [these] neighborhoods." They killed neighborhood dogs and left their carcasses in shantytown roads as a reminder of their power over life and death. Edward Murphy's oral histories suggest that these "arresting and provocative tactics left their mark indelibly on residents' sensibilities."[12]

The junta's "operation cleanse" also sought to "erase all traces of the Left" and leftist cultural expression. In fact, the nascent regime decreed all public forms of expression illegal and punishable by death. Assemblies, especially marches and demonstrations, were strictly forbidden; political parties were banned or suspended; and elections, even in youth clubs, were prohibited under pain of death.[13] The junta's forces patrolled the city's streets, publicly shaved men's hair and beards, slashed women's pants, and outlawed miniskirts, asserting military control over body and action.[14] Andean instruments and sounds, associated with the left-wing musical movement known as the nueva canción, were banned. Political posters, murals, and graffiti were criminalized. Military officers supervised santiaguinos who whitewashed walls, painted over murals, ripped down posters, and burned books on the streets. Many more residents destroyed their own books, art, and record covers in fireplaces or buried them in their backyards in an attempt to hide them from cadets, neighbors, or informants who might intrude into private space.[15]

Local municipalities undergirded these efforts: the municipality of Las Barrancas, now Pudahuel, ordered the "cleansing and exterior cleaning" of buildings and walls. It decreed the "elimination" of "slogans, posters, graffiti, and any other political or party propaganda, so that the *población* [would take] on a generally orderly and hygienic quality."[16] The junta outlawed the "fashions and colors" that spoke to the "Popular Unity's imaginary," censored means of expression and circulation, and dismantled the networks that supported visual and cultural producers. It also sought to "reconstruct" a "new" social and cultural reality, represented symbolically in orderly spaces, white walls, and clean streets and in the schools and settlements that were renamed for the anniversaries and heroes of nationalist, military struggles.[17] Santiago's mayor, Maria Eugenia Oyarzún, ordered that a similar campaign of order and cleaning be undertaken every July and September 10 and prohibited "the use of black or other violent colors on exterior walls, so as to not perturb an overall harmony."[18] Military officials "celebrated how they were able to put an end to much of the extraordinary, public phenomena that had marked the tumult of the UP period." Multiple newspaper articles charted a macabre geography of erasure in downtown Santiago, including the famous murals authored by artists and brigades along the Mapocho River walls.[19]

Pinochet's regime sought to actively "eradicate politics" and fashion a society structured around the traditional family. They achieved a broad erasure of public life but only by also and urgently rebuilding and politicizing the family and the everyday in equally potent ways. The military quickly moved to reestablish traditional gender and class norms and roles after the coup, and did so by acting directly on individual bodies. Gender scholars have studied how the regime mobilized violence and terror to regulate or discipline "bodily comportment, gender dynamics, and the regulation of living spaces."[20] For those detained, interned, or disappeared, torturers "exercised a power based on the physical and often sexual domination of the tortured, a power that humiliated the sense of self-worth and dignity of the victim."[21] They coupled extreme, deadly physical violence that included electric shock, burns, and beatings with rituals of humiliation that ranged from forced nudity to rape to submersion in water and excrement.[22]

Electric shock was used on genitalia, material proof that military authority "could penetrate and wound the most intimate, private area of the body."[23] Physical and psychological attacks on gendered bodies and identities became routine. Women suffered violence in distinct ways. In documenting the regime's "widespread and systematic use of torture against Chileans through its network of approximately 1,200 torture centers," the National Commission on Political Detention and Torture paid special attention to the widespread use of sexual violence against and torture of women. Women "made up roughly 14 percent of the 27,255 ex-prisoners who gave confirmed testimony to the Commission. They were typically subjected to a variety of sexual tortures, from systematic harassment to gang rape."[24] Many were raped in front of partners, family members, and other soldiers in an attempt to destabilize affective networks and play on victims and citizens' gendered identities. As the sociologist Julieta Kirkwood reminds us, political violence was tied reciprocally to the reassertion of patriarchal authority in public and private.[25]

The metaphor of surgical extirpation and the reality of physical and symbolic violence underwrote a regime of terror that included both spectacular and direct experience of violence. But the real threat of violence and its particular application in the form of semisecret acts in violation of basic human rights created a deep and destabilizing sense of uncertainty. The regime's assertion that the country was in a "'state or time of war'" justified its reliance on disappearance and torture in clandestine detention centers alongside direct, spectacular, and public violence. This particular combination of "precise counterinsurgent tactics and more furious sentiments and aesthetics" was crucial to the military's ability to fashion what Primo Levi defines as a "gray zone" of terror and Benjamin and Agamben call an ongoing "state of emergency."[26] The disappearance of people was so effective precisely because of the destabilizing fear that one's family member might be alive, in pain. The arbitrary and uncertain played a significant role in the "reorganization" of political and social worlds. The proliferation of semisecret sites of incarceration, interrogation, and disappearance; the torture of parents and children; and the "disappearance" of "subversives" and sporadic "reappearance" of bodies remade both the political and social worlds. It redefined public space, transformed city streets into sites of terror and uncertainty. Military authority was buttressed by terror. It relied on the macabre way in which terror, fear, and grief became "normalized" by the military's "shock treatment" in ways that destroyed and reshaped individual lives.[27]

The National Stadium played a crucial role in maintaining and projecting this sense of "terror-as-usual." As I have examined elsewhere, the stadium had been a laboratory for different "rituals of rule" since its inauguration in 1938.[28] The junta continued this tradition in a very different historical context. Under military rule, the stadium was only the most visible and public of a network of clandestine and semiclandestine torture centers, where the drive for political hegemony was felt in the bodies of the thousands who were apprehended and which illustrated the paralyzing promise of pain for those who had not yet been caught. Within its walls, modern technologies created scientific, electrified forms of torture. Torture transformed the stadium into a veritable "space of death," in which a violent reality was built up around bodies that were torn down through physical and psychological violence.[29] The military's violence was not only rational and precise but also random and unpredictable. Detainees ranged from former political leaders to those unfortunate enough to appear in someone's Rolodex or to be caught out in public by a random patrol. Marcelo Suárez-Orozco examines torture as a "perverse poly-semantic ritual" that can be explored as "meaningful text" without obscuring its devastating and brutal experience. For him, information was neither the ultimate justification nor the goal of torture. Pain itself was the point, the vehicle through which to force "complicity" or "cooperation," to transform anger into shame, to enact the ultimate act of symbolic violence.[30]

Torture acted as a bridge between the public spectacle of violence and the workings of violence on the self through the body. Violence created the fiction of an ordered public world distinct from the private and individual and simultaneously shattered the possibility of a retreat to the safety of the home.

The stadium was only one of many sites in the military state's ongoing efforts to reach into private spaces and individual lives. It lay, then, at the center of "a regime of systematic violence and fear" that the junta assembled "so that the old ways of understanding, organizing, and practicing politics could be annihilated and replaced by technocratic and authoritarian governance." Stern defines this process of annihilation as policide, which speaks to him of destruction *and* reconstruction. Policide implies "a 'war' to destroy the old ways," but this war was only "the precondition for building the new order."[31] In this concluding chapter I examine the ways in which the military regime engaged, destroyed, rebuilt, and transformed the political and urban landscape that the first five chapters of this book explore. I also want to suggest how we can bridge and connect the seemingly distinct histories of democracy and dictatorship. The chapter begins with a reexamination of the book's central themes in the immediate aftermath of Allende, but it ends with a look at visual practices, and especially street photography in dictatorship, as a source through which to understand both continuity and change in Chilean politics and aesthetics.[32]

RETHINKING URBAN CONFLICT IN DEMOCRACY AND DICTATORSHIP I: ARCHITECTURE

The history of the UNCTAD building is also the history of urban politics in changing political climes. The book's initial chapter introduced the story of the building's birth, how it was imbricated with the architectural and political currents of the time, and how citizens shaped it through use and transit. It suggested the different ways in which the military regime transformed what had been a study in utopian modernity, of transit and movement as emblematic and indeed generative of participatory, socialist democracy. The junta turned the building into the seat of military rule, the headquarters of the Executive and the Ministry of Defense. It wrapped the structure in "protective" bars, sealing it from the surrounding city. The transformation of the building was at the center of the military's attempt to "sanitize," "order," and thereby obliterate political ferment. Scholars have read this symbolic attack as closure, as an erasure and eradication of a democratic government and practice, as the symbol of military authority cemented.

The politics of repression can most fruitfully be understood in relation to the politics it attempted to eradicate. The original UNCTAD structure was significant to the regime precisely because it was so important to the Popular Unity political landscape. The performance of erasure was an engagement with the persistent legacies of Popular Unity politics. The military's reappropriation of public spaces established, even relied on, the close relationship between democracy and dictatorship. A close look at the military's Ritoque detention center, built along the coastal fringe outside the port city of Valparaíso just north of the experimental Open City architectural school, reveals a similarly intimate connection between democracy and dictatorship.[33]

The dialectic between Ritoque and the Open City illustrates the close relationship and ongoing tension between a modernist experiment in architecture and design and the military's innovative use of violence and terror to remake the political landscape. These were diametrically opposed projects with surprising harmonies. They utilized a similar or parallel repertoire to create real and imaginary spaces but with very different ends. The Open City was founded in 1971 as an experimental site that drew equally on architecture and poetry, where teachers and students participated in "collective events that recall surrealist practices." Participants reimagined architecture as a collective, open-ended, "improvised process" by allowing poetic acts and ritual performances to shape the "design, construction, and sometimes destruction" of evolving architectural projects. These were theatrical performances that served as the basis for "the design and construction of buildings, sculptures, and installations" on the campus, part of a "slow, additive process" of experimentation and construction "that makes it difficult to attribute specific authorship." The Open City's "idiosyncratic experimentation" resonated in and was echoed by the type of architectural innovation, collective construction, and emphasis on fluid, transformative use and circulation that were so important to the symbolism of the UNCTAD.[34]

This fluidity stood in marked contrast to the detention and torture center the regime established a few miles south of the Open City. The Ritoque camp held a heterogeneous population of detainees, opposition leaders, educators, and activists among them. Miguel Lawner was a prisoner in Ritoque. Lawner recorded the camp's dimensions and structures, walking the camp's perimeters and buildings, drawing its structures and the lives the prisoners led inside them, diagrams he memorized, destroyed, and recreated after being freed from the camp and escaping into exile.

Lawner also described everyday life in the camp. Ritoque inmates gave classes in their respective fields: "nuclear physicists taught advanced mathematics, farmers explained land cultivation, mechanics showed how to dismantle a car engine." The playwright Óscar Castro staged plays featuring fellow prisoners, amateurs and actors alike. They became weekly occurrences. Ana Maria León writes, "Castro would write plays, performing them in front of the camp authorities for approval and then change emphasis and intonation in the actual performance. Engineers and mechanics helped with special effects, using an economy of means and material improvisation similar to the works of the Open City." These plays were creative and therapeutic. "Victims of torture," for example, "would reenact their experiences, only to be rescued by comic book heroes."[35] One particularly poignant, ongoing performance was named *The Town of Ritoque.* In the play, prisoners imagined Ritoque as the nation's one free town, "protected from the rest of Chile by barbed wire." This was an inverted urban fantasy in which prisons reimagined camp space, complete with street names, "a City Hall, Fire Department, a Music Band, a Priest[,] . . . a Post Office[,] . . . [and] a town plaza." It was a world in which prisoners themselves "decided who should play each role, a hierarchy distinct from their internal organization."[36] Prisoners "used acronyms and anagrams to invent code words and make allusions to their political situation, and created narratives that paralleled but did not directly describe their experience of arrest and torture." These strategies allowed them to criticize guards, interfere with torture sessions, and maintain records of who was interned and how they resisted.[37]

The complicated relationship established between performance and design, practice and structure, reveals surprising parallels between the Open City and the concentration camp at Ritoque. The latter was, in its barbed-wire fences, torture sessions, and forced imprisonment, an attempt to eradicate the open-ended experimentation and egalitarian ethos that was shaped in the former. Yet, paralleling the performance of architectural students and Ritoque prisoners, León suggests that the coup did not silence or eradicate but instead transformed the experience and practice that characterized democratic exchange in surprising ways. The coup's radical violence instantiated a process of silencing that existed alongside an ongoing if paradoxical engagement with the practices Chilean citizens had honed in democracy.

Open City members protected their freedom by turning inward and away from the political promise at the heart of the school's history of formal experimentation, even as Ritoque prisoners were using performance and experiment to transform the restricted arena into a site of uncertain but potent and creative association. A critical reappraisal of the themes that structure this book allows us to explore these surprising connections, continuities, and tensions in ways that destabilize traditional periodizations that present the coup as an unbridgeable rupture that separates distinct periods. It instead suggests that a history of urban politics in the Popular Unity can include and incorporate the history of military repression after Allende's overthrow.

Scholars have recently rethought the arc of twentieth-century Chilean history beyond traditional tropes and periodizations. Historians have long noted that Chilean political history is fundamentally marked by a political peace unrivaled in Latin America. The coup emerges as an unprecedented, unthinkable aberration in the context of this exceptionalist history of peaceful political transitions.

Others trace a *longue durée,* to subvert the myth of Chilean exceptionalism.[38] Lessie Jo Frazier and Florencia Mallon transform class conflict, race, and gender inequity into prisms that refract the narrative of twentieth-century history in new ways. They fasten on the persecution and massacre of laborers, multiple forms of gendered violence and patriarchal control, and the repression of indigenous communities as fundamental factors that rupture but are obscured by this exceptionalist narrative. Mallon's *Courage Tastes of Blood* is a rich history reread through the prism of Mapuche struggles. It "modifies our understating of Chilean history" and interrupts "many of the well-known narratives of twentieth-century Chilean history—[including] the gradual incorporation of workers and popular sectors into a national-level practice of coalition politics; the unique characteristics of the Chilean compromise state; the unique experiment with social inclusion represented by the agrarian reform decade of 1964–1973; the military coup of 1973 as a bloody rupture in an otherwise effective consolidation of Chilean democracy."[39] In short, Mallon's recognition of state-sponsored violence allows her to rethink the relationship between the state (which "seems to set the rule of the game [and] . . . establishes the structure, institutions, and political discourses within which people must struggle to exist") and local communities (who "push the boundaries of these discourses, structure, and institutions").[40]

RETHINKING URBAN CONFLICT IN DEMOCRACY AND DICTATORSHIP II: GENDER

A more focused history of the Popular Unity also prompts us to rethink the coup as an aberration or rupture in a history of peaceful, democratic transform of power. Coupling politics and gender, we can see how the latter was always a language of political debate that allows us to bridge democracy and dictatorship, to think about continuity within change. Alongside these broad reconceptualization of the history of state formation and engagement from below, labor historians remind us that gender has remained a crucial if changing political language across the rupture of the coup.[41] Gwynn Thomas contends that political battles "were often fought on and through specific understandings of the relationships among the family, the state, and citizens" under Allende and after his ouster. Toward the end of Allende's rule, and especially after the March 1973 congressional elections showed that the Popular Unity would not be legally ousted, anti-Allende women "publicly and repeatedly called for military intervention." One of the most spectacular and compelling performances of the Popular Unity's failed masculinity was enacted by the group El Poder Femenino, which organized a series of protests at the homes of constitutionalist military leaders and military barracks, throwing chicken feed, presenting chicken feathers, and singing children's songs about chicks to prod the military to "intervene in politics and protect the women's families, or be considered a coward."[42] Recalling her experience in the empty pots protest, Carmen Sanz argued that the iconic march was a performance that instantiated and directed political unrest.

> They began scaring us off by throwing pellets and rocks[;] . . . they took up positions in what is now the Diego Portales [Gabriela Mistral] building, which was being built at the time, and from there they began to throw rocks. That was like lighting a fire. . . . That's what woke the men up, it was like, "Hey, where are you guys?" After that people began to understand. We had to push the military men to take this burden off of us. And we threw chicken feed at any military man who passed by, as a way of telling him that he was a coward, a chicken.[43]

In the course of Allende's thousand days, women's "public actions helped make a military coup against the civilian government 'thinkable.'"[44] "One of the tragic ironies in Chile," Pratt suggests, "is that the dictatorship took advantage of the near vacuum in political discourse and party structures in regards to women, not because the regime particularly cared about them, but because it saw patriarchal values as the key to the one thing it could not dictate for itself: legitimacy."[45] Subsequently, the military state sought refuge and legitimacy in these gendered languages. "Your voice . . . for us the voice of the *patria* that called us to save her," Pinochet himself claimed. It was "the Chilean women who 'risked their lives and abandoned the tranquility of their homes to implore the intervention of the military institutions.'"[46] "By constantly invoking the March of the Empty Pots," Lisa Baldez suggests, "[Pinochet] ensured it would have a permanent place in public memory."[47]

Indeed, Thomas argues compellingly that the "connection between the military regime's strategy and previous struggles becomes evident when examining how the leaders of the junta incorporated the mobilization of anti-Allende women and their arguments about how Allende had endangered Chilean families."[48] The military engaged, complicated, and reimagined gendered political mobilization. Motherhood, for instance, was reentrenched as a politicized and political language but one that underwrote a traditional, conservative image of family as the basis for military authority. The regime brutalized women, upheld patriarchal authority in the household, enacted restrictions on women's rights over their own bodies, and spoke in gendered languages of self-"sacrifice" and "surrender" as "proper" gendered behavior. Nevertheless, and in many cases simultaneously, activists fought to assert an alternative form of gendered protest and built spaces and mechanisms with which to continue to protest and resist; opened unexpected sites of debate over power, gender, and sexuality; and "eventually emerged as leaders of a movement that ended Pinochet's rule."[49] The Chilean feminist scholar Julieta Kirkwood perfectly summarized this tension: "We were very brave: heretics by dint of shamelessly, openly turning everything around."[50]

Activists established new, gendered associational cultures and institutional frameworks in defense of human rights after the coup.[51] Most famously, the Association of the Families of the Detained-Disappeared, created after the killing of almost 120 MIR activists, organized female family members in the aftermath of murder and disappearance. They politicized traditional motherhood as a means of organizing for the release and protesting the treatment of detained and disappeared family members and citizens throughout the Southern Cone. As Pieper Mooney claims, women also transformed familiar practices of gendered political association into bases for new political identities. The Vicariate of Solidarity, headed by Cardinal Raúl Silva Henríquez, became "the primary source of refuge and help for victim of human-rights abuses throughout the dictatorship."[52] It also sponsored *arpilleras,* women's groups that embroidered tapestries depicting everyday scenes as a means of critiquing the ubiquity of military repression.[53] The Vicariate then added an academic arm, the Academy of Christian Humanism in 1975 ("which provided safe meeting spaces for human rights groups and study circles"), and continued to support the work of the Women's Studies Circle (which "helped transform the vary nature of women's quest for rights" by convening gatherings where women from diverse backgrounds and neighborhoods could converse and develop new ways of organizing and thinking about gender and politics under dictatorship).[54] Dialogues about motherhood, sexuality, education, and nutrition opened new, often surprising terrains of debate regarding the limits of gender politics.[55] Studying these debates has allowed scholars of gender to trace a "remarkable trajectory of a new rights discourse and women's rights practice in Chile," one that "shows how middle-class women's feminist organizations and women's groups in Santiago's poor neighborhoods transformed motherhood as a political tool that enabled women to engage politics as *women*—and not as mothers—first."[56]

For women's groups like the Women's Studies Circle, motherhood was not a "fixed, essentialized identity" but a potent means of organizing "a new political praxis" that connected a range of political and social issues to state violence and critiques of patriarchal authority. In 1979, Santiago feminists, all members of the Circle, convened a meeting of over three hundred women "from different neighborhoods and brought with them a wide range of educational and personal experiences . . . to further the 'struggle against all forms of discrimination and oppression against women.'"[57] In 1982, pobladoras organized into the unified Movement of Shantytown Women (MOMUPO). Facing deep inequities at home and in public, and poignantly aware of the connections between patriarchal authority and state-sponsored violence, women were "active agents whose voice shaped" the process of political resistance. Their actions demonstrated how women could and did seize interpretive power and transform some symbols of resistance including, most spectacularly, "the banging of pots and pans, first introduced by the conservative women who had protested the Allende government."[58]

Women's groups played a crucial role in the massive protest movements of the early 1980s, when they called for "democracy in the nation and at home" and turned the empty pot into the paradigmatic symbol of the failure of the military regime's political and economic program. During the 1988 plebiscite, more "than 1.9 million women, or 51 percent, supported the 'No' campaign, as did 58 percent of male voters. From that moment, women's demands for rights appeared in a new light, connected to the right of equal citizenship under elected government." Then, over the "the course of five, intensely active months of mobilization, forty-eight organized gatherings afforded women from all walks of life the opportunity to listen to presentations, read documents, and discuss what they saw as major challenges to women's rights," building a campaign in which "women's rights discourse and the formulation of demands were no longer marginal quests."[59] Gender remained a plastic political discourse: gender equality was largely reinterpreted as women's rights rather than motherhood rights, but it remained at the heart of and was the basis for renewed and stubborn public protest, resignified and reappropriated political action, and an ongoing contest over the terms, limits, and means of politics.

Of course, gendered political practice and performance was not limited to women's actions and (re)invention of femininity; it included a critical engagement with masculinity. There is a long tradition of studying politics and class in relation to masculinity in Chile. Gabriel Salazar and Sonia Montecino have investigated mobility, legitimacy, race, and masculinity in the nineteenth-century "huacho"; Jorge Pinto and Thomas Klubock have studied the "lacho" and "roto macanudo" in twentieth-century mining communities as transgressive figures who engaged and reacted to discourses of working-class respectability and familial responsibility that buttressed company, state, and leftist party discipline;[60] Karin Rosemblatt, Elizabeth Hutchinson, Heidi Tinsman, and Gwynn Thomas have traced the corollary development of state, party, and gender narratives that articulated tropes of familial responsibility, proper femininity, and legitimate and energetic masculinity. In this book I chart the gendered urban politics that reshaped the landscape of political practice and citizenship through the Allende period and beyond. My investigation of the march of the empty pots and the truckers' strike sheds light on the constructions of legitimate femininity and disciplined masculinity as emergent and flexible political languages that were crucial to the setting of limits of legitimate political action. These languages remained salient if transformed under Pinochet.

Recently, Mallon has traced the complicated masculinity that MIR members adopted from this longer history of "gender rebelliousness . . . that had already taken shape in popular political culture." She examines how MIRista masculinity intersected with global and hemispheric traditions of gendered political ideologies, including, most significantly, the Cuban revolutionary narratives on the one hand and conservative, homophobic notions that drove the party to expel known homosexuals members from its ranks on the other.[61] Mallon finds that "dramatic forms of romantic and revolutionary masculinity" continued under the dictatorship. "If we plant our feet firmly on the ground," she writes, "we can see how [individual] experience and subjectivity give the lie to the dramatic forms" of masculinity the MIR constructed.[62] These were powerful, complicated constructions that influenced those Miristas who refused to "seek political asylum" and those many more "who survived [and] did so by going into exile." The individual experiences and subjectivities that Mallon traces belie the universality of heroic masculinist constructions. She instead shows how these constructions influenced and informed those who did not fulfill masculinist revolutionary ideals.[63]

The history of the cordones industriales is flecked with these contradictions between ideal and practice. Cordones were laboratories of creative political practice in democracy but also, and because of it, they were direct targets of military repression before and after the coup. Peter Winn recounts how he watched from his window while "troops, aided by tanks and helicopter gunships, reduced the *cordones industriales* one by one" and labor activists were "transformed from vaunted leaders to hunted 'subversives.'"[64] Masculinist discourse might have underwritten the trope of heroic armed struggle favored by the MIR, the more radical branch of the Socialist Party headed by Carlos Altamirano, and other more traditionally "revolutionary" groups, but this discourse, and especially the language and specter of failed masculinity resulting from the inability to ward off an armed military force, also informed the recollections of many more who lived through dictatorship.[65] Mallon relates a conversation with José Cárdenas: "I can tell you that I'm not ashamed of having such a romantic idea of Che, even today, because it allows me to hold on to a sensibility, an ability I still have to feel awe, to be affected by the things happening around me, the things I live today on a daily basis."[66] Ideals rooted in gendered constructions shape the structures of feeling, sensibilities, experiences, and recollections of political actors in democracy and dictatorship.[67] The persistence of these constructions reveals not only their complexity but also the multiple, changing, sometimes contradictory forms in which gender continued to be politicized in ways that cut through and across traditional historical political periods.

RETHINKING URBAN CONFLICT IN DEMOCRACY AND DICTATORSHIP III: VISUAL CULTURE

The intersection of urban politics and visual culture offers some final insights into a political history that is rooted in the Popular Unity but opens up into and encompasses the initial moments of the dictatorship. This book presents visual culture as a means by which myriad actors engaged in the struggle over public space and thereby transformed themselves into political citizens with political voice. Drawing equally from urban, visual, and performance studies, *Ephemeral Histories* suggests that visual practices, and especially ephemeral visual practices, had lasting effects. They allowed multiple groups an opportunity to claim public spaces and present complex political argument, to engage in ongoing political debates that took place directly on city streets and walls and that created an alternative geography of political practice in the city center, peripheries, and poblaciones. Graffiti, posters, and murals were therefore immediately targeted for erasure. Yet, as I point out in the introduction, these erasures did not signal an end to the visual as political practice. Ephemeral forms of public writing and art became the basis for continued if clandestine forms of urban politics, debate, and association. Santiaguinos were able to rebuild networks of political association and establish clandestine political practices by drawing on, altering, and reimagining the very ephemeral practices they had sharpened in the democratic exchange that had characterized the Popular Unity's thousand days. Erasure set the condition in which new forms of visual culture and new scopic regimes emerged after the coup. It paradoxically offers a window onto the tense interplay of persistence and change that characterized the early years of military rule and that animated urban politics but is obscured by scholars' emphasis on the coup as a single moment of rupture and violence.

Clandestine photographic practices drew on a history of creative experimentation that went hand in hand with the exploration and veneration of the objective gaze. The archive of the state press, Quimantú, is particularly instructive, for it allows scholars to compare the editorial marks on the press's photographs with the images published in its myriad illustrated magazines. The illustrated journal *Documentos Gráficos* saw only four issues published through 1973. Its third issue "chronicled" the relationship between photography, the city, and the complex dynamics of urban protest. The *Quimantú* journal exposed this relationship between class, place, and politics in a special issue titled "Classes of Marches."[68] Turning their attention to the competing April 1972 marches for and against Allende, the *Documentos Gráficos* staff editorialized: "Santiago has witnessed two massive marches. The first, on April 12, was called by the opposition to protest the 'loss of liberty.' More recently, on April 18, workers organized in support of the government to prompt it to forge ahead with its promises. . . . [W]e are not here interested in the numbers. We would instead like to analyze WHAT CLASS of people attends these marches, how they arrive there, what do they look like, how they act, etc."[69] This methodology was predicated on the evidence provided by the camera lens. Here, the staff articulated a clear definition of photographic indexicality: "We could write hundreds of pages about these topics. We prefer to let our photographs speak for us. The reader can in this way form his or her own judgment. Photos reveal reality as it is."[70] Pulling the veil from reality "as it is" rendered text and commentary superfluous: "We have added captions at the foot of these images. These are the comments that any person would make having seen both marches. . . . [T]he most important thing[,] . . . and this should not be forgotten, is that photographs never lie."[71] The objectivity of the lens was rendered clear and simple. Captions described rather than interpreted. Presenting the objectivity of photography as an organizing trope allowed *Documentos Gráficos* to play on and naturalize powerful arguments regarding gender and class.

The magazine's editors juxtaposed images of well-dressed older women driving their vehicles to the city center to stills of humbly dressed working-class protesters hanging off overflowing buses or simply walking, en masse, to their destination.[72] Its photo-essay was framed by questions—"How do people move?" and "What distinguishes one from another?"[73] These inquiries set up a clear dichotomy between marchers in terms of class. The photograph's caption reads, "The most exclusive group of wealthy Chileans attended the march organized by the opposition. Since every family owns two or three cars, they did not have difficulty reaching the stage located at the corner of Avenida Grecia and Salvador."[74] Intertwining photo and text, the journal made a powerful and cogent argument regarding the importance of place and class, written in the language of material symbols ranging from dress to the "work tools" that the working class carried as a "banner."[75] Invoking the unquestioned "fact" of the objective lens, it fashioned a contrast between marchers, highlighting the importance of transportation and movement through the city. This piece rendered the women's desire, ability, and "right" to move through the city as they pleased as a sign of class privilege and proposed to show them what they were: political and class interlopers in a scene that now "belonged" to the "popular government."[76]

To this point, *Documentos Gráficos* remains very much in line with a traditional definition of photography's indexicality. But the organization of the press's photographic archives tells a more complicated story. The photographs are not categorized by photographer. They are instead organized according to categories and practices: "volunteer labor," "strike," and so on. Images include women at Mother's Centers; posters and public art; the happiness of children; and middle-class youth side by side with the president and politicians—effectively outlining or imaging a legitimate political subject and a broadly inclusive national body. These photographs chart myriad complex political practices, including mass marches and protests and the associative culture of women's groups and communal pots. The photographs collected in the archive populated illustrated magazines like *Documentos Especiales, Nosotros los Chilenos,* and, most significantly, *Ahora Gráfico, Mayoría,* and *Documentos Gráficos.*

The plasticity of this classification system and of individual photographs is clearly seen in the juxtaposition of archived and public images. Each archival print contains notes on the size and shape of each photograph to be published, information on cropping, and suggestions regarding their projected placement in each magazine, all recorded in pencil on the reverse side of the image. The significance of this juxtaposition is clearest in a close reading of *Documentos Gráfico*'s protest series. The journal's marriage of text and image frames the protest in simple, dichotomous terms: the Popular Unity versus the opposition; joy versus hatred; surface versus action behind the scenes. Yet these categories, and the series of images that accompanied them, point to a struggle over the political narrative and significance of protest. If the opposition's march played on politicized motherhood as the main point of the protest, the magazine sought to wrestle the narrative of gender into the language of class conflict. By editing its images, *Documentos Gráficos* countered marchers' claims to represent both family and nation by instead highlighting the class distinctions *between* women. The images were chosen and shaped to highlight the same material culture that protesters had politicized in the march of the empty pots, in their use of pots, pans, pins, and other symbols. They also sought to resignify faces, bodies, and bodily comportment. In a section simply titled "Faces," photographs and text together establish a key distinction between two "typical faces that require no further comment. The first shows a right-wing woman. . . . In the second, a homemaker who attended a pro-government march. These photographs do all the talking."[77] The commentary supposes that class is indelibly written onto these different women's bodies, superseding motherhood as a universal, political construct.

These texts treat photographs as evidence, as a transparent record of the material culture of debate. But these pages formed part of a complex process through which narratives of gender, class, and politics were creatively intertwined. In one photograph, reproduced in *Documentos Gráficos*' third issue, a man in a suit strides resolutely through a street strewn with the material remnants of protest, a newspaper tucked under his arm. The accompanying caption notes that his is a figure "most representative of the march of the wealthy," an emblem of capital and class distinction that marks the protest as of the "bourgeoisie."[78] If class was elevated to counter the potential for gendered solidarity, the foregrounding of bourgeois masculinity here defines the politics of protest. Yet the photograph has been radically cropped. Santiago's Museo Histórico contains the original image, in which a line of women protesters is beside the suited man, and the composition of the image leads the eye across the marching women and to the suited figure. The published version undercuts the tension between class and gender that animated this composition and wrests the narrative squarely into the realm of class.

As these early examples suggest, the relationship between urban practice, political discourse, and visual culture was continually contested. By juxtaposing these sources, we can perceive the flexibility and malleability of political discourse and the complex relationship between streets and national political debates, here mediated by material and visual languages that historians often ignore. Presenting the photographic archive as a complex site of historical recollection, Roberto Tejada finds that photographs are not transparent representations of a historical moment, or simple vehicles for the construction of a singular national narrative. Rather, they "render inoperative the conventional historiographical narratives, because the positivist value of a photograph as a mere visual document is so often betrayed by its inadequacy or failure to represent a categorical conclusion."[79] Examining archives and sequences of photographs in context allows us to draw out shared themes and shifting relationships between images and contradictory narratives that develop between them.[80] Tejada's is, among other things, a radical reinterpretation of the role and potential of the photographic archive. Similarly, we see here that the Quimantú photographs could be pieced together in innovative forms, and photographers and editors did just that. This single example suggests that the archive is not the arena of monolithic officiality counterpoised to performance, action, or product but is itself a site of creative construction where the organization of images into categories, and where the selection, intervention, and manipulation of photographs generates political discourse.[81]

This lesson serves us well when we look at street photography after the coup. Street photography became the paradigmatic form of documenting and commenting on human rights abuses and repression on the city's thoroughfares. Yet clandestine photographers' personal archives reveal that they too built a flexible, creative photographic practice. Their creative engagement with tropes of objectivity and transparency paradoxically formed the foundation for open-ended and subjective aesthetic play even in moments of extreme repression.[82] Their photographs fashion an alternative way of thinking about city, space, and secretive movement through city streets. They present the urban world as site, scene, and stage for political practice in tyranny. In the context of military censure, these photographic collections complement, engage, and critique traditional sources of political history: properly contextualized, they serve as evidence of repression, but they are also themselves innovative praxis, a way of knowing and arguing about politics that was rooted in democracy but reimagined in dictatorship.

It is no surprise, then, that Chilean scholars have recently begun to explore the "correlation between Chilean political history and the history of photography."[83] A handful of young photographers gravitated to symbolic sites of violence in order to photograph the aftermath of the overthrow of Allende, turning to the streets to document repression and resistance. Both international journalists and Chilean photographers entered the sites that the military regime had recast as symbolic centers of unquestioned authority and terror and produced haunting explorations of the connection between public space, state violence, and political hegemony. Photographs of the presidential palace erupting in flames, the nation's stadiums transformed into internment camps ringed by barbed wire, and armed soldiers patrolling checkpoints quickly became emblematic of state violence and were reproduced throughout the globe.

Scholars writing in the 1980s and 1990s drew a relatively strict distinction between "documentary photography" and "more reflexive" works that introduce the photographic referent in Chilean art.[84] The latter, these scholars claim, attempted to "deconstruct the myth of photographic objectivity" and the illusion of the photograph's transparency. More recent analyses have charted the eruption and institutionalization of documentary photography in the late 1970s and 1980s to challenge the idea that there existed a clear line between "documentary" and "experimental" photography. This simple distinction, they write, masked a deceptively complex dialectic. Understanding this tension requires rethinking the very "definition of 'documentary' and the indexical quality of the photographic sign" and recognizing the interconnection between "documentary" and "creative" photography.[85]

As we have seen, the military's reliance on the threat and reality of political repression radically altered the urban landscape, giving new significance to "unauthorized" forms of inhabiting public space and, in the case of the "disappeared," lending deadly significance to a person's sudden absence from public and private spaces. The visual medium and language that photographers chose reflected this change in the relationship between politics, presence, and public space. Military violence was meant to control public association in order to circumscribe the open-ended process of meaning-making found in political posters and murals and rupture the playful, creative interrogation of cinematic language favored by documentary filmmakers.[86] Urban photographers seized on the objective authority of the lens to document and comment on political violence as it was happening, proposing the transparency of the fixed photographic image in response to the crippling uncertainty that was the defining characteristic of military terror-as-usual.[87]

But they were also aware, as we should be, of the photograph's multiple and contradictory applications. Street photographers fashioned a new "scopic regime" under dictatorship but did not fully capitulate to the objectivity of the lens as a tool of ensured veracity in a context of a "state of siege." They seized on photography's claim to truth without ignoring the potential for creativity and play, and without forgetting what they had learned in democracy. Even seemingly objective visual practices created alternative mechanisms through which to keep memory "obstinate" and creative political debate active.[88]

Christian and Marcelo Montecino produced stunning photographs, including haunting images of the La Moneda in ruins and the National Stadium transformed into a concentration camp. Marcelo Montecino's personal collection contains a small selection of photographs authored by his brother, Christian, who was killed shortly after the coup. One series of images examines the Popular Unity's final celebrations. These are photographs of overflowing streets, Socialist Youth marching in disciplined formation, parading with sticks instead of guns over their shoulders—images that prefigure the Left's inability to wage armed resistance against military might. In each of these photographs, and in the tension between them, public art appears as a form of political practice in and of itself and, seen across the rupture of the coup, of a potential political world eradicated.[89]

The Montecinos gravitated back to the same city streets after the coup.[90] Their photographs of tanks rolling through the early mist of Santiago's main thoroughfares were taken surreptitiously, using spectators, who they leave blurry in the foreground, as cover. But their most striking series contrasts the destruction of the presidential palace with depictions of people beginning to resume a semblance of normal life amid the new reality of state-sponsored repression. One of Marcelo Montecino's trademark images shows a young couple embracing, looking back at the photographer while La Moneda lies crumbling in the background, personal pleasure or emotional comfort set against the backdrop of radical political and social crisis. In a second example, the photographer has moved closer to the building itself. The window from which Allende addressed crowds of onlookers lies shredded by missiles. A young cadet guards the palace walls, which are scarred by bullets. In the next, La Moneda's neoclassical facade, long an emblem of Chile's "democratic" parliamentarian legacy, provides the backdrop for passing crowds, once again free to move about the city center during the day. Their sideways glances and expressions betray fear, shock, and surprise. Their emotions are masked but evident. Finally, the photographer focuses directly on details of the building's destruction. The Chilean shield, wrought in iron and hanging over the palace's shattered entrance, displays the national motto, "By Reason or Force." The message is clear: the process of reasoned political debate has been resolved by the exercise of force.

When seen in series, these photographs provide a critical commentary on violence and everyday life and link military authority with repression.

The juxtaposition of these powerful symbols (the facade, shield and signs of destruction) gives new meaning to each isolated sign; the framing, manipulation, and juxtaposition of the images are creative acts that lay beneath the lens's objectivity. This is a testimonial series that acknowledged but pushed the limits of impartiality in order to articulate powerful, critical claims regarding the new connections the military established between public space and political hegemony.

The Montecino brothers' work inside the National Stadium offers persuasive examples of the seizure of public space. Marcelo Montecino entered the stadium on September 20, 1973, as part of a group of international photographers invited by the military junta to tour the camp. His photographs of the field and bleachers and of the guards and prisoners scattered throughout the stadium's "open" spaces present a stark contrast between uniformed, armed soldiers standing alert behind wire fences that separate them from the disheveled prisoners dressed in the same clothes they had worn when they were taken, an eclectic mix of rough woolen sweaters and, interspersed throughout, dress shirts and tailored suits. One poignant photograph is shot from within a group of guards, across the playing field and through a wire fence dotted with hanging clothes, evidence of the days and nights spent in the stadium.

Marcelo Montecino's pictures of the soldiers watching over the structure's interior spaces, under the bleachers, and posted in passageways that lead to areas off limits to the press are equally shocking. His images of prisoners seem to have been taken quickly, with the purpose of recording prisoners' fearful and incredulous looks in order to testify to the reality of terror kept hidden within the structure's walls. His photographs of the military linger on the expressions of officers and cadets, individualizing these figures. The cadets are young recruits, teenagers and young adults with questioning expressions that stand in contrast to the older soldiers' dark glasses and smug expressions. They hint at the pervasive violence within and beyond stadium walls.

In contrast, David Burnett's photographs of the National Stadium leave soldiers out of focus, indistinct but recognizable by their uniforms, helmets, and boots. Burnett fastens instead on the faces of prisoners, carefully framing them among the symbols of military power. By placing these symbols in the foreground of his images, Burnett suggests that our experience of his photographic space, our comprehension of depth and perspective in his images, is informed by or filtered through the persistent threat of violence. His images provide a rudimentary visual language of danger, fear, and power, in which these emblems of authority stand in stark contrast to prisoners' wide-eyed helplessness, the experience of terror made shocking, inescapable, corporeal reality.

Together, these photographers present the stadium not only as the site of terror-as-usual but also as an overarching symbol of human rights abuse.[91] Their images embody a new paradigm of representation that could document a nebulous and uncertain reality without losing sight of photography as a creative, analytical act.[92] They intimate that the military's authority was predicated, especially in the early stages of the dictatorship, on the threat of violence as a defining characteristic of everyday reality, a means of restructuring the public sphere and the experience of urban life. They were part of a broader process of resistance to military might and show us that military authority routinely met with citizens' stubborn attempts to reconvene a once-vibrant political culture in surprising places. Street photography, then, became a creative testimonial form.

In arguing for a creative testimonial form, I hope not to undermine the significant truth claim of the photograph or the key social and political role that this truth claim played in the context of military repression. Rather, I am inspired by Alicia Partnoy's analysis of the creative value of testimonial literature as an act of witnessing and evidence of survivors' value "as subjects with valuable contributions to critical and theoretical discussions."[93] Responding to Beatriz Sarlo's critique of testimony as analytical practice, Partnoy argues stridently that what "concerns me about these words and Sarlo's statements is the belief that survivors are unfit for theoretical reflection unless they undergo traditional academic training and do not refer directly to their experience."[94] Partnoy is here trying to undermine the purported opposition between experience and theoretical insight, between truth and substantial and creative analytical scholarship. "The challenge that Sarlo and many scholars in the United States and Latin America seem to share," she concludes, "involves the ability to train their imagination to go visiting without tying it to the leash of truth. In my view, that leash is a limit imposed by self-interest: the preservation of academia as the only realm where knowledge can be produced." Partnoy's critique introduces a way of thinking about testimonial genres that does not discount the political role of public memory (as her own extensive testimony against violence and complicity in Argentina indicates) while simultaneously opening space for the creative potential of purportedly "objective" registers.[95]

I adapt this perspective to suggest that photography not only records an external reality; it also serves as a creative, analytical, and argumentative practice. It is an act of recollecting and reconstructing a potent visual language in which narratives of violence and struggle are formed around complex visual symbols. In turn, the practice and display of these photographs allowed a range of individuals to seize meaning-making technologies to leave a trace of repression and resistance, and also formulate an alternative narrative and analysis. Regular citizens also used this double-edged tool in creative ways. Family members of the disappeared in Chile and Argentina, for example, publicly displayed cherished, private family photographs of their loved ones in an attempt to reassert the place of these absent individuals in a public and material world. In so doing, they reinscribed their presence in public and reclaimed public, symbolic spaces, such as the central square or the stadium, as a realm of political dissent. Street photography should be placed alongside public protest, ephemeral forms of public art, and documentary film as acts of creative political citizenship.

Claudia Calirman's analysis of Brazilian art in the first and most repressive years of the dictatorship is emblematic of scholars' attempts to rethink the relationship between art, production, and creativity, and especially their ability to tease out the significance of ephemeral practices in contexts of state sponsored violence.[96] Calirman finds that political repression paradoxically stimulated creative, even "anarchic practices."[97] The need for secrecy, speed, and subversion spurred innovative forms of visual and political expression. "Body art, media-based art, and conceptual practices," inspired by international trends, addressed "a very specific and local situation, creating new hybrid forms that embraced both a political tone and a strong drive toward artistic innovation and visual excellence." Artists turned the necessity of clandestine practice into the basis for radical innovation; rather than "confront the system overtly, they invented ways to get around it, discovering novel methods of questioning authority, both that of the regime and that of the prevailing art institutions of the time."[98]

Nelly Richard sees the Chilean "escena de avanzada," a heterogeneous group of artists who experimented with new discursive, conceptual strategies, as the most significant example of Calirman's general thesis. Richard, best known for her rich study of Chilean conceptual art under dictatorship, builds a seminal analysis of the "novel methods of questioning authority" that avanzada conceptual artists established under threat of repression. Richard's early work calls into being—by documenting, narrating, and naming—the avanzada scene.[99] The group shared certain beliefs in the politically destabilizing effect of the body and body art, the political importance of ephemeral urban "action" under repressive rule, and open-ended critique of modes of representation and political and social frames.

Richard focuses on photography as support for the avanzada's deconstructive action. "The introduction of photography" in these artists' work "coincide[s] with the end of that period of silence after the 1973 coup, when the artists had to carefully rethink the meaning of their practice in . . . a more explicit or actively critical way."[100] Richard here establishes, by way of example, a marked contrast between Adriana Valdés (who focuses squarely on the potential of photography under dictatorship as "a form of evidence and proof of accusation") and the avanzada artists' deconstructive practices in regard to photographic indexicality.[101] Eugenio Dittborn, for instance, incorporated photography into his paintings, mediated through the "grammar of collage and montage (with its techniques for cutting, fragmenting, juxtaposing, dissociating)." He effectively deconstructed photography's claim to truth and transparency through montage and collage, which emphasize fission, disconnection, and surprising pairings. Cutting, drawing on, and superimposing images allowed Dittborn to "underscore the material violence" that fractured otherwise coherent images or subjects and introduced photography into a new context "proper to a culture of fragments." He effectively complicates the indexicality of the photograph by inserting it in new aesthetic and urban contexts and thereby "activates" its potential as a generative figure around which to organize a critical language.[102]

Dittborn's work with identity card images recontextualizes these *fotos carné* by pairing them with painting and writing. They transform the carné's nominal role from "signs of identification" (indexical material that could allow the regime to identify and track its subjects) into a means by which artist and viewer could achieve a critical deconstruction of photographic objectivity and arrive at what Richard calls a "disidentification of signs." He neither relies on nor quickly dismisses the purported transparency of the photograph. He instead proposes a "theoretical-visual investigation into the question of photography,"[103] transforming the photograph from technical recourse into theoretical figure, a vehicle through which to rethink the very limits and function of photography.[104]

In her analysis of Dittborn, then, Richard successfully rescues the *dobleces,* or double function of the photograph under dictatorship, where photography is always about the affirmation of presence in the face of the shadowy reality of disappearance and uncertainty of terror, yet also reminds us of the illusion of the organic totality of the very form that, in its purported transparency, is "used to sustain representation discourses."[105] Her analysis is compelling and opens the door to reading photography as the foundation of a more flexible, critical, and creative testimonial genre. However, Richard's historical narrative and analysis of Dittborn depends on an understanding of the coup as a radical rupture, a discrete "event" with a clear before and after, a point dividing democracy from dictatorship. This assumption prompts her to argue that visual artists working under dictatorship believed in "naïve" discourses of transparent representation while dictatorship-era conceptual artists were forced to create subtler, more creative and self-reflexive practices.[106] This periodization structures her analysis of politics and aesthetics.

Although I draw on Richard's compelling and exciting analyses, I want to subtly alter her fundamental periodization. I argue that those practices that Richard terms "naive" were already critical and creative before the coup and that they served as a foundation for the type of deconstructive action that Richard locates squarely and stridently in the years of harshest military repression. This book understands different experiments with visual culture, including both journalistic street photography and Dittborn's deconstructionist works, as part of longer history that crosses the schism introduced by the coup. [107] This final chapter proposes an alternative chronology that connects dictatorship and democracy.

PHOTOGRAPHY, EPHEMERA, AND RESISTANCE: "CHALKBOARD CITIES"?

Military violence did not quiet the production of political meaning in public spaces during the Popular Unity. The junta used violence to *redefine* legitimate or proper ways of being in space along political, classed, and gendered lines. Being on the street was already a fundamentally political act, especially after the coup. In dictatorship, it was a dangerous act, and a potentially revolutionary one.

If images of La Moneda or the National Stadium were shared by solidarity movements worldwide, another set of images told a more local story of the stubborn conflict over public space and public expression that took place after the coup. Newspapers published telling photograph of "patriots" whitewashing walls that had been covered by political murals only days before. Koen Wessing's image of a suited man turning back to look over his shoulder at a small group painting over rayados in the city while overseen by police cradling machine guns, a photograph that graces this book's cover, speaks to the tangible, immediate attention paid to public art and public writing. The power of this image stems from a particular play of presence and absence: the whitewash is an opaque yet expressive symbol, lending extra significance to the forms of visual expression that it covered. It is part of the story, not its end.

Ephemeral public art was politically significant precisely because it was ephemeral, because it could be torn down and repainted daily, a metaphor

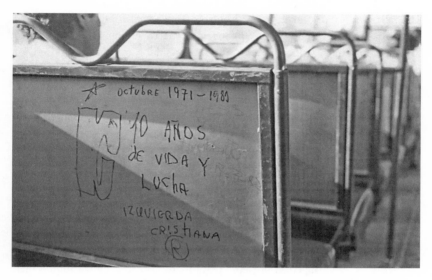

FIGURE 12. "IC: 10 años de vida y lucha." Graffiti on back of bus bench. Photograph by Kena Lorenzini. Black and white. Reproduced courtesy of the author. Kena Lorenzini, *Marcas crónicas: Rayados y panfletos de los ochenta* (Santiago: Ocho Libros, 2010), 104.

for and a vehicle driving this fluid political process forward. It became even more important after the coup, when the military's urgent attempt at erasure was effective but not complete. Small pockets of armed resistance persisted, especially in outlying shantytowns. Underground networks and solidarity campaigns sprang up throughout the country and across the globe. As Kena Lorenzini's photograph suggests (fig. 12), activists in Santiago scrawled graffiti on bus seats, where they became mobile messages of resistance winding their way through the city. They offered new languages of political contention and bolstered new, clandestine geographies of political practice and association.[108] These small examples and actions illustrate the lasting significance of public expression. As the anthropologist Pedro Araya writes, "Resistant practices progressively opened space for new possibilities for political organization that led to the rebuilding of networks of sociability and political resistance."[109] Ephemeral forms of visual practice continued to rally resistance to the military government even in moments of harshest repression.

Public art emerges again and again as a transgressive act, a remnant of past political action and identity whose attempted erasure constitutes a radical political act and whose continued presence speaks to obstinate resistance.

The first wave of organized mass protests against the dictatorship shook the regime in the early 1980s. Between 1982 and the 1988 plebiscite that toppled Pinochet, and in the midst of these protests, Rafael Karque hid hundreds of political pamphlets in a shoebox in his house. Juan Pablo Rojas and Roberto Aguirre uncovered this collection and published it in a public exposition and accompanying catalog.[110] In their introduction to the catalog, Rojas and Aguirre chart the proliferation of these ephemeral written documents despite mounting repression organized under a 1975 statute decreeing it a crime "to be found holding flyers, pamphlets, or advertisements that serve to spread a political message." This statute and the threat of repression "did not stop people from frequently papering the streets and sidewalks of the city with these pamphlets, many of which form part of [Karque's] collection." Rather, military censorship meant that ephemera such as pamphlets were the only means of articulating political claims or organizing multitudinous gatherings. Although until now they have not been considered viable scholarly sources, this collection presents pamphlets as material "through which to reconstruct the political history of the nation."[111]

In the early 1980s, Kena Lorenzini took to Santiago streets to photograph, as Guadalupe Santa Cruz writes, "the surface or skin of the city." She trained her camera on the circulation of public writing in pamphlets and graffiti. The relationship between city and subject animates Lorenzini's work. She returned again and again to city walls covered, inscribed, or intervened with "the censored word." Her collection, *Marcas crónicas*, begins with a series of five images of bathroom doors and walls that, while bereft of people, suggest a fascinating, vibrant dialogue in semipublic spaces. The first image is the inside of a bathroom door, with a relatively straightforward expression of disgust: "Merry Christmas for All but One . . . Death to the Jackal." The second is a more complex exchange. Words are scrawled on the bathroom wall in pencil and permanent ink. Simple tags, insults, and opposition party acronyms that cover the wall are scratched out and painted over. The final image charts the development of the dialogue in another stall. "Viva Pinochet" has been scrawled out and "Asesino" has been added, creating the critical phrase "Pinochet Asesino." The "Viva" of the next "Viva Pinochet" has again been crossed out, and the sentiment has been transformed again. It reads simultaneously "Fuck Pinochet" or "Viva Pinochet . . . In Exile." "In Exile" has again been scratched out. Though too blurry to be read, whole paragraphs of writing follow the phrases.

Lorenzini charts a similar, palimpsestic dialogue in public space. On one wall, the original, "Join the Communist Youth," is superseded by an aggressive commentary: "Join the Communist Youth . . . The Same Drunks as

Always, and Assassins." This sentence is written over the Socialist Party insignia, under which someone has scrawled the hammer and sickle. Lorenzini's images present public debates written throughout the city. One sentence often follows another horizontally. But most often one iteration is simply scrawled over another. In a fascinating image, Lorenzini records the phrase "Juan Pablo Hermano, Llévate al Tirano," which calls rhythmically on the pope to use his visit to remove Pinochet. A single painted arrow leads the reader's eye around a ninety-degree turn to another writer's sentiment: "And forgive us for his hate."[112]

Lorenzini's photographs study how public art and public words circulate in the city in diverse ways. Entire walls are covered in statements of political position or debates about proper practice. These are not images of beauty but instead a city where the "surface" or "skin" has become a site of continual conflict, expression, and erasure. In others, "official" public pronouncements have been disfigured or resignified. In one of the most fascinating photographs, someone has used the cover of a commonplace act, the commemoration of young love, to articulate political sentiment. The assertion of coupledom written on the back of a bus seat, "Marisol y Humberto, 17–3–82," is overlaid by the announcement "Izquierda Cristiana's 10 years of existence (1971–1989)." The furtive action of a passenger holding only a pen has transformed the bus into a mobile advertisement of political resistance and persistent political association.[113]

Lorenzini's photographs also reveal a keen eye for how surprising visual and textual strategies (including but not limited to irony, double meanings, and humor) fashion evanescent publics. The ephemeral nature of public writing, along with the intersection of textual and visual strategies, helped to set the conditions of possibility for an ongoing, clandestine dialogue. Her photographs are carefully composed and curated to show the palimpsestic layering of texts that instantiates the "myriad play on words, reversals, or displacements of meaning" that characterizes clandestine urban politics. "Toque de queda" (state of siege) becomes "toque de cacerolas" (which refers to the ubiquitous pots and pans protests); "hombre" (man, as in "Büchi is the Man") becomes "hambre" (hunger) with the stroke of a brush; "votar" (to vote) is transformed into its Spanish homonym "botar" (to throw out, depose).[114] One statement reflects or alters another; textual devices like plays on words and visual tactics like superimposition, juxtaposition, and montage dislocate the familiar, create new political languages and slogans, or highlight inconsistencies in official rhetoric.

In one image, an advertisement lauding the military's purported ability to foster economic success is utterly disfigured by splattered paint, graffiti, and

FIGURE 13. "NO Más Pin8." Graffiti on city of Santiago billboard advertisement. Photograph by Kena Lorenzini. Black and white. Reproduced courtesy of the author. Kena Lorenzini, *Marcas crónicas: Rayados y panfletos de los ochenta* (Santiago: Ocho Libros, 2010), 61.

printed pages averring simply, "Enough! Pinochet Lies!" Another reveals an official placard claiming, "The Country Deserves . . . ," where the conclusion has been covered over, replaced by the ubiquitous "No" repeated again and again, painted on scraps or streams of paper (*papelografo*) and pasted over billboards, scrawled on walls and advertisements, or spray painted over street signs. The juxtaposition of paint and paper over public texts and existing words pieces together an altogether new message, "The Nation Deserves a No [Vote]."[115] In another photograph of an advertisement taken on the edges of the city, a baby carriage appears in the foreground, with text that claims, "Today's Reality: More Health"; over the text someone has scrawled "NO Pin8" ("Pin8" is the colloquial, critical shorthand for Pinochet). But this text does not simply cover, disfigure, or obliterate. The new "NO" is superimposed on and precedes the original "More," resulting in a new phrase that references the ubiquitous cry of resistance, "No Más . . . ," and would be read as "No More Pin8" (fig. 13).[116]

In a final, related photograph, a billboard extolling the benefits of Pinochet's export economy has been splattered with paint. "No" has been spray painted above, though the "o" has been written as a heart; below, the Communist Youth have painted their initials (fig. 14). The billboard's text

FIGURE 14. "No al plan patronal . . . " Paper, paint and graffiti on billboard.
Photograph by Kena Lorenzini. Black and white. Reproduced courtesy of the
author. Kena Lorenzini, *Marcas crónicas: Rayados y panfletos de los ochenta*
(Santiago: Ocho Libros, 2010), 81.

has been covered by paper that reads, "No to employer's plan, No to unemployment, No to misery, and No to dictatorship." Another papelografo
screams, "Enough! Pinochet Lies." The advertisement has been fully transformed by multiple moments of public writing and overwriting.[117] Altering
words already painted on public advertisements, traffic signs, and walls
was a key tactic that proved political debate could continue in an otherwise
censored public arena.

Writing itself refashioned the experience of the city and the political
potential of urban citizenship, effectively locating the practice of political
citizenship back on city streets.[118] Fleeting forms of public writing produced
both city and citizen. "Those words were the city," Santa Cruz avers.[119]
Clandestine writing brought together "a community that exists in and for
that writing." It reclaimed spaces of public presence and dialogue that had
been fractured and shut down by violent repression and disappearance; the
ephemeral circulation of words, texts, and images in dictatorship "convened" new political publics that could exist if only temporarily in the clandestine sites and spaces that created fissures in the dictatorship.[120]

Pamphlets and flyers played an especially important role in organizing
new political publics and cultivating new networks of association. Texts

FIGURE 15.   Whitewashed graffiti on exterior house wall. Photograph by Kena Lorenzini. Black and white. Reproduced courtesy of the author. Kena Lorenzini, *Marcas crónicas: Rayados y panfletos de los ochenta* (Santiago: Ocho Libros, 2010), 105.

called passersby to meetings or marches (e.g., "The General Strike Is Coming, Pinochet Will be Going"). Pamphlets might call for strikes, provide time and place, and delineate the reasons for protest, often in great detail. Some featured handwritten text, cartoons, or photocopied images.[121] Others communicated information, statistics, and political analysis. Public sphere scholars have been more comfortable developing their paradigm of fluid democratic exchange in the nineteenth and early twentieth century, in political contexts closer to Habermas's original ideal. My research on ephemeral forms of public art and public writing suggests a different possibility. It illustrates that, far from breaking down in contexts of dictatorship, public sphere theory and the analysis of political publics is even more significant in dictatorship. In fact, a study of how public writing supported and sanctioned clandestine arenas and networks of political resistance shines light on the fluidity of the mechanisms by which publics were formed and reformed in the fissures of military repression, in the interstices and through the act of erasure.

Sensitivity to ephemeral forms of debate reveals a complex view of layered urban space. This book takes as its object of study the physical or material city. This history of the city (re)made and (re)mapped by the circulation of people, protesters, pamphlets, rayados, images, and other ephemera is also the history of an urban public coming together in seemingly innocuous practices, even if only for a moment.[122] Lorenzini argues that rayados "as a whole spoke to something concrete, to the possibility that a *marca crónica* inscribed on a wall or a fragment of city space, could pierce the barriers that impeded our freedom of expression."[123] Similarly, Santa Cruz claims that clandestine public writing is always a meditation on the practice of erasure—a performance that paradoxically opens the possibility of ongoing debate in the interspaces of a burgeoning repressive apparatus. Lorenzini's work ultimately explores the crucial role that public writing and public images could play in protecting and rebuilding political citizenship under duress. Far from merely documenting reality, Lorenzini's images are a reflection on "a new way of seeing the city" that includes the visible and invisible, marked and erased, circulated and silenced.

Lorenzini charts the chronology of and the process by which public texts formulate a live public debate that relies on the fluidity, instability, and ephemerality of public writing under the threat of censure. Even the erasure of public texts creates the sense of ongoing political practice, as the ugly evidence of censure only creates dangerous curiosity about what lies under whitewash.[124] Whitewash is not an end to the conversation but another layer that lends new meaning to the ongoing exchange. A number of Lorenzini's images explore the complexities of erasure, examining how words and images shine through thin layers of cover, how new words are scratched into the paint, and how the spectacle of erasure itself shapes public life under repression. Figure 15 is evocative only because whitewash has made spectacle of a persistent sphere of political association organized in plain sight. Yet, unlike the other photographs of erasure, which focus squarely on the wall and the text mediated by coats of white or black, this one creates a contrast between thick paint covering political expression, dripping ominously to the floor, and two smiling women deep in conversation on city streets. It hints at the many ways in which the ephemeral practices that were utilized and developed in democracy took new forms under dictatorship and ultimately helped buttress a vibrant, clandestine public sphere of political debate.

Epilogue

Ephemeral Histories: Erasure and the Persistence of Politics

The spaces of political participation that workers, students, and pobladores fought for during the Popular Unity were brutally and quickly closed after the military coup. Public art was an immediate target of erasure, a crucial node in the military's project to cover the remnants of the Popular Unity, prohibit public gathering, and wash the walls clean of the "epic, contestatory, commemorative" register of the past.[1] Their aim was the total eradication of politics. They were not wholly successful.

Most Brigada Ramona Parra murals and the photographic evidence of their existence were destroyed immediately after the coup. Images of people whitewashing public walls, painting over murals, ripping down posters, and burning books in the streets stand in stark contrast to an urban world that was made into a site of political debate and social change under Allende. Muralists conceived of their work as inherently ephemeral. But precisely because they employed a variety of materials that included household paint and car oil, their murals often outlived the thin coat of whitewash or paint used to cover them. A mural painted over in a night would sometimes begin to show the next morning as the sun slowly burned through the outer layer.

This tension between ephemerality and persistence, erasure and obstinacy animated a reinvention of the Mapocho riverbed as a site of repression and resistance. These complex tropes were organized around a resilient tradition of clandestine public art. The charging waters of the Mapocho River spilled over into city streets in the aftermath of heavy rains that struck in the early 1980s. As it calmed and sunk back into its basin, the river revealed a public secret: the intricate murals drawn by artists, workers, students, and members of the surrounding shantytown communities in the last days of Allende's government emerged from under the layers of whitewash that had covered them for close to a decade. The reappearance of these collective works of mural art celebrating the role of the Left in Chilean politics was particularly shocking after the military junta had disposed of cadavers in the river's waters.

In studying these often-overlooked forms rooted in democracy but remade in response to radical repression, this book illustrates how clandestine visual practices ultimately helped a range of citizens maintain and recreate networks of political association and identity that had been shattered by continued political violence. Yet chroniclers place this reappearance, and subsequent reactions, at different points in history, ranging from the late 1970s to the early 1980s. The writer Pedro Lemebel positions the reappearance as an event in a nebulous time in the decade after the fall of Allende: "Years after the coup, the murals painted along the Mapocho riverbank reappeared from under the military's stucco of enforced forgetting. They returned, time and time again, like the party's leftovers, pale, bleached sunflowers stubbornly searching out the light. . . . [They] reemerged fleetingly, under full state of siege, and graphically presented the events that had been covered by official whitewash."[2] Others, more precise, locate the reappearance of the murals in 1983, amid the rise of student and other street protests, as well as the reemergence of brigadas as public political players. What lies behind this slippage?

As Portelli reminds us, "errors" in recollection are not simple inconsistencies. They are, instead, instructive of a particular way of remembering and organizing the past.[3] Whatever the differences between these narratives, subjects remember the "event" of the Mapocho mural reappearance in moments of greatest repression and burgeoning instances of resistance. These errors point to the fact that these in situ performances anchor a larger argument regarding ephemeral art and the persistence of political resistance. Here, again, memory, muralism, and visual practices intersect: their narration of the murals' reemergence shows that practitioners continued to understand public art as a means of and a vehicle for rehearsing political identity and action, and the ways in which artists and activists claimed city spaces, including riverbed walls, was a tenacious form of political contest. Visual practice, material culture, and the repertoire of urban action remained the stuff of political argument and laid a new foundation for complex forms of political resistance. We can read these competing memories, the disjuncture between them and the errors that distinguish them, "against the grain" to garner insight into how memory continued to be organized in and around urban politics and visual culture in democracy and dictatorship. This is not memory versus forgetting but memory as competing remembrances filtered through and structured around public action.[4]

Taking public forms of political expression as the object of study has allowed me to analyze the process of political debate as it spilled into and was fought out in the streets by a range of different actors. I have shown that urban politics in the postwar period was related to but not determined by parties, unions, or other "traditional" sites and forms of politics "from above." Gendered and classed symbols, languages, and narratives were articulated on the city's streets and walls—in public protests and marches, posters and murals, and documentary film and photographs. These were also taken up in congressional debates, where they underwrote and buttressed traditional political strategies. They shaped political arguments, justified impeachment attempts, and supported tactics to block or hinder the Popular Unity's constitutional road to socialism. Combining archival, textual, and visual analyses with oral history, and bringing this hybrid methodology to bear on the study of the politics of public space, I have examined how Chilean political conflict was carried out and political discourse written and rewritten in democracy and again in dictatorship.

This perspective and methodology offers new insight into the study of political change. It draws out the complexities of state formation in Chile and during the Popular Unity. Scholars often describe Allende's presidency and overthrow as the "inevitable" outcome of growing polarization, which progressed teleologically toward a violent resolution. However, studying everyday forms of mobilization and unpacking the visual and material culture of political debate in public space points us to the ways in which Left and Right political strategies and discourse developed not in contradistinction but in relation to each other. We cannot examine either side of this conflict in isolation but instead as dialectically related camps.

My study of political change in turn reveals the intimate connections between politics from below (on the streets) and politics from above (in Congress). It broadens our understanding of who participated in political debate and how they did so. It helps us question or expand what we consider "political" acts, and how we consider the relationship between traditional political organization and association and the alternative sites, forms, and spheres of public political debate. I hope to have suggested a path and opened a space in which to investigate how things like design, image, and color became key components of political conflict, arguing that how people inhabit and transit through the city are important components of this political process. I have proposed an analysis of political practice, tactics, and dialogue that includes overlapping publics, multiple sites, and multiple instances of appearance, erasure, and reappearance. I hope that this method and perspective—in its cross-disciplinary interests, its respect for ephemeral documents, and its attention to political process and action—can provide new insight into political change in and beyond Allende's Chile.

Notes

INTRODUCTION

1. These are, of course, rough (and conservative) figures. I examine this literature more closely in my concluding chapter. See, recently, Steve J. Stern, *Remembering Pinochet's Chile: On the Eve of London 1998* (Durham, NC: Duke University Press, 2004), 168–71; Edward Murphy, *For a Proper Home: Housing Rights in the Margins of Urban Chile, 1960–2010* (Pittsburgh, PA: University of Pittsburgh Press, 2015), 290 nn. 10–11, 20–22; Patricia Verdugo, *Pruebas a la vista: La caravan de la muerte* (Santiago: Editorial Sudamericana Chilena, 2000).

2. Peter Winn, *Victims of the Chilean Miracle: Workers and Neoliberalism in the Pinochet Era, 1973–2002* (Durham, NC: Duke University Press, 2004), 19.

3. Eliana Parra, in conversation with Murphy, *For a Proper Home*, 137.

4. See, e.g., Mauricio Vico and Mario Osses, *Un grito en la pared: Psicodelia, compromiso político y exilio en el cartel chileno* (Santiago: Ocho Libros Editores, 2009).

5. Many struck spoons together in workplace lunchrooms or banged pots and pans in their homes late into the night, an appropriation of the symbolism of the empty pots protest, here reinterpreted as an aural remonstration against military repression and curfew.

6. Pedro Araya, "*El Mercurio* miente: Siete notas sobre escrituras expuestas," *Revista Austral de Ciencias Sociales* 14 (2008): 157–71.

7. Alan Angell, "Chile since 1958," in *Chile since Independence*, ed. Leslie Bethell (Cambridge: Cambridge University Press, 1993), 129–202 [154].

8. Peter Winn, *Weavers of Revolution: The Yarur Workers and Chile's Road to Socialism* (New York: Oxford University Press, 1986), 58.

9. See Winn, *Weavers of Revolution*, 58; Simon Collier and William F. Sater, *A History of Chile, 1808–2002* (Cambridge: Cambridge University Press, 2004), 269; Angell, "Chile since 1958," 131. As I discuss below, these hard-fought, gradual openings exist alongside a continued history of political and social violence or inequity that belies any simple "exceptionalist" discourses and their penchant for dividing "peaceful" democracy from violent repression.

For earlier periods, see James Wood, *The Society of Equality: Popular Republicanism and Democracy in Santiago de Chile, 1818–1851* (Albuquerque: University of New Mexico Press, 2011); and Jody Pavilack, *Mining for the Nation: The Politics of Chile's Coal Communities from the Popular Front to the Cold War* (University Park: Pennsylvania State University Press, 2011).

10. See for this period Mario Garcés, *Tomando su sitio: El movimiento de pobladores de Santiago, 1957–1970* (Santiago: LOM Ediciones, 2002); Mario Garcés and Pedro Milos, eds., *Memorias para un nuevo siglo: Chile, miradas a la segunda mitad del siglo veinte* (Santiago: LOM Ediciones, 2000); and Murphy, *For a Proper Home.*

11. For a masterful summary of left-wing politics, see Winn, *Weavers of Revolution*, 54–69. See also Gabriel Salazar, *Violencia política popular en las "grandes alamedas": Santiago de Chile, 1947–1987: Una perspectiva histórico-popular* (Santiago: Ediciones SUR, 1990); and Gabriel Salazar, "Sobre la situación estratégica del sujeto popular," in *Unidad Popular: Treinta años después,* ed. Rodrigo Baño (Santiago: LOM Ediciones, 2003), 209–26.

12. Collier and Sater, *A History of Chile,* 290, 292, 294–96. See also Peter Hakim and Giorgio Solimano, *Development, Reform and Malnutrition in Chile* (Cambridge: Cambridge University Press, 1978), 8.

13. Thomas Klubock finds that male and female workers "located their independence in their capacity to move from one sector of the economy to another in deeply rooted patterns of labor transience." Nitrate and copper mines, subject to the vicissitudes of the international market and the cyclical labor demands that it engendered, were only one node in a network that connected mines, fields, and the urban shantytowns where workers and their wives and families settled during times when opportunities ebbed elsewhere. Thomas M. Klubock, *Contested Communities: Class, Gender, and Politics in Chile's El Teniente Copper Mine, 1904–1951* (Durham, NC: Duke University Press, 1998), 47.

14. Shantytowns were sites and products of ongoing urban mobilization. As Angell finds, "The urban labour force in unions doubled in the six years of the PDC government. Peasant unions grew rapidly to include more than 120,000 members by 1970. Shantytowns became organized and increasingly militant in this period. The number of strikes increased from 564 in 1964 to 977 in 1969 (and to 2,474 in 1972). In the countryside where there had been only 3 strikes in 1960 and 39 in 1964, there were 648 strikes in 1968 and 1,580 in 1970. Seizures of farms, urban land sites for housing and factories also increased. In 1968, 16 farms were invaded by their workers; in 1970 there were 368 invasions. In the same period the number of urban land seizures rose from 15 to 352, and the number of factory seizures from 5 to 133." Angell, "Chile since 1958," 154–55.

15. Winn, *Weavers of Revolution,* 68–69.

16. Ibid.

17. For Winn, the battle of the poster and paintbrush is emblematic of the Left's success in harnessing emergent political groups. Winn's is a brilliant examination of the Yarur textile factory and workers' ability not only to seize

the industry but also to enter into negotiations with representatives of an embattled state and ultimately shape the cadence of its project for political change. Winn, *Weavers of Revolution*, 12.

18. Winn, *Weavers of Revolution*, 68–69.

19. Peter Winn, *La revolución chilena* (Santiago: LOM Ediciones, 2003), 91.

20. Esther Gabara, "Gestures, Practices, and Projects: [Latin] American Re-visions of Visual Culture and Performance Studies," *E-misférica* 7, no. 1 (2010), hemisphericinstitute.org/hem/en/e-misferica-71/gabara.

21. Winn, *Weavers of Revolution*, 68–69.

22. As Eric Zolov argues, political histories written "in the shadow of the Cold War" have treated culture as distinct from and a backdrop to "questions of political mobilization, state-sponsored violence, and the actions of insurgency and counterinsurgency organizations." This book takes up culture as a site of investigation in its own right, opening up new questions, approaches, materials, and methods to the study of politics in democracy and dictatorship. Eric Zolov, "Introduction: Latin America in the Global Sixties," *The Americas* 70, no. 3 (January 2014): 349–62 [351].

23. Henri Lefebvre, *The Production of Space* (Oxford: Blackwell, 1991); Edward Soja, *Thirdspace: Journeys to Los Angeles and Other Real-and-Imagined Places* (Oxford: Blackwell, 2012); Mary Ryan, *Women in Public: Between Banners and Ballots, 1825–1880* (Baltimore, MD: Johns Hopkins University Press, 1990).

24. See also James Holston, *Insurgent Citizenship: Disjunctions of Democracy and Modernity in Brazil* (Princeton, NJ: Princeton University Press, 2009).

25. Recently, scholars of state formation have drawn from language that parallels Lefebvre's and Soja's seminal arguments regarding public space. They contend that the state and the public space do not simply exist, but are "produced" (and, I would add, produced together). Following analysts of (social) space, then, scholars of state formation suggest that the state is not a fixed entity but a fluid historical construction.

26. Craig Calhoun, Richard Sennett, and Harel Shapira, "*Poiesis* Means Making," *Public Culture* 25 (2013): 195–200 [199]. Emphasis added.

27. Ibid.

28. This argument draws on the emergent field of visual studies, which "conceives 'vision' not as a naturally given optical faculty, but rather as an historical, shifting assemblage of technical and social forces that shape—without mechanically determining—the perceptual, cognitive, and psychic lives of subjects in their relation to the world." My goal in examining *poiesis* is to juxtapose this view of visual culture to a study of the production of urban space as political practice. See, e.g., Meg McLagan and Yates McKee, Introduction to *Sensible Politics: The Visual Culture of Nongovernmental Activism* (New York: Zone Books, 2012), 9–26 [12].

29. The phrase "a ganar la calle" is from a Patricio Aylwin speech, cited in Patricio Garcia F. and Luis Muñoz, eds., *Los gremios patronales* (Santiago:

Quimantú, 1972), 25. The idea that the public sphere is rooted in messy conflicts that redefine the terms and limits of politics is Hilda Sabato's. Hilda Sabato, "On Political Citizenship in Nineteenth-Century Latin America," *American Historical Review* 106, no. 4 (October 2001): 1290–1315 [1314]; see also Ryan, *Women in Public.*

30. My research suggests that Chilean urban politics stands as a significant example of the process defined by Henri Lefebvre and developed by Edward Soja by which the "appropriation of the social spaces of everyday life is an essential precondition for the political empowerment of subordinated social groups" (Ryan, *Women in Public,* 22; see also Henri Lefebvre, *The Production of Space* [Oxford: Blackwell, 1991]; Edward Soja, *Thirdspace: Journeys to Los Angeles and Other Real-and-Imagined Places* [Oxford: Blackwell, 2012]). Studies of the public sphere, political citizenship, and public space can complement traditional political histories and their focus on elections, voting patterns, and state building. This book suggests an avenue for weaving these perspectives together, grounding political citizenship in public practice and showing how these actions inform and enrich national politics.

31. See, e.g., Nancy Fraser, "Rethinking the Public Sphere: A Contribution to the Critique of Actually Existing Democracy," *Social Text,* no. 25–26 (1990): 56–80; Mary P. Ryan, *Civic Wars: Democracy and Public Life in the American City during the Nineteenth Century* (Berkeley: University of California Press, 1997); Pablo Piccato, "Public Sphere in Latin America: A Map of the Historiography," *Social History* 35, no. 2 (2010): 165–92.

32. See the essays collected in Craig J. Calhoun, ed., *Habermas and the Public Sphere* (Cambridge, MA: MIT Press, 1992), where, it should be noted, Habermas himself accepts and engages many of these revisions in his own contribution to the volume.

33. Pablo Piccato, introduction to *Actores, espacio y debates en la historia de la esfera pública en la Ciudad de México* (Mexico City: Instituto Mora, 2005), 5, 47.

34. Ryan, *Women in Public.* See esp. chap. 3, "Gender and the Geography of the Public," 92; and chap. 4, "The Public Sphere: Of Handkerchiefs, Brickbats, and Women's Rights," 130–70.

35. Ryan, *Women in Public.* See also Mary Ryan's article on gender and public action: "Gender and Public Access: Women's Politics in Nineteenth-Century America," in Calhoun, *Habermas and the Public Sphere,* 259–88 [268]: "Sometimes these proliferating public groupings met at merchants' exchanges, mechanics halls, grand hotels, or neighborhood saloons. Often the meetings spilled out into the streets. Just as often the designated spot for assembly was a public thoroughfare, street corner, or town square. Wherever their location, these invitations to popular assemblies were steeped in a language of publicness."

36. Sabato, "On Political Citizenship in Nineteenth-Century Latin America," 1314. See also Piccato, "Public Sphere in Latin America," 174–76; Elias J. José Palti, "Recent Studies on the Emergence of a Public Sphere in Latin

America," *Latin American Research Review* 36, no. 2 (2001): 255–66; Calhoun, *Habermas and the Public Sphere;* Fraser, "Rethinking the Public Sphere"; Ryan, *Civic Wars.*

37. Piccato, "Public Sphere in Latin America," 174–76.

38. This articulation is a reformulation of James Holston's argument that, contrary "to so much nineteenth- and twentieth-century social theory about the working classes, members of those classes became new citizens not primarily through the struggles of labor but through those of the city—a process prevalent . . . throughout the global south." For Holston, the "experience of the city is, therefore, critical to the insurgence of a new formulation of citizenship," mainly through the "performance of citizenship" in the "commonplace public encounters." As "the urban poor gained political rights, became landowners, made law an asset, created new public spheres of participation, achieved rights to the city, and became modern consumers . . . the lived experiences of the peripheries became both the context and the substance of a new urban citizenship. In turn, this insurgence of the local transformed national democratization." Holston, *Insurgent Citizenship*, 9, 15, 23.

39. Hilda Sabato, *The Many and the Few: Political Participation in Republican Buenos Aires* (Stanford, CA: Stanford University Press, 2001); Sarah Chambers, *From Subjects to Citizens: Honor, Gender, and Politics in Arequipa, Peru, 1780–1854* (University Park: Pennsylvania State University Press, 1999); Ryan, *Women in Public.*

40. An ever-widening range of young scholars have recently examined political conflict in a series of unexpected places. See, e.g., Brenda Elsey, *Citizens and Sportsmen: Fútbol and Politics in Twentieth-Century Chile* (Austin: University of Texas Press, 2011); Murphy, *For a Proper Home;* Alison J. Bruey, "Organizing Community: Defying Dictatorship in Working-Class Santiago De Chile, 1973– 1983" (PhD diss., Yale University, 2008); Clara Han, *Life in Debt: Times of Care and Violence in Neoliberal Chile* (Berkeley: University of California Press, 2012); Clara Han, "Memory's Manifestations: Salvador Allende in La Pincoya," *NACLA* (Fall 2013), https://nacla.org/article/memory%E2%80%99s-manifestations-salvador-allende-la-pincoya (last accessed September 10, 2015); Joshua Frens-String, "A New Politics for a New Chile," *NACLA* (Fall 2013), https:// nacla.org/article/new-politics-new-chile (last accessed September 10, 2015).

41. Instructive in the analysis of juxtaposition, collage/montage, and the city is Nicolas Whybrow's reading of Walter Benjamin, Bertol Brecht, and Michel de Certeau against each other "to provide and produce" theories of urbanism. Nicolas Whybrow, *Street Scenes: Brecht, Benjamin and Berlin* (London: Intellect Books, 2005), 55. On urban palimpsest, see Andreas Huyssen, *Present Pasts: Urban Palimpsests and the Politics of Memory* (Stanford, CA: Stanford University Press, 2003).

42. Huyssen's theorization of the urban palimpsest is predicated on the imbrication of memory and temporality, which, he argues, "have invaded those spaces and media that seem stable and fixed," including cities, monuments, architecture, and sculpture. It is by understanding "urban space as lived space"

that he is able to transcend distinctions between text and material, literary and concrete. Huyssen introduces the transitory to the fixed, the fluid to the material. "We have come to read cities and buildings as palimpsests of space," he writes, "monuments as transformable and transitory, and sculpture as subject to the vicissitudes of time." Huyssen delights in reading "intertextually, constructively, and deconstructively at the same time." Through this lens, the palimpsest becomes not only a literary trope, but a material reality that speaks to the sites where text and space, concrete and evanescent, and past and present intersect and build on one another. I am inspired by this complex reading of urban palimpsests here, though my research on Allende's Chile suggests a methodology one step broader. Despite his drive to destabilize the concrete, Huyssen traces a historical trajectory by which the open, fluid city-as-text and palimpsest gives way to a corporate, fixed city-as-image. My research suggests that in Allende's Chile the city in image formed the foundation for a complex, fluid, and creative performance, challenging any distinction between the textual and visual, the fluid and fixed. Huyssen, *Present Pasts*, 7, 63.

43. Michael Frisch, "Oral History and the Digital Revolution: Toward a Post-Documentary Sensibility," in *The Oral History Reader*, ed. Robert Perks and Alistair Thompson (London: Routledge, 2006), 16. Looking at oral history in a digital age, Frisch contends that digital technologies reduce all data to a common currency and, in so doing, create a potential equivalency between visual, oral, aural, and textual information. Where oral historians are too often confined by the unavoidable tension between "cooked" transcript and "raw" original, digital technologies allow investigators to fashion a "web" of information—whether "interviews, music, and performance, or other field documentation"—that anyone can democratically access, order, and share to make their own meaning. This fluidity, Frisch argues, is where real innovation occurs, for it displaces the emphasis from documentary product to democratic process. Michael Frisch, "Three Dimensions and More: Oral History beyond the Paradoxes of Method," in *The Handbook of Emergent Methods*, ed. Sharlene Hesse-Bibe and Patricia Leavy (New York: Guilford Press, 2010), 1–38 [37]. See also Michael Frisch, "American History and the Structures of Collective Memory: A Modest Exercise in Empirical Iconography," *Journal of American History* 75, no. 4 (March 1984): 1117–29.

44. Frisch, "Three Dimensions and More," 15, 17.

45. Ibid., 17.

46. See especially Steve J. Stern, *Remembering Pinochet's Chile: On the Eve of London 1998* (Durham, NC: Duke University Press, 2004), for an epistemological investigation of memory and the telling of the past.

47. Oral histories of the period are structured by fear, omission, regret, or triumph; yet these narratives also shed light on the process of politicization. My understanding of memory and oral histories leaves room for contradictory stories or overlapping narratives. It finds meaning in these sometimes-conflicting tales and especially in their narrative structure and form and the events that anchor these structures. I read history telling as a performance, a means of

claiming or seizing a voice in the present. Oral narratives are nonlinear tales that feature multiple stories, overlapping narratives, and contradictory meanings structured by the "event" defined by the visual practice in the past. See, e.g., Daniel James and Mirta Zaido Lobato, "Family Photos, Oral Narratives, and Identity Formation: The Ukrainians of Berisso," *Hispanic American Historical Review* 84, no. 1 (2004): 5–36; Ruth Finnegan, "A Note on Oral Tradition and Historical Evidence," *History and Theory* 9 (October 1970): 195–201; and Florencia Mallon, "Editor's Introduction," in *When a Flower Is Reborn: The Life and Times of a Mapuche Feminist*, by Rosa Isolde Reuque Paillalef (Durham, NC: Duke University Press, 2002), 17.

48. Of course, archival research, visual studies, and oral history have their internal limitations, and scholars have fruitfully examined how archival records can be shaped by and re-create repression practices. Yet these very limitations can also lead scholars to find new instances and avenues of political analysis. Political repression, for instance, lent even greater significance to transgressive visual practice and ephemeral performance of resistance fashioned in democracy but honed in dictatorship. See, e.g., Diana Taylor, *The Archive and the Repertoire* (Durham, NC: Duke University Press, 2003); Kristen Weldt, *Paper Cadavers: The Archives of Dictatorship in Guatemala* (Durham, NC: Duke University Press, 2014); Michel-Rolph Trouillot, *Silencing the Past: Power and the Production of History* (Boston: Beacon Press, 1997).

49. See Huyssen, *Present Pasts.*

50. As I lay out in the conclusion, the political history of twentieth-century Chile is often written around the exceptionalism of Chilean democratic transfer, unbroken until the "shocking" eruption of military violence on September 11, 1973. If studies of Chilean politics, political violence, and the public sphere often ended or began with the coup, reproducing the idea that military violence drew a "natural" break between dissimilar historical periods, recent scholars increasingly frame the studies across the rupture of the coup. The narrative of Chilean exceptionalism obfuscates a more complicated history that includes episodes of state-sponsored political violence and repression that range from a massacre of workers at Iquique in 1904 to the massacre and disappearance of hundreds of rural people in Ranquil in the 1930s to the exclusion and persecution of Communist Party members during the Carlos Ibáñez and Gabriel González Videla regimes and the history of systematic persecution of Mapuche peoples—all of which ultimately frames the dictatorial violence of Augusto Pinochet's regime. The violence of the coup emerges here not as an aberration in this otherwise unblemished story of democratic politics but as part of a significant history of state-sponsored repression and marginalization of ethnic, class, and gender others that shapes Chilean politics. See, e.g., Brian Loveman, "The Political Architecture of Dictatorship: Chile before September 11, 1973," *Radical History Review* 124 (January 2016): 11–41 [12, 31]. Florencia Mallon, *Courage Tastes of Blood: The Mapuche Community of Nicolás Ailío and the Chilean State, 1906–2001* (Durham, NC: Duke University Press, 2005), 236; Lessie Jo Frazier, *Salt in the Sand: Memory, Violence, and the Nation-State in*

Chile, 1890 to the Present (Durham, NC: Duke University Press, 2007); Murphy, *For a Proper Home;* Marian E. Schlotterbeck, "Everyday Revolutions: Grassroots Movements, the Revolutionary Left (MIR), and the Making of Socialism in Concepción, Chile, 1964–1973" (PhD diss., Yale University, 2013).

Many of the urban strategies I study in this book, especially those that mobilized women and entrepreneurs, created enduring means of political participation taken up again and again in democracy and dictatorship. Among others, Nancy Scheper-Hughes and Philippe Bourgois propose a relationship between political, structural, symbolic, and everyday violence in peacetime and in war, a continuum in which seemingly distinct forms of violence reflect and produce one another in a nonlinear and mimetic fashion. Nancy Scheper-Hughes and Philippe Bourgois, "Introduction: Making Sense of Violence," in *Violence in War and Peace: An Anthology,* ed. Nancy Scheper-Hughes and Philippe Bourgois (Malden, MA: Blackwell, 2003), 1–30.

51. Alejandro Velasco's new book finds a correlation rather than a contradiction between popular, even illegal repertoires of protest and democratic political participation. *Barrio Rising,* he writes, "engages a literature that identifies the blend of institutional and extra-institutional mobilization characteristic of urban popular politics not as exceptional but rather as an essential element of democratic life." He reads "urban popular protests that straddle legal and extralegal, institutional and noninstitutional means . . . as the radical realization of the promise of democratic participation, accountability, and citizenship." His work proposes a relationship rather than clash between popular urban protest and democratic practice. It "sheds light on the counterpoint of street protest and electoral politics that over the course of decades shaped popular understandings of democracy that live on today." Alejandro Velasco, *Barrio Rising: Urban Popular Politics and the Making of Modern Venezuela* (Oakland: University of California Press, 2015), 12–13, 17. See too Brodwyn Fischer, Introduction to *Cities from Scratch: Poverty and Informality in Urban Latin America,* ed. Brodwyn Fischer, Bryan McCann, and Javier Auyero (Durham, NC: Duke University Press, 2014), 1–8 [7].

52. Calhoun, Sennett, and Shapira, "*Poiesis* Means Making," 199.

53. This is an adaptation of Diana Taylor's seminal argument regarding performance: "Recognizing performance as a valid focus of analysis contributes to our understanding of embodied practice as an episteme and a praxis, a way of knowing as well as a way of storing and transmitting cultural knowledge and identity." Taylor, *The Archive and the Repertoire,* 278.

54. Charles Tilly, "The Rise of the Public Meeting in Great Britain, 1758–1834," *Social Science History* 34, no. 3 (Fall 2010): 291–99. On the theatricality of urban politics and the symbolic reappropriation of city space as a political act, see Alicia del Campo, "Theatricality of Dissent: Human Rights, Memory, and the Student Movement in Chile,"*Radical History Review,* no. 124 (January 2016): 177–91 [178].

55. Jadwidga Pieper-Mooney makes a parallel argument: "Under the UP government, the militant motherhood in the making would be strikingly dif-

ferent from the references to motherhood maternal activists had used early in the century." Women carved out spaces of political association and languages of political participation that engaged the tension between politics, class, and gender identities, while masculinity became a means of organizing or shaping political participation "from below." At the same time, "anti-Allende women also established a lasting presence of women on the political arena—and prepared fellow Chileans for a reinterpretation of women's citizenship rights." Under dictatorship, women not only organized as mothers and grandmothers to fight for detained family members, politicizing motherhood in new ways, but also built everyday strategies of survival and resistance and engaged in public protest and conflicts over national politics and everyday forms of patriarchy alike, all attempts to build and expand a complex gendered politics. Jadwiga Pieper-Mooney, *Politics of Motherhood: Maternity and Women's Rights in Twentieth-Century Chile* (Pittsburgh, PA: University of Pittsburgh Press, 2009), 104, 158–59, 161–62.

56. See, e.g., Michael Taussig's concept of "space of death," Primo Levi's articulation of "gray zones" of terror, and Scheper-Hughes and Bourgois on "everyday violence," all of which explore the ambiguities and indecipherability of terror. See Scheper-Hughes and Bourgois, *Violence in War and Peace.*

CHAPTER 1

1. The advisory committee was made up of the architects José Covacevich, Juan Echeñique, Hugo Gaggero, Sergio González, and José Medina. See Daniel Talesnik, "Monumentality and Resignification: The UNCTAD III Building in Chile," in *Latin American Modern Architectures: Ambiguous Territories,* ed. Patricio del Real and Helen Gyger (New York: Routledge, 2013), 135–52 [136–37].

2. Talesnik, "Monumentality and Resignification," 136–38.

3. Ibid., 138.

4. Ibid.; David F. Maulen de los Reyes, "Proyecto Edificio UNCTAD III: Santiago de Chile (junio 1971–abril 1972)," *Revista de Arquitectura* 13 (2006): 80–91 [86].

5. Talesnik, "Monumentality and Resignification," 140.

6. Ibid., 148. See also Paulina Varas Alarcón and José Llano Loyola, *275 días: Sitio, tiempo, contexto y afecciones específicas* (Santiago: Centro Cultural Gabriela Mistral, 2011).

7. José Covacevic, in conversation with José Llano Loyola, cited in Varas Alarcón and Llano Loyola, *275 Días,* 271.

8. Miguel Lawner, "Ante el ataque al edificio Diego Portales," *El Clarín de Chile,* August 8, 2007, aparienciapublica.blogspot.com/2007/08ap_ataque.al .edificio.diego.portales.html (last accessed August 6, 2015).

9. Allende, cited in Talesnik, "Monumentality and Resignification," 145.

10. Georg Schollhammer, cited in Miguel Lawner, letter to the editor, *El Mercurio,* August 14, 2007. See also *Crónica Digital,* August 17, 2007, www .cronicadigital.cl/2007/08/17/cronica-2007-p8771/ (last accessed September 12,

2014); Miguel Lawner and David Maulen, "UNCTAD III Santiago de Chile, 06/1971–04/1972," *Documenta 12*, February 4, 2008.

11. Lawner, letter to the editor, *El Mercurio*, August 14, 2007.

12. Ibid.; and Lawner, "Ataque al edificio Diego Portales."

13. Here Talesnik draws from a contemporary article in the magazine *Quinta Rueda*, which I examine later in this chapter. Talesnik, "Monumentality and Resignification," 145.

14. Lawner argued in his open letter to *El Mercurio*, "The military government ended the intense cultural activity that found a home in the buildings with a stroke of the pen and radically intervened in its architecture." Lawner, "Ataque al edificio Diego Portales." Luis Hernán Errázuriz writes: "In effect, the military coup imposed diverse restrictions and the exercise of force in the nation's political and cultural life, which led to the disarticulation of the Popular Unity and the democratic system by acts that Carlos Catalán and Giselle Munizaga summarize as the closing of a vast network of cultural organization, the suspension of the artistic-cultural organisms tied to the Left and Center's political parties[,] . . . and the unrestricted control of state power and systematic practice of repression and exclusion of progressive artists." Luis Hernán Errázuriz, "Política cultural del régimen militar chileno (1973–1976)," *Aisthesis, Revista Chilena de Investigaciones Estéticas* 40 (November 2006): 62–78 [67]; Luis Hernán Errázuriz, "Dictadura militar en Chile, antecedentes del golpe estético-cultural," *Latin American Research Review* 44, no. 2 (2009): 136–57, cited in Talesnik, "Monumentality and Resignification," 148, 148 nn. 21–23; and Luis Hernán Errázuriz and Gonzalo Leiva Quijada, *"El golpe estético": Dictadura militar en Chile, 1973–1989* (Santiago: Ocho Libros, 2012).

15. Varas Alarcón and Llano Loyola, *275 Días*, 94.

16. Talesnik, "Monumentality and Resignification," 148.

17. Ibid.; Varas Alarcón and Llano Loyola, *275 Días*, 94.

18. See Talesnik, "Monumentality and Resignification," 147–48. On "invented traditions," see Eric Hobsbawm and Terence Ranger, eds., *The Invention of Tradition* (Cambridge: Cambridge University Press, 1983), 1.

19. See Jorge Wong, "La maratónica construcción del edificio UNCTAD III," July 21, 2008, www.consejodelacultura.cl (last accessed August 5, 2015); *El Mercurio*, Sección Arquitectura, *Cuerpo Artes y Letras*, August 12, 2007.

20. *El Mercurio*, Sección Architectura, *Cuerpo Artes y Letras*, August 12, 2007. See esp. Christián De Groote, "Demolería el edificio entero," E3. See also in the same section, Mathias Klotz, "Desgraciadamente llegaron los bomberos"; Martín Hurtado, "Es un edificio desubicado en su contexto"; Cristian Boza, "Es una plataforma lineal, de suyo fea"; and Jorge Swinburn, "Podría tener más trasparencia hacia la Alameda."

21. Lawner and Maulen, "UNCTAD III Santiago de Chile, 06/1971–04/1972."

22. Lawner, "Ataque al edificio Diego Portales." Lawner's letter is written in response to the *El Mercurio* series.

23. Lawner and Maulen, "UNCTAD III Santiago de Chile, 06/1971–04/1972."

24. See Mario Garcés Durán, *Tomando su sitio: El movimiento de pobladores de Santiago, 1957–1970* (Santiago: LOM Ediciones).

25. Ibid. See also Edward Murphy, *For a Proper Home: Housing Rights in the Margins of Urban Chile, 1960–2010* (Pittsburgh: University of Pittsburgh Press, 2015); Alison J. Bruey, "Organizing Community: Defying Dictatorship in Working-Class Santiago de Chile, 1973–1983" (PhD diss., Yale University, 2008); Rodrigo Hidalgo Dattwyler, *La vivienda social en Chile y la construcción del espacio urbano en el Santiago del siglo XX* (Santiago: Pontificio Universidad de Chile, Centro de Investigaciones Diego Barros Arana, 2005).

26. Alfonso Raposo Moyano and Marco Valencia Palacios, "Práctica política del diseño urbano: Notas sobre la vida institucional y labor de la corporación de mejoramiento urbano, CORMU, 1966–1976," *Boletín del Instituto de la Vivienda* 18, no. 49 (January 2004): 112–43 [115].

27. Ibid., 113.

28. This parallels Gilbert M. Joesph and Daniel Nugent, "Popular Culture and State Formation in Revolutionary Mexico," in *Everyday Forms of State Formation: Revolution and the Negotiation of Rule in Modern Mexico*, ed. Gilbert M. Joseph and Daniel Nugent (Durham, NC: Duke University Press, 1994), 3–23.

29. In 1965, the Frei government created the Ministry of Urbanism and Housing, which housed a series of semi-independent institutions that included the Corporation of Housing (CORVI) and, eventually, the CORMU. I am indebted to the generous advice of David F. Maulen de los Reyes here. Pers. comm., May 1, 2015.

30. Raposo Moyano and Valencia Palacios, "Práctica política del diseño urbano," 118.

31. Daniela Sepúlveda Swatson, "La vivenda social en el período de participación popular, 1964–1973," in Ministerio de Vivienda y Urbanismo, *Chile: Un siglo de políticas en vivienda y barrio* (Santiago: MINVU, 2004), 126–79 [168].

32. Raposo Moyano and Valencia Palacios, "Práctica política del diseño urbano," 129–30. Recent journalistic pieces have traced the history of the San Borja towers, highlighting the subterranean web of pipes that provide the extant towers with potable water and steam heat belowground and the network of pedestrian walkways that would have linked the towers above. See, e.g., "Remodelación San Borja, el gran sueño urbano de Santiago," *La Tercera*, March 28, 2015, http://masdecoracion.latercera.com/2015/03/28/01/contenido/10_4698_9 .shtml (last accessed August 5, 2015); "Foto reportaje: La desconocida red de túneles con agua potable que está bajo Santiago Centro," *El Desconcierto*, July 25, 2015; Pepa Valenzuela, "Torres San Borja: Rascacielos clase media," April 14, 2012, https://pepaperiodista.files.wordpress.com/2012/04/torres.jpg (last accessed August 5, 2015).

33. Raposo Moyano and Valencia Palacios, "Práctica política del diseño urbano," 129–30. What was actually completed was only a fraction of this "first step": 7 hectares, 1,476 residents distributed in 12 towers and 120 or 125 apartments.

34. Ibid., 135–36.

35. MINVU, *Fundamentos y estructura del Plan habitacional* (Santiago: MINVU, 1971), cited in Edmundo Haramoto, "Políticas de vivienda social: La experiencia chilena de las tres ultimas decadas," in *Vivienda social: Reflexiones y experiencias,* ed. Modesto Callados N. et al. (Santiago: Corporación de Promoción Universitaria, 1983): 75–131 [101].

36. Haramoto, "Políticas de vivienda social," 107–9.

37. Emilio T. Sessa, "Arquitectura de vivienda social y construcción de la ciudad: Una mirada actual del Concurso Internacional: 'Área de remodelación en el centro de Santiago de Chile'—U.I.A. 1972," *Revista de Urbanismo,* June 24, 2011, 14–15, 17. See also Raposo Moyano and Valencia Palacios, "Práctica política del diseño urbano," 131; Haramoto, "Políticas de vivienda social"; Sepúlveda Swatson, "La vivenda social en el período de participación popular."

38. Christian Bartlau, "La monumentalidad incompleta del conjunto UNCTAD III o la fusion de fuerzas creadoras sin la posibilidad de proyectarse en el tiempo," in Allende and Illanes, *Trabajo en utopía,* 79.

39. Haramoto, "Políticas de vivienda social," 109–10, 129–30.

40. Raposo Moyano and Valencia Palacios, "Práctica política del diseño urbano," 141. In redrawing Santiago's urban fabric, Popular Unity "aspired to provide a rhetoric, a concrete symbolism [*simbolización*] that could be felt or experienced in the everyday." Carol Illanes, "'Así nació el gigante': Obra total y psicodrama social en la construcción del UNCTAD III," in Allende and Illanes, *Trabajo en utopía,* 82.

41. Vicente Gámez Bastén, "El pensamiento urbanístico de la CORMU (1965–1976)," *Urbano* 9, no. 13 (May 2006): 9–18 [13]. See also Vicente Gámez Bastén and Galith Navarro Bello, "La transformación del paisaje metropolitano y la idea de cinturón verde en el Plan Regulador Intercomunal de Santiago (1960–1994)," *Revista Electrónica DU&P: Diseño Urbano y Paisaje* 1, no. 3 (2004), www.ucentral.cl/du&p/pdf/002.pdf, last accessed March 4, 2016.

42. Gámez Bastén, "El pensamiento urbanístico de la CORMU," 14.

43. Ibid.

44. Ibid., 13. See also Jorge Wong and M. Rosa Giulano, "Concurso Internacional, área de remodelación en el centro de Santiago, Chile," *AUCA* 24–25 (1973): 23.

45. Wong and Giulano, "Concurso Internacional," 24–25.

46. Salvador Allende, "First Annual Message to the National Congress," in *Salvador Allende Reader: Chile's Voice of Democracy,* ed. James D. Cockcroft (Melbourne: Ocean Press, 2000), 89–113 [93].

47. See Hugo Palmarola Sagredo, "Productos y socialismo: Diseño industrial estatal en Chile," in *1973: La vida cotidiana de un año crucial,* ed. Claudio Rolle (Santiago: Planeta, 2003), 225–93.

48. Eden Medina, *Cybernetic Revolutionaries: Technology and Politics in Allende's Chile* (Cambridge, MA: MIT Press, 2011), 108. Increasing workers' spending power was concomitant with an emphasis on increasing national industrial production. Popular Unity economists argued that nationalized key industries and worker authority in the workplace would increase efficiency and

take advantage of the latent potential of Chilean production. This vision was initially successful, as workers reached historic heights of income, status, and organization. The first-year economic policies led to a 30 percent rise in real wages and close to a 10 percent displacement of national income from capital to labor. Escalating inflation, accompanied by widespread shortages exacerbated by internal boycott and hoarding and international pressure and an "invisible blockade," eroded these gains, but structural changes in Chilean industry had other far-reaching effects.

49. Ibid., 108; Eden Medina, "Designing Freedom, Regulating a Nation: Socialist Cybernetics in Allende's Chile," *Journal of Latin American Studies* 38 (2006): 571–606; and Palmarola Sagredo, "Productos y socialismo."

50. Medina, *Cybernetic Revolutionaries*, 112–14.

51. See also Illanes, "'Así nació el gigante,'" 79.

52. "Destruido ha sido el mito de la neutralidad aséptica de la tecnología," *Revista INTEC* 1 (December 1971): 5.

53. José Valenzuela, "Apuntes sobre la política de acción del INTEC," *Revista INTEC* 1 (December 1971): 22.

54. Gui Bonsiepe, "Vivisección del diseño industrial," *Revista INTEC* 2 (June 1972): 43.

55. Ibid., 49. Allende had historically viewed food and nutrition, especially infant nutrition, as political and social issues. Food and nutrition continued to serve as crucial proof of the consequences of dependent capitalism and the need for a socialist modernity. See Cockcroft, *Salvador Allende Reader*, 43, 71.

56. Valenzuela, "Apuntes sobre la política de acción del INTEC," 11: "Systematic technological transformation, in which INTEC played a leading role, could drive larger political and economic changes. According to the state and INTEC members alike, the remaking of systems of production and consumption would ensure a transition from a society 'disfigured by the sores of dependent capitalism' to a modern, developed nation. Individual INTEC projects sought to develop the production of consumer goods, even as the Industrial Design Group attempted to design fluid integration of a national industry."

57. Medina, "Designing Freedom, Regulating a Nation," 589. Also, as Medina suggests based on her research on the cybermetrician Stanford Beer's papers and according to Beer's own recollection, Allende demanded that Beer consider "the political implications of the project and insisted that the system behave in a 'decentralizing, worker-participative, and anti-bureaucratic manner.' These words stayed with Beer and convinced him that the system needed to be more than a toolbox for technocratic management; it needed to create social relations that were consistent with the political ideals of the Allende government," including the eventual leadership of "the people." Eden Medina, "Cybernetic Revolutionaries," *Cabinet* 46 (Summer 2012): 21–27 [23–24].

58. *Revista INTEC* 4 (June 1973): 41.

59. Their focus was squarely on the "standardization of the measurements of containers [and] . . . better use of raw materials . . . substituting for the non-economical hodgepodge of the present." *Revista INTEC* 2 (June 1972): 49–50.

60. Ibid., 60.

61. Ibid. Emphasis in original.

62. Ibid.

63. For Bonsiepe and his team, for instance, rational use of industrial technology and design was fundamental to Chile's unique form of socialist modernity, as long as it was not used "to replicate other countries' development . . . but rather to shatter the many forms of technological and cultural domination." Their opponents drew on a parallel discourse to challenge the legitimacy of the Popular Unity platform. The opposition argued that Popular Unity economics were antithetical to national development and contrary to its citizens' access to the benefits of modernity. The commonalities between the "Left" and the "Right" are striking, and they both exist parallel to and mitigate the growing schisms between political groups. Valenzuela, "Apuntes sobre la política de acción del INTEC," 11.

64. Especially those associated with everyday experiences of consumption and eating.

65. *Revista INTEC* 2 (June 1972): 49–50.

66. Palmarola Sagredo, "Productos y socialismo," 225–93.

67. Ibid.

68. *Revista INTEC* 3 (December 1972): 34–35.

69. Ibid. See also Valenzuela, "Apuntes sobre la política de acción del INTEC," 22.

70. *Revista INTEC* 3 (December 1972): 38.

71. Ibid., 51–67. This team was composed of Gui Bonsiepe, Guillermo Capdevila, Alfonso Gómez, Gernando Schultz, Rodrigo Walker, and Werner Zemp. Werner Zemp was almost solely responsible for the design of the china.

72. *Revista INTEC* 1 (December 1971): 51–67. The "system's components" included a chair, with two variations; a table, which would seat six adults or four adults and four children; a bench, for two children; a single bed, which could be transformed into a bunk-bed; a queen-size bed; a bedside table; and a set of shelves. For these details, see *Revista INTEC* 1 (December 1971): 53. *INTEC Magazine* editors wrote, "With these designs, we mean to contribute to the rationalization of households' equipment and to achieve the basis for standardization and 'typification'" (52–53).

73. *Revista INTEC* 1 (December 1971): 51–67.

74. Ibid. The connections between INTEC designs for CORVI houses and UNCTAD furnishings come through clearly in reading *AUCA*, where INTEC's contributions to CORVI houses emerge as "designs that will rationalize household furnishings." These designs were based on a four-part scheme: "(1) anthropometric studies, (2) dimensions of architectural blueprints, (3) technological factors, (4) factors of rationalization." *AUCA* 23 (1972): 19.

75. My analysis is influenced by the work of Arturo Escobar, *Encountering Development: The Making and Unmaking of the Third World* (Princeton, NJ: Princeton University Press, 1995); "Power and Visibility: Development and the Invention and Management of the Third World," *Cultural Anthropology* 3,

no. 4 (1988): 428–43; "Discourse and Power in Development: Michel Foucault and the Relevance of His Work to the Third World," *Alternatives* 10, no. 3 (1984): 377–400.

76. Allende, in Cockcroft, *Salvador Allende Reader*, 214.

77. "Furniture design is here done in tandem with a team made up of architects and aided by artists . . . [which leads to] an exhaustive understanding of interior structure, and achieving full harmony among building materials, be these rugs, curtains, fabrics, etc." *Revista INTEC* 3 (December 1972): 71. See too Lawner and Maulen, "UNCTAD III Santiago de Chile, 06/1971–04/1972"; Varas Alarcón and Llano Loyola, "Sitio, tiempo, contexto y afecciones específicas," 18.

78. *AUCA* 19 (December 1970): 7.

79. Ibid.

80. Ibid.

81. Ibid.

82. Ibid.

83. Ibid.

84. *AUCA* 23 (1972): 17.

85. Ibid.

86. This aesthetic also referenced iconic late nineteenth-century, French-inspired, exposed-steel structures such as the Estación Central and Viaducto Malleco.

87. *AUCA* 23 (1972): 17.

88. Ibid. A second design for a piece that was again multifunctional and could serve as desk space, shelving, and entertainment unit in one built on these common principles. "The present work," the article argued, "responds to . . . the growing need for new solutions to finding livable interior spaces structured around industrialized, multifunctional, and space-defining furniture." The proposed design, therefore, would have to be uniform yet adaptable, industrially built yet individualized, capable of fitting into the changing context of everyday life dictated by the particularities of Chilean modernity yet able to create the conditions for "contemporary life—dynamic, functional, spatial and richly mutable."

89. *AUCA* 23 (1972): 19.

90. Ibid.

91. See David Maulen and David Molina Neira, "Arquitectura heterárquica a través de la mediación informática," *La forma moderna en Latinoamerica*, blog at http://laformamodernaenlatinoamerica.blogspot.com/2012/12/arquitectura-heterarquica-traves-de-la.html (last accessed November 29, 2015).

92. Christian Bartlau traces the relationship between the CORVI and UNCTAD furnishings through a close reading of the *AUCA* issue devoted to the UNCTAD. The issue opens with "the plan [*planimetría*] and image of the Placa [lower structure]. . . . Then it shows the tower, with all its accompanying graphics, and finally, the 'equipamiento,' the furniture designed by Carlos Garretón. Each of these . . . is represented in plans, bisections, and elevations. These appear as equally important. . . . There is almost no heirarchy between

'heavy' structure, 'light' works, and furniture, which form part of the art built into the buildings' design. Each of these elements was equal in importance." Bartlau, "La monumentalidad incompleta del conjunto UNCTAD III," 64.

93. *AUCA* 22 (April 1972): n.p.

94. Maulen and Molina Neira, "Arquitectura heterárquica."

95. "Vista panorámica del moderno y gigantesco edificio construido por la firma DESCO para la UNCTAD III," *El Mercurio*, April 13, 1972.

96. *AUCA* 22 (April 1972): n.p.

97. Ibid.

98. Ibid.

99. "UNCTAD: Un piso cada 50 horas. Trabajadores chilenos baten records en la construcción del gigantesco edificio," *Revista Ahora* 25 (October 5, 1971); reprinted in Allende and Illanes, *Trabajo en utopía*, 166.

100. "Avances y debilidades de la Unidad Popular: Discurso de Pedro Vuskovic en la Asamblea Nacional de la Unidad Popular, 8 de enero de 1971," Archivos Salvador Allende, www.salvador-allende.cl/Unidad_Popular/Vuskovic%20 Asamblea%20UP%201971.pdf (accessed January 23, 2008); Felipe Herrera, "Reflexiones en torno a UNCTAD III," in *Edificio sede para UNCTAD III: Centro cultural metropolitano de Santiago* (n.p.: n.p.,1972).

101. Herrera, "Reflexiones en torno a UNCTAD III."

102. Andres Guzmán, "Así nació el gigante," *El Mercurio, Suplemento UNCTAD III*, April 11, 1972.

103. "Hemiciclo mundial," *El Mercurio*, April 12, 1972.

104. Marcos Valencia, "Las remodelaciones urbanas de CORMU en Santiago," in Varas Alarcón and Llano Loyola, *275 Días*, 75. Cited also in Illanes, "'Así nació el gigante,'" 79.

105. Marcos Winograd summarized these fundamental questions and tensions that, in his mind, animated Chilean urban and architectural planning during the Popular Unity and are broached by the UNCTAD buildings: "It is possible to put forward the idea of a city-in-a-building, to modify the traditional scale of the checkerboard urban design. It is possible to insert a structure of the most absolute modernity and sociability without losing but rather reinforcing the feeling of peace, scale, individuality, restraint offered by the sequence of piazzetas, open spaces, fountains, sculptures found in the Villavicencio exit." Marcos Winograd, "Impresiones sobre el concurso y sobre nuestro funcionamiento," *AUCA* 24–25 (November 1973).

106. Winograd, "Impresiones sobre el concurso y sobre nuestro funcionamiento."

107. See *Edificio sede para UNCTAD III*. In his "anti-memoir" of the period, for example, Mark Cooper recalls the neighborhood, Villavicencio Street and its emblematic café-bar, the Casa de la Luna Azul, where he met the socialist photographer Orlando Jofré at his "regular table." See Marc Cooper, *Pinochet and Me: A Chilean Anti-Memoir* (London: Verso, 2001), 29.

108. *AUCA* 22 (April 1973). *Revista Educación* characterizes the structure as an "edificio 'alero'" that incorporated pedestrians in a way reminiscent of

colonial-era galleries. "En inauguración de la UNCTAD Allende descubre la realidad actual del continente y formula las perspectivas de desarrollo," *Revista Educación,* no. 39 (May 1972); reprinted in Allende and Illanes, *Trabajo en utopía,* 156–57.

109. See Herrera, "Reflexiones en torno a UNCTAD III."

110. Ibid.

111. Winograd, "Impresiones sobre el concurso y sobre nuestro funcionamiento."

112. *Revista Educación* portrayed the building not only as an "edificio ciudad" but also as an "edificio-túnel" and "edificio 'plaza,'" reflecting its various iterations as public spaces and spaces of transit. "En inauguración de la UNCTAD Allende descubre la realidad actual del continente y formula las perspectivas de desarrollo."

113. *El Mercurio* columnist "Geminis" argued that "prohibiting a group of citizens from marching in front of [UNCTAD building] doors contrasts with the open mind" and the tradition of open circulation that characterize the space in front of the UN headquarters in New York.

The contrast with New York highlighted that the Santiago of Popular Unity was to the writer a "closed city" in which movement through space was circumscribed and political expression therefore curtailed. Railing against what were for him symptomatic restrictions on marchers' trajectories, Geminis instead proposed an "open city," a modern urban center defined by unrestricted movement and unrestricted expression, "a city that is surrounded neither by walls nor prohibitions, where that freedom allows one to know, without any intermediary, the true voices of public opinion and the opinions of the man of the street."

Ironically, Popular Unity officials were elaborating an image of the UNCTAD building as the centerpiece of a fluid city center, the product of a concrete project of simultaneously democratizing space and social relations, even as march organizers and press pundits argued that the city of the UNCTAD was one where movement of people, goods, and ideas were under attack by an increasingly repressive Marxist government. These discursive and rhetorical struggles over the definition of the city in terms of physical movement and public expression reveal the surprisingly intimate connection between opposition and government discourse. In the context of growing political polarization, supporters and opposition proposed diametrically divergent visions that were, paradoxically, written in similar terms; each side's representations of mobility, modernity, and expression used coeval languages for very different ends. Geminis, "La vía pública no es territorio internacional," *El Mercurio,* April 13, 1972.

114. Miguel Lawner, Letter to the Director of *El Mercurio,* August 14, 2007.

115. Lawner to Pia Montalegre, "Jardín para el pueblo: El imaginario de la Unidad Popular en el Parque O'Higgins" (MA thesis, Pontificio Universidad Cátolica de Chile, 2010), cited in Matías Allende, "UNCTAD II y la imagen enaltecedora de una nación," in Allende and Illanes, *Trabajo en utopía,* 23.

116. *Chile Hoy,* November 3–9, 1972, cited in Margaret Power, "La Unidad Popular y la masculinidad," trans. Moisés Silva, *La Ventana,* no. 6 (1997): 250–70.

117. "bien vistos" in the original. Juan Tralma, interviews by author, June and November 2004. Edward Murphy beautifully treats dignity and affect as significant historical subjects. Murphy, *For a Proper Home,* 243, 255, 262.

118. Luis Ulíbarri, "Fotos estilo UNCTAD," *Quinta Rueda,* December 1972.

119. See Anita Mannur and Martin Manalansan, "Dude, what's that smell? The Sriracha shutdown and immigrant excess," *From the Square,* NYU Press blog, www.fromthesquare.org/?p=5903 (accessed April 8, 2015). For a fascinating examination of "synesthesia," see William B. Taylor, *Magistrates of the Sacred* (Stanford, CA: Stanford University Press, 1998), 550 n. 7.

120. Lawner and Maulen's piece draws a parallel narrative, pitting the UNCTAD's spatial and social project against the military government's repressive reaction and equating the dictatorship's fragmentation of public space with its violent repression of its opponents and their political expression. These narratives draw an important connection between public space and the foundations for the formation of the political; and, in drawing out these connections between public space and public sphere, they contextualize the military's use of radical violence to fracture and fragment political debate by censuring public space. See Lawner and Maulen, "UNCTAD III Santiago de Chile, 06/1971–04/1972."

121. This is a reformulation of Diane Davis's insights into Mexico city's downtown core, a built environment that, she argues, creatively reestablished the "physical preconditions necessary for the emergence of [a] public sphere." Diane Davis, "Whither the Public Sphere: Local, National, and International Influences on the Planning of Downtown Mexico City, 1910–1950," *Space and Culture* 7 (2004): 195.

122. Medina, *Cybernetic Revolutionaries,* esp. chaps. 4 and 6.

123. Ibid., 108.

124. Beer was a leading cybernetics expert recruited in 1971 by Fernando Flores, who played a crucial role in the Cybersyn project. Medina, *Cybernetic Revolutionaries.*

125. See Medina, "Designing Freedom, Regulating a Nation," 588–90.

126. Medina, *Cybernetic Revolutionaries,* 115.

127. Ibid., 116.

128. This argument draws on the emergent field of visual studies, in which visual practices and representation do not only reflect but also in fact create or shape politics, citizenship, and other forms of social reality. See, e.g., Meg McLagan and Yates McKee, Introduction to *Sensible Politics: The Visual Culture of Nongovernmental Activism* (New York: Zone Books, 2012), 9–26 [12]. CHECO was "an ambitious effort to model the Chilean economy and provide simulations of future economic behavior. Appropriately, it was sometimes referred to as 'Futuro.'" The simulator's predictive potential allowed it to act as the "government's experimental laboratory," a symbolic parallel to Allende's view of Chile as a localized "social laboratory." Medina, "Designing Freedom, Regulating a Nation," 107–8, 116.

129. As Medina relates, the "designers paid great attention to ergonomics and concerned themselves with such questions as the best angles for a user to read a display screen. . . . They studied aspects of information visualization and wondered how they could use color, size, and movement to increase comprehension or how much text could be displayed on a screen while maintaining legibility." Medina, "Designing Freedom, Regulating a Nation," 108, 115.

130. See also Illanes, "'Así nació el gigante,'" 77: "An "alternative modernity" was being proposed, says Javier Pinedo, inspired by Marxism's fundamental questions, the material reality of production."

131. "Trabajadores chilenos . . . ," *Revista Ahora* 25 (October 5, 1971); reprinted in Allende and Illanes, *Trabajos en utopía*, 166.

132. Talesnik, "Monumentality and Resignification," 139.

133. "Trabajadores chilenos . . . ," *Revista Ahora* 25 (October 5, 1971); reprinted in Allende and Illanes, *Trabajos en utopía*, 166.

134. Ibid., 167–68.

135. Ibid.

CHAPTER 2

1. Margaret Power, *Right-Wing Women: Feminine Power and Struggle against Allende, 1964–1973* (University Park: Pennsylvania State University Press, 2002), 163. Similarly, Lisa Baldez finds that the march was a performance that created a new form of political activism (a "feminine revolution") and helped "catapult" the opposition's political leaders into swift action to depose Allende's government. Lisa Baldez, *Why Women Protest: Women's Movements in Chile* (New York: Cambridge University Press, 2002), esp. chap. 4, "Catapulting Men to Action: The March of the Empty Pots," 76–97. See also Gwynn Thomas, *Contesting Legitimacy in Chile: Familial Ideals, Citizenship, and Political Struggle, 1970–1990* (University Park: Pennsylvania State University Press, 2011), chaps. 2–4, conclusion; Michelle Mattelart, "Chile: The Feminine Version of the Coup d'état," in *Sex and Class in Latin America: Women's Perspectives on Politics, Economics and the Family in the Third World*, ed. June Nash and Helen Icken Safa (New York: Bergin, 1980), 279–301; Temma Kaplan, *Taking Back the Streets: Women, Youth, and Direct Democracy* (Berkeley: University of California Press, 2004).

2. Laura Putnam finds in her study of migrant mobility in the Jazz Age that "subaltern" political identities have historically been formed in both traditional print-centered public spheres and "performative" arenas that included jazz clubs and other public and semipublic spaces. As discussed in chapter 1, Popular Unity architects, urban planners, and protesters sought to transform Santiago's city center into an expansive if contested arena of political and social exchange. In contrast, the empty pots protest seized control of these same spaces but in a way that suggested a fundamentally conservative vision of its limits. Laura Putnam, *Radical Moves: Caribbean Migrants and the Politics of Race in the Jazz Age* (Chapel Hill: University of North Carolina Press, 2013).

3. See esp. Craig J. Calhoun, ed., *Habermas and the Public Sphere* (Cambridge, MA: MIT Press, 1992).

4. Charles Tilly expands on the idea of "repertoires" of contention and methods for a political history that take forms of political association and debate as their subject. Charles Tilly, "The Rise of the Public Meeting in Great Britain, 1758–1834," *Social Science History* 34, no. 3 (Fall 2010): 291–99.

5. Heidi Tinsman, *Partners in Conflict: The Politics of Gender, Sexuality, and Labor in the Chilean Agrarian Reform, 1950–1973* (Durham, NC: Duke University Press, 2002), 206.

6. Heidi Tinsman, "Good Wives and Unfaithful Men: Gender Negotiations and Sexual Conflicts in the Chilean Agrarian Reform, 1964–1973," *Hispanic American Historical Review* 81 (November 2001): 599, 615. Also see Thomas Miller Klubock, "Writing the History of Women and Gender in Twentieth-Century Chile," *Hispanic American Historical Review* 81 (August–November 2001): 515–18; Elizabeth Quay Hutchison, "From 'La Mujer Esclava' to 'La Mujer Limón': Anarchism and the Politics of Sexuality in Early-Twentieth-Century Chile," *Hispanic American Historical Review* 81, no. 3–4 (August–November 2001): 519–54; Karin Alejandra Rosemblatt, "Charity, Rights, and Entitlement: Gender, Labor, and Welfare in Early-Twentieth-Century Chile," *Hispanic American Historical Review* 81, no. 3–4 (August–November 2001): 555–86.

7. Annie G. Dandavati, *Engendering Democracy in Chile* (New York: Peter Lang, 2005), 19.

8. Heidi Tinsman, *Buying into the Regime: Grapes and Consumption in Cold War Chile and the United States* (Durham, NC: Duke University Press, 2014): 234–36. Here Tinsman also cites Valeria Redondo, "Los significados de la participación de mujeres dirigentas en organizaciones de Comprando Juntos," in *Mujer y organizaciones de consumo en América Latina: Seminario Taller*, ed. Margarita Fernández and Pamela Allen (Santiago: Programa de Empleo y Trabajo, 1995), 207. Yet "anti-Allende women established a lasting presence of women on the political arena—and prepared fellow Chileans for a reinterpretation of women's citizenships rights." Jadwiga Pieper Mooney, *Politics of Motherhood: Maternity and Women's Rights in Twentieth-Century Chile* (Pittsburgh, PA: University of Pittsburgh Press, 2009): 104–5. See also Baldez, *Why Women Protest*.

9. Then, during military rule, they sometimes lasted months or years at a time, stocked by individuals, the church, and international organizations, and they soon "developed into a space of political critique," organizing a vibrant public that "discussed problematic employers, the fate of imprisoned loved ones, and the shared hardship of surviving on low wages and through the winter off-season." Tinsman, *Buying into the Regime*, 234–36.

10. Pieper Mooney, *Politics of Motherhood*, 104.

11. Redondo, an anthropologist, concludes that during the dictatorship "communal organizations organized around consumption were important participatory spaces, because of the number of people who took part but also because they gave popular women a site of heightened purpose [*convocatoria*]."

These spaces, she argues, were "relevant": though it was not unprecedented that women would participate in the resolution of everyday economic problems, these actions were now arranged into "organizations with permanence, a permanence that has allowed them, to a greater or less extent, to consolidate their institutional order, generating collective and individual growth in their participants because they produced economic and noneconomic resources." Redondo, "Los significados de la participación de mujeres dirigentas," 208, 214–16. In other words, these acts, which had been fleeting during the Popular Unity, were commonplace and institutionalized during the hardest times of the dictatorship.

12. I study urban contests rooted in concrete, often-violent protests and performances through the lens, and as part of, public sphere scholarship. On the significance of performance for the creation and policing of public spheres, see Jill Lane, *Blackface Cuba, 1840–1895* (Philadelphia: University of Pennsylvania Press, 2005), 107, 120, 135; and esp. Putnam, *Radical Moves*, 195, 233.

13. Mary Ryan, *Women in Public: Between Banners and Ballots, 1825–1880* (Baltimore, MD: Johns Hopkins University Press, 1990), 131.

14. "Mujeres realizan marcha de las cacerolas vacías," *El Mercurio*, November 30, 1971.

15. Raquel Sellan, quoted in "Mujeres realizan marcha de las cacerolas vacías."

16. Ibid.

17. "Mujeres realizan marcha de las cacerolas vacías."

18. Pieper Mooney, *Politics of Motherhood*, 116–17.

19. See Power, *Right-Wing Women in Chile*, 164 and n. 96. See too Margaret Power, "Class and Gender in the Anti-Allende Women's Movement: Chile 1970–1973," *Social Politics* 7, no. 3 (Fall 2000): 289–308 [298].

20. Pieper Mooney, *Politics of Motherhood*, 105.

21. It also shaped popular imaginings of the city's economic landscape. See, e.g., Enrique Lafourcade, *Palomita Blanca* (Santiago: Editorial Zig-Zag, 1971), 78, 81–82, 85–86, 111, 113–14.

22. Teresa Donoso Loero, *La epopeya de las ollas vacías* (Santiago: Editora Nacional Gabriela Mistral, 1974), 58. See also, e.g., "Muertas de hambre," *El Clarín*, December 3, 1971.

23. "Protesta femenina," *El Mercurio*, December 2, 1971.

24. Ibid.

25. Contradicting Habermas's original contention that violence should be bracketed from the public sphere, Donoso Loero's recollections place aggressive conflict at the heart of this emergent gendered public.

26. Of course, others asserted repeatedly that members of the paramilitary group Patria y Libertad, armed with clubs and protected by their white helmets, accompanied female protesters, provoked onlookers, and instigated violent clashes.

27. Lisa Baldez's sources include original interviews of participants and the opposition press. Baldez, *Why Women Protest*, 78–79.

28. "Informe de Comisión," Cámara de Diputados, January 5, 1972, Sesión 38, Legislatura Extraordinaria, 1971–1972; reproduced in *Acusación Constitucional, Ministro del Interior señor José Tohá González* (Biblioteca del Congreso Nacional de Chile, n.d.), 65.

29. Nina Donoso, "¡¡Las Mujeres Protestamos!!," *El Mercurio,* December 5, 1972.

30. In turn, Teresa Donoso Loero's memoirs transform her experience in this chaotic scene into a crucible that defined her political transformation, will, and patriotic belief: "In the epic of the empty pots each one lived her own heroic deed: each woman held her own corner, her street, and her agony. A woman fell in Lira Street, on the side of the Universidad Católica, asphyxiated: I picked up the flag she let go as she was falling. Another one fainted, losing her footing with a cardboard banner in her hands: I picked that one up too." As her comrades fell around her, Donoso Loero's narrative became one of personal and ideological perseverance. Donoso Loero, *La epopeya de las ollas vacías,* 30.

31. "Pedíamos solamente comida," *La Tribuna,* December 3, 1971. Murphy illustrates how the racialized trope of "hordes" unfolds historically. Murphy, *For a Proper Home,* 46, 243.

32. "Cubanos fueron los provocadores," *La Tribuna,* December 3, 1971.

33. "'Amar al marxismo obliga a odiar a los no marxistas,'" *La Tribuna,* December 3, 1971.

34. "Cubanos fueron los provocadores," *La Tribuna,* December 3, 1971.

35. It became a node around which people on the ground, in the press, and in Congress argued the merits and limits of proper political practice and urban expressions of citizenship. If, as Craig Calhoun argues, public sphere historiography has privileged "contestation and resistance" and has featured a "celebration of counterpublics," political historians should also be aware of the ways in which those "protagonists of counterpublics" like the empty pots protesters often sought "integration into a more general public" or could support the very definitions of the general public that invalidated their ongoing participation in these publics. Marchers made use of the political potential of evanescent public behavior to articulate novel political identities and yet used these practices to also buttress traditional or conservative public spheres and political structures. Craig Calhoun, "The Public Sphere in the Field of Power," *Social Science History* 34, no. 3 (2010): 301–35 [308]. On this question, see too Geoffrey Eley, "Nations, Publics, and Political Cultures: Placing Habermas in the Nineteenth Century," in Calhoun, *Habermas and the Public Sphere,* 289–339 [306].

36. For a fascinating discussion of narrative "tropes" and how these organize complex political debates, see Mariana Torgovnick, *Gone Primitive: Savage Intellects, Modern Lives* (Chicago: University of Chicago Press, 1991).

37. Mary Ryan and, more recently, Laura Putnam examine how an awareness of the public and of the language of publicness is crucial to the formation of public spheres in the nineteenth and twentieth centuries. Mary Ryan, "Gender and Public Access: Women's Politics in Nineteenth-Century America," in Calhoun, *Habermas and the Public Sphere,* 259–88 [268]; see also Putnam, *Radical Moves,* 233–34. In Chile, protesters themselves debated the critical

questions that underwrite current theoretical debates on the public sphere and invoked the language of the public, rational communication, and violence in their discussions.

38. Pieper Mooney, *Politics of Motherhood*, 132–33.

39. Pieper Mooney, *Politics of Motherhood*, among other works, traces the long, twentieth-century history of women's participation in politics, including the changing ways in which Popular Unity interpreted motherhood, sexuality, and domesticity as political categories.

40. Pieper Mooney, *Politics of Motherhood*, 132–33.

41. In the December 19 edition of *El Mercurio*, march organizer Silvia Pinto made a direct connection between the minister of the interior's impeachment for the violent repression of women marchers and the minister of the economy's inability to control the price and availability of staple goods. "In sum," Pinto editorialized, "a minister is responsible for the fact that pots are empty, and we accuse him of having violently put down the women's protest against the lack of foodstuffs." Silvia Pinto, "El 'Yo Acuso' de la oposición," *El Mercurio*, December 19, 1971.

42. "Acusación constitucional en contra del Ministro del interior señor José Tohá González," Cámara de Diputados, Legislatura Extraordinaria, 1971–1972, Sesión 38, January 6, 1972, Discusión; reproduced in *Acusación Constitucional, Ministro del Interior señor José Tohá González*.

43. Reproduced in *La Tercera* and *El Clarín*, December 8, 1971.

44. *La Prensa*, January 7, 1972.

45. Ibid.

46. Pinto, "El 'Yo Acuso' de la Oposición," *El Mercurio*, December 19, 1971.

47. Cámara de Diputados, Sesión 24a, December 3, 1971; reproduced in *El Clarín*, December 8, 1971.

48. Ibid. In contrast, in the title of a piece published in *La Tribuna*, December 3, 1971, march organizers claimed that "all we asked for was food for their families."

49. Ibid.

50. Instead, Popular Unity ruled because of its citizens' freely given support, not by force. "Freedom means equality," Tohá stated, "but equality in legal as well as in economic terms." The issue of freedom of assembly and expression was, in this light, not a simple constitutional or legal question but one that must be addressed at its social roots. Cámara de Diputados, Legislatura Extraordinaria, 1971–1972, Sesión 38, 6 de enero, 1972, Discusión; reproduced in *Acusación Constitucional, Ministro del Interior señor José Tohá González*, 142.

51. Ibid., 134.

52. Ibid., 144.

53. "Mujeres se tomaron La Moneda para respaldar a Allende," *Puro Chile*, December 8, 1971.

54. As Foucault argues, lists are powerful tools of categorizing and relating disparate events and, therefore, of creating the image of a discursive unity. See Michel Foucault, *The Order of Things: An Archaeology of Human Sciences* (London: Routledge, 1994).

55. Cámara Diputados, Sesión 24a, December 3, 1971; reproduced in *El Clarín*, December 8, 1971.

56. "Presidente Allende: 'Si Quieren Plebiscito, Tendrán Plebiscito,'" *El Mercurio*, December 20, 1971.

57. Kristin Ross articulates a powerful definition of the "afterlife" of a political event: "I use the term . . . to mean simply that what has become known as 'the events of May '68' cannot now be considered separately from the social memory and forgetting that surround them. That memory and that forgetting have taken material forms, forms whose history I trace in this book. The management of May's memory—the way in which the political dimensions of the event have been, for the most part, dissolved or dissipated by commentary and interpretations—is now, thirty years later, at the center of the historical problem of 1968 itself." Kristin Ross, *May '68 and Its Afterlives* (Chicago: University of Chicago Press, 2002), 1. Though I am fascinated by how memory and forgetting take material forms, and how the present informs the past, I am interested here in the immediate afterlife of the women's march, in how its meaning was debated, and in how this ongoing public debate shaped and reshaped its continued significance for politics under Allende and beyond.

58. "La marcha democrática de hoy," *El Mercurio*, April 12, 1972.

59. Ibid.

60. *El Mercurio*, April 11, 1972.

61. Ibid.

62. *El Mercurio*, April 12, 1972.

63. "Instrucciones para la Marcha de Chile por su Democracia," *El Mercurio*, April 12, 1972.

64. Ibid.

65. "Esta tarde Marcha la Democracia," *El Mercurio*, April 12, 1972.

66. Ibid.

67. "La Marcha," *El Mercurio*, April 12, 1972.

68. "Imponente defensa de la libertad," *El Mercurio*, April 13, 1972. In this way, one could see how, in every street, there were groups of people who carried small Chilean flags and chanted slogans for democracy, the fatherland, and freedom.

69. "Instrucciones," *El Mercurio*, April 12, 1972.

70. The Partido Nacional published an ad that asked readers, "Be Firm Alongside Chile," and made an explicit link between democracy and progress in its contraposition of "Capacity for Rule" and "Democracy for Progress." "Instrucciones," *El Mercurio*, April 12, 1972.

71. "¡Enarbole esta página como símbolo de patriotismo!," *El Mercurio*, April 12, 1972.

72. "La Marcha," *El Mercurio*, April 12, 1972.

73. "Avasalladora concentración: Así marchó la democracia," *El Mercurio*, April 13, 1972.

74. Ibid.

75. Ibid.

76. Ibid.

77. Ibid.

78. Ibid.

79. Allende cultivated this image at the inauguration of the UNCTAD building, holding a gathering for its construction workers that featured "meat pies and red wine," the traditional cuisine of Independence Day celebrations and (working-class) Chileanness.

80. "Avasalladora concentración," *El Mercurio,* April 13, 1972.

81. "Llamado femenino," *El Mercurio,* April 12, 1972.

82. Ibid.

83. "To preserve order, we urge protesters to leave ample time for travel and to proceed to the proper meeting place, depending on the area in which you live or work." "Instrucciones," *El Mercurio,* April 12, 1972. Where one lived or worked would determine where (and how) one marched.

84. The paper's enthusiasm regarding this "monumental" protest, scheduled to coincide with the opening days of the UN meeting, was tempered by the government's refusal to allow protesters to march past the UNCTAD building, effectively barring participants from the city center. This decision, attributed to Intendente Joignant, was controversial. "La Marcha," *El Mercurio,* April 12, 1972.

85. Enrique Lafourcade's *Palomita Blanca* may be read as an exploration of space and mobility and modernization.

86. "En concentración de ayer: UP forzó su poder de masas," *El Mercurio,* April 19, 1972.

87. "They began to organize marches from [the building's] very doors. Groups began to come together, filling the columns that marched first on the city center, then turning toward Matta and Grecia Avenues." "En concentración de ayer," *El Mercurio,* April 19, 1972.

88. "En concentración de ayer," *El Mercurio,* April 19, 1972.

89. Ibid.

90. Daniel James, "October 17th and 18th, 1945: Mass Protest, Peronism, and the Argentine Working Class," *Journal of Social History* 21 (1988): 441–61.

91. "Allende enviará acta para expropiación ITT," *El Mercurio,* April 19, 1972.

92. See Mary Ryan's foundational argument regarding the centrality of the language of publicness itself: "Just as often the designated spot for assembly was a public thoroughfare, street corner, or town square. Wherever their location, these invitations to popular assemblies were steeped in a language of publicness." Ryan, "Gender and Public Access," 268.

93. "Allende enviará acta para expropiación ITT," *El Mercurio,* April 19, 1972.

94. Ibid.

95. Ibid.

96. Ibid.

97. For example: "Today, the people are government, and that is the reason we are carrying out our program, wiping out the monopolistic clans and putting an end to privileges." Ibid.

98. Elias J. José Palti, "Recent Studies on the Emergence of a Public Sphere in Latin America," *Latin American Research Review* 36, no. 2 (2001): 255–66.

99. Charles Tilly, "The Rise of the Public Meeting in Great Britain, 1758–1834," *Social Science History* 34, no. 3 (Fall 2010): 291–99.

100. This is close to Pieper Mooney's arguments regarding "militant motherhood" as a form of gendered argument that developed in innovative ways in the postwar period—away from traditional arguments regarding motherhood and domesticity. Pieper Mooney, *Politics of Motherhood*.

CHAPTER 3

1. "Balazos y Cadenas en Villa Olimpica por las cacerolas," *La Prensa*, August 26, 1972.

2. Ibid. Debates over the politics of food, consumption, and everyday experience were ultimately complex discussions about the shape and form of legitimate political conflict.

3. This articulation of the "repertoire" of action is borrowed from Diana Taylor, *The Archive and the Repertoire: Performing Cultural Memory in the Americas* (Durham, NC: Duke University Press, 2003).

4. For instance, the Far Right Partido Nacional announced its decision to adopt a "position of integral opposition" in the wake of the strike, a plan that would "encompass many arenas . . . spread from the streets and the structures of civil society to state institutions." Sandra Castillo Soto, *Cordones industriales: Nuevas formas de sociabilidad obrera y organización política popular (Chile, 1970–1973)* (Concepción, Chile: Ediciones Escaparate, 2009), 71, 73.

5. See, most recently, Edward Murphy, *For a Proper Home: Housing Rights in the Margins of Urban Chile, 1960–2010* (Pittsburgh, PA: University of Pittsburgh Press, 2015); Alison J. Bruey, "Organizing Community: Defying Dictatorship in Working-Class Santiago de Chile, 1973–1983" (PhD diss., Yale University, 2008); Rodrigo Hidalgo Dettwyler, "¿Se acabó el suelo en la gran ciudad? Las nuevas periferias metropolitanas de la vivienda social en Santiago de Chile," *Revista EURE* 33, no. 98 (May 2007): 57–75; Mario Garcés, *Tomando su sitio: El movimiento de pobladores de Santiago, 1957–1970* (Santiago: LOM Ediciones, 2002). Boris Cofre, *Campamento nueva la Havana: El MIR y el movimiento de pobladores, 1970–1973* (Santiago: Ediciones Escaparate, 2007). Cf. James Holston, *Insurgent Citizenship: Disjunctions of Democracy and Modernity in Brazil* (Princeton, NJ: Princeton University Press, 2009).

6. Franck Gaudichaud, *Poder popular y cordones industriales: Testimonios sobre el movimiento popular urbano, 1970–1973* (Santiago: LOM Ediciones, 2004), 34. See also Augusto Samaniego, "Octubre al rojo: Fulgor y agonía de 'la Unidad de los Trabajadores,'" *Contribuciones Científicas y Tecnológicas, Área Ciencias Sociales* 130 (April 2002): 1–22.

7. Peter Winn, *Weavers of Revolution: The Yarur Workers and Chile's Road to Socialism* (New York: Oxford University Press, 1986). See also Peter Winn, *Tejedores de la revolución: Los trabajadores de Yarur y la vía chilena al socialism* (Santiago: LOM Ediciones, 2004).

8. Castillo Soto, *Cordones industriales*, 23. See also Francesco Penaglia, "Desde la matriz estado céntrica al autonomismo: Una perspectiva histórica de lo político, social e identitario," *Revista Búsquedas Políticas* 2, no. 1 (2013): 21–36 [29].

9. Cordones were part of a wider experiment in the form and shape of political participation in which changing "forms of marking a public presence on city streets" went hand in hand with shifting practices and identities of political citizenship. Castillo Soto, *Cordones industriales*, 29. Castillo Soto here draws on Helia Henriques Riquelme, "El movimiento de trabajadores," in *Unidad Popular: 30 años después*, ed. Rodrigo Baño (Santiago: LOM Ediciones, 2003), 187–208.

10. See, e.g., James Holston and Arjun Appadurai, "Cities and Citizenship," *Public Culture* 8, no. 2 (Winter 1996): 187–204.

11. Simon Collier and William F. Sater, *A History of Chile, 1808–2002* (Cambridge: Cambridge University Press, 2004), 348.

12. Ibid., 349.

13. Ibid., 348–49.

14. Congress passed a bill to restrict automatic weapons ownership to the police and armed forces and gave the military the right to seek and confiscate firearms, which Allende passed into law and went into effect in October 1972. Ibid., 349–51.

15. See Gaudichaud, *Poder popular y cordones industriales;* and Dolores Mujica and Gabriel Muñoz, "El siglo XX del movimiento obrero: Breve introducción a la historia de la clase trabajadora en Chile (1850–1990)" (Biblioteca de Historia Obrera, n.d.).

16. The term *gremio* refers to professional schools, small owners' organizations, and white-collar syndicates. I keep it in the original to encapsulate the complexities of the grouping.

17. Paul E. Sigmund, *The Overthrow of Allende and the Politics of Chile, 1964–1976* (Pittsburgh, PA: University of Pittsburgh Press, 1977), 184–85.

18. In 1975, the Church Report found that the CIA authorized $8 million to support the overthrow of Allende, including funds given to the opposition paper *El Mercurio* and support to the gremios and their striking members. More recently, Peter Kornbluh has dedicated himself to uncovering and analyzing once-classified U.S. documents, including material evidence of government interference in Chilean politics during the Popular Unity and during the dictatorship. Peter Kornbluh, *The Pinochet File: A Declassifed Dossier on Atrocity and Accountability* (New York: New Press, 2003). Scholars have debated the significance of Nixon's and Kissinger's involvement against the Popular Unity and the weight of CIA "covert action" in Chile—and while many emphasize U.S. action in Chile as well as throughout Latin America and the Caribbean, many others recognize this influence while claiming that "the real 'destabilization' of Chile was the work of Chileans." Collier and Sater, *A History of Chile,* 355. One of the best recent treatments of this issue is Tanya Harmer, *Allende's Chile and the Inter-American Cold War* (Chapel Hill: University of North

Carolina Press, 2014). The trucker's strike offers one of the clearest instances in which national politics and foreign interests intersected.

19. Collier and Sater, *A History of Chile*, 349. Alan Angell writes: "In some ways as impressive as the growth of the popular sectors and their organizations was the parallel expansion of the *gremios*. These were associations of non-manual employees and professional groups, ranging from doctors, lawyers and architects to lorry owners, small shopkeepers and taxi-drivers. Small shopkeepers organized a *gremio* of some 160,000 members (claimed to be close to 90 per cent of the national total). Lorry owners, many of them running only one vehicle, could call on 25,000 members. The twenty or so professional associations, or *colegios,* including such large organizations as those of the 20,000 accountants or the 7,000 doctors, formed a confederation during the UP period." Alan Angell, "Chile since 1958," in *Chile since Independence,* ed. Leslie Bethell (Cambridge: Cambridge University Press, 1993), 173.

20. Collier and Sater, *A History of Chile,* 1349.

21. "Afirmaron dirigentes máximos," *La Tercera,* August 22, 1972. These organizations are the Confederación del Comercio Detallista and the Cámara Central de Comercio, respectively.

22. Ibid.

23. Ibid.

24. For the strike's impact outside of Santiago, see Marian Schlotterbeck, "Everyday Revolutions: Grassroots Movements, the Revolutionary Left (MIR), and the Making of Socialism in Concepción, Chile, 1964–1973" (PhD diss., Yale University, 2013).

25. "PARO FUE TOTAL: Zona de Emergencia," *El Mercurio,* August 22, 1972. The paper alluded to the national ramifications of the mobilization. But press coverage of the strike focused on the city center as the "liminal" arena that bridged the movement's purported roots in neighborhood organizations and its potentially national ramifications.

26. "Afirmaron dirigentes máximos." *La Tercera,* August 22, 1972.

27. The gremios and their supporters relied on other familiar tactics of public protest. Members of the opposition renewed their banging of pots and pans in order to express their dissatisfaction.

28. "PARO FUE TOTAL," *El Mercurio,* August 22, 1972. DIRINCO was the government organism responsible for maintaining the price, flow and distribution of goods.

29. There were also "clashes in places such as Bilbao, Bandera, areas of the municipality of Ñuñoa, in San Pablo, and Villa Portales in Quinta Normal." "PARO FUE TOTAL," *El Mercurio,* August 22, 1972.

30. Ibid.

31. "Until 1 A.M., in different parts of the capital, women and youngsters demonstrated against price increases and in support of shop owners. The din of empty pots could be heard in the Villa Frei, in sectors of Providencia from Manuel Montt to Pintor Cicarelli to Mapocho. Young people in Providencia set barricades aflame and threw stones at police vehicles and buses." Ibid.

32. *El Mercurio,* September 2, 1972.

33. Ibid.

34. "Declaran partidos de oposición: Gobierno se pone al margen de la ley," *El Mercurio,* October 7, 1972.

35. "Solidarity among *gremios* is now the only effective tool left against the Unidad Popular's march toward the absolute control of the country's sources of subsistence." "Llamado a los hombres libres," *El Mercurio,* October 9, 1972.

36. He was here following in a tradition of fomenting gendered political "shame" that included the march of the empty pots, women's protests before "passive" military generals, and so on. Ultimately, Fontaine envisioned a "Great Coalition of Liberty" capable of supporting "those peoples burdened by the arbitrary and twisted manipulation of the Constitution and the law with resolution and efficiency." "Llamado a los hombres libres," *El Mercurio,* October 9, 1972.

37. "Significiado del paro del transporte," *El Mercurio,* October 12, 1972.

38. "Así se generó el paro que conmocionaría a todo el país," *El Camionero,* October 1972, 2. See also "En apoyo a transportistas de Aysén: Paro nacional indefinido de la Confederación de Dueños de Camiones," *El Camionero,* October 1972, 4.

39. "En apoyo a transportistas: Doce mil dueños de camiones inician un paro indefinido," *La Prensa,* October 10, 1972.

40. See Patricio Garcia F. and Luis Muñoz, eds., *Los gremios patronales* (Santiago: Quimantú, 1972), 27–28.

41. *El Camionero,* October 1972.

42. "Masiva protesta de la oposición," *La Tercera de la Hora,* October 11, 1972.

43. Ibid.

44. Ibid.

45. "As suggested months ago by Senator Carmona (Christian Democrat), the opposition's public gatherings were greatly significant because these protests are a necessary response to the totalitarian promise the Marxist parties have made to 'win the battle for the streets.'" Patricio Aylwin, in Garcia F. and Muñoz, *Los gremios patronales,* 25.

46. Ibid.

47. Garcia F. and Muñoz, *Los gremios patronales,* 27–28.

48. "From this moment on, the government declared war not only on the truck owners' *gremio,* as it initially thought, but on all *gremios* and all nationalist organization populated by free men." "¡Policía política allana sede camionera deteniendo a los dirigentes nacionales de la Confederación!," *El Camionero,* October 1972.

49. *El Camionero,* October 1972.

50. "No 1: A los transportistas del país," *El Camionero,* October 1972, 14.

51. Ibid. While the *gremio* inhibited the movement of goods and people throughout the country, its actions encouraged dialogue regarding the movement, the effects of its strike, and the political significance of consumption and commodities.

52. "Cierre del comercio. cifras oficiales: Valparaíso: 80%. Viña del Mar: 90%," *La Estrella de Valparaíso,* October 13, 1972.

53. Sigmund, *The Overthrow of Allende,* 184–86.

54. "Chile protestó en silencio," *El Mercurio,* October 25, 1972.

55. Ibid.

56. Ibid.

57. Ibid.

58. "Ante el desafío del fascismo," *Las Noticias de Última Hora,* October 13, 1972.

59. "Salvador Allende: Llamó a la cordura y a la reflexión . . . ," *Las Noticias de Última Hora,* October 13, 1972.

60. "Por orden del gobierno: Jefes de FF.AA. asumieron control de doce provincias," *La Tercera de la Hora,* October 13, 1972.

61. *El Mercurio* would later claim that in the face of an almost complete paralysis the Popular Unity sent its supporters into the streets to create the illusion of movement and normalcy. Differences of interpretation notwithstanding, this debate points to the symbolic and material importance that circulation, movement, and physical presence on city streets acquired in the context of the strike, the state's reaction to the protest, and worker's efforts vis-à-vis this complicated struggle. "Chile protestó en silencio," *El Mercurio,* October 25, 1972.

62. This debate over the definition of public violence had a longer history, which included the *marcha de las ollas vacías.*

63. Peter Winn, *La revolución chilena* (Santiago: LOM Ediciones, 2013), 106.

64. "El significado del paro," *El Mercurio,* October 12, 1972.

65. "Declaración del consejo general del Colegio de Abogados," *El Mercurio,* October 17, 1972.

66. "El papel de Joan Garcés como asesor de Allende," *El Mercurio,* October 14, 1972.

67. Ibid.

68. Joan Garcés, *Revolución, congreso y constitución: El caso Tohá* (Santiago: Quimantú, 1972), 218.

69. Ibid.

70. Garcés's argument challenged the opposition's claims that repressive control over public space and other forms of public violence negated the government's institutional legality. Instead, he saw public clashes as a necessary part of a larger struggle over political and social change. This argument recalled Tohá's own defense of "public order" as tantamount to equality in everyday social relations carried out in the public sphere (see chapter 2).

71. Garcés, *Revolución, congreso y constitución.*

72. *Diario Sesiones Senado Ordinaria, Sesion 97ª,* September 14, 1972, 4561–62.

73. For the Popular Unity, Aylwin contended, "elected government is only part of the power system." Instead, their ultimate "goal is to conquer Parliament,

the courts, mass media, and, above all, economic power and total control of grassroots organizations in order to complete the revolution." Ibid., 4568–69.

74. Garcia F. and Muñoz, *Los gremios patronales*, 37–38.

75. In James D. Cockcroft ed., *Salvador Allende Reader: Chile's Voice of Democracy* (Melbourne: Ocean Press, 2000), 66.

76. Ibid.

77. Allende was trying to protect the distance between a fractured downtown (which had become a stage of conflictive political debate) and an industrial ring around the city (which contributed to Popular Unity stability by engaging in disciplined production while staying away from direct political confrontation).

78. See Cockcroft, *Salvador Allende Reader*, 66. This articulation of masculinity is intimately related to the forms of gender and familial discourse as the basis for disciplined political organization analyzed for the twentieth century by Elizabeth Q. Hutchinson, *Labors Appropriate to Their Sex: Gender, Labor, and Politics in Urban Chile, 1900–1930* (Durham, NC: Duke University Press, 2001); Karin Alejandra Rosemblatt, *Gendered Compromises: Political Cultures and the State in Chile, 1920–1950* (Chapel Hill: University of North Carolina Press, 2000); Thomas M. Klubock, *Contested Communities: Class, Gender, and Politics in Chile's El Teniente Copper Mine, 1904–1951* (Durham, NC: Duke University Press, 1998); Heidi Tinsman, *Partners in Conflict: The Politics of Gender, Sexuality, and Labor in the Chilean Agrarian Reform, 1950–1973* (Durham, NC: Duke University Press, 2002); and Gwynn Thomas, *Contesting Legitimacy in Chile: Familial Ideals, Citizenship, and Political Struggle, 1970–1990* (University Park: Pennsylvania State University Press, 2011).

79. Gaudichaud, *Poder popular y cordones industriales*, 34; Sebastian Leiva, "El MIR y los Comandos Comunales: Poder popular y unificación de la movilización social," *Cyber Humanitatis* 30 (Fall 2004).

80. Peter Winn, "The Pinochet Era," in *Victims of the Chilean Miracle: Workers and Neoliberalism in the Pinochet Era, 1973–2002*, ed. Peter Winn (Durham, NC: Duke University Press, 2004), 18.

81. Angell, "Chile since 1958," 172–73.

82. Allende recognized and referenced these spaces and strategies. But he also spoke to the state's ambivalence to these changing structures and its struggle with the potential of violence contained within urban action and, as of this moment, increasingly epitomized by the burgeoning cordones.

83. More militant left-wing groups, including the Movimiento de Izquierda Revolucionaria (MIR) and a radical wing of the Socialist Party, which favored extraparliamentary tactics, had a presence in the cordones. However, the shape and structure of cordones' political organization cannot be explained simply by participants' party affiliations. Winn, "The Pinochet Era," 18; Winn, *Weavers of Revolution*, 139–43 passim; and Peter Winn, "Chile's Revolution from Below," in *Problems in Latin American History*, ed. John Chasteen and James Wood (New York: SR Books, 2005), 247. See also Samaniego, "Octubre al rojo," 1–2; and Leiva, "El MIR y los Comandos comunales."

84. Winn, *La revolución chilena*, 113. A special thank you to Peter Winn for suggesting I make continued reference to the national scope and weight of the strike and do so in reference to this example.

85. Peter Winn, *Tejedores de la revolución: Los trabajadores de Yarur y la vía chilena al socialism*, trans. Victoria Huerta and Paula Sálazar (Santiago: LOM Ediciones, 2004), 199.

86. See Taylor, *The Archive and the Repertoire*, 20, 50–51.

87. The Interdisciplinary Center for Urban and Regional Development (CIDU) completed a comprehensive report, replete with details, charts, and tables, on the urban and rural populations, the density of industrial settlement in Maipú, and the socioeconomic and employment history of workers, housewives, students, and retirees who lived in the comuna. Its research speaks to the dense network of local community organizations that participated in increasingly contentious tactics in an effort to push for change. María Cristina Cordero, Eder Sader, and Mónica Threlfall, *Consejo comunal de trabajadores y Cordón Cerrillos-Maipú: 1972. Balance y perspectivas de un embrión de poder popular*, Documento de Trabajo N° 67, CIDU–Universidad Católica de Chile, Santiago, August 1973, 58–73, esp. 61. Sandra Castillo Soto provides a close analysis of the CIDU document. See Castillo Soto, *Cordones industriales*. See also Bryan Seguel, "Prácticas de movilización y de subjetivación política en el desarrollo del poder popular en Chile, 1967–1973," in *Poder popular, militancias y movimientos sociales durante el Estado de Compromiso, Chile, 1965–1973*, ed. Matías Ortis and Bryan Seguel (Concepción: Escaparate, 2014).

88. Samaniego, "Octubre al rojo," 13.

89. *La Nación* reported that "workers from about forty factories stopped their work and took to the street to erect barricades with the purpose of calling authorities' attention to the issue." "Obreros de Maipú se tomaron camino a Melipilla y Pajaritos," *La Nación*, July 1, 1972, 3.

90. "El Cordón Cerillos," *Trinchera*, November 29, 1972, 4.

91. Samaniego, "Octubre al rojo," 13.

92. Cited in Gaudichaud, *Poder popular y cordones industriales*, 306. As Pablo Muñoz, member of the Socialist Party and the CUT's health department, explained, "The *cordón* occupied an organizing territorial space for the working class. . . . [T]he *cordón* was born, then, as a territorial organization that was close by, an organization that was very much a neighborhood association" (306).

93. Ibid. Guillermo Rodriguez, member of the extraparliamentary leftist group, the MIR, and of the Cordón Cerillos, paints a similar picture of the cordones as an emerging form of organization engaged, with some success, in small, localized attempts at challenging the strike: "In October, I believe the ability of the Cordón to strike back was nonexistent. At that time, the cordón undertook only small actions, small groups went out to open stores closed by strikers. . . . [T]his coincides with mobilizations in Bata. . . . At a certain point all the industries were seized to prevent them from stopping. These gave the Cordón other influence" (306–7). He concluded with a short description of the

schism that developed between the government and the cordones when the Popular Unity agreed to return almost half of the industries it had nationalized as part of a plan to restore political stability after the strike (307).

94. Castillo Soto, *Cordones industriales*, 183.

95. Cordero, Sader, and Threlfall, *Consejo comunal de trabajadores y Cordón Cerrillos-Maipú*, cited in Castillo Soto, *Cordones industriales*. See also the oral histories collected in Gaudichaud, *Poder popular y cordones industriales*.

96. Hernán Ortega, interview by Sandra Castillo Soto, Santiago, September 21, 2006. See Castillo Soto, *Cordones industriales*, 152.

97. Castillo Soto, *Cordones industriales*, 215.

98. Ibid., 229; Franck Gaudichaud, "La Central Única de Trabajadores, las luchas obreras y los Cordones Industriales in el periodo de la Unidad Popular en Chile (1970–1973): Análisis histórico critica y perspectiva," 20, www.rebelion.org/docs/13779.pdf (last accessed March 4, 2016). Winn points to this transformation in his treatment of generational tensions within the Yarur factory. He finds that shop floor strategies, an intergenerational dialogue regarding "proper" political action that took place throughout the factory, and the circulation of messages in informal spaces, break rooms, and bathrooms created new forms and languages of connection and led to tense debates among workers. See Winn, *Weavers of Revolution*, 137–39.

99. Castillo Soto, *Cordones industriales*, 27, 136; See also Samaniego, "Octubre al rojo."

100. Castillo Soto, *Cordones industriales*, 230–35, draws insightful examples from rich oral histories. He contends that urban actions, including tomas, were mechanisms by which "diverse popular agents brought together under the unifying category of 'the people' . . . gradually acquired . . . a space of popular sociability . . . [and] sought to fashion a new form of social praxis" (241–43). See also Cordero, Sader, and Threlfall, *Consejo comunal de trabajadores y Cordón Cerrillos-Maipú*, cited in Castillo Soto, *Cordones industriales*, 138–39.

101. Cancino, cited in Castillo Soto, *Cordones industriales*, 252.

102. "Convocatoria del Cordón Santiago Centro ¡¡Tiemblen momios!!," *Tarea Urgente* 8 (July 13, 1973): 3; Hugo Cancino, *Chile: La problemática del poder popular en el proceso de la vía chilena al socialismo, 1970–1973* (Aarhus, Denmark: Aarhus University Press, 1988); Soto Castillo, *Cordones industriales*, 252.

103. Hernán Ortega, September 21, 2006, interviewed by Castillo Soto, *Cordones industriales*, 253. Castillo Soto's thoughts are succinctly presented earlier in the chapter (249).

104. Ibid. Cf. Winn's emphasis on intergenerational tension and cooperation in Allende-era labor movements. Winn, *Weavers of Revolution*, esp. chaps. 2 and 6.

105. Ian Roxborough, *Estado y revolución en Chile* (Mexico City: El Manual Moderno, 1979), 249–50, cited in Castillo Soto, *Cordones industriales*, 252–53. See also Cancino, *Chile*, 303: "Workers saw in the *Cordones* a space more ample and flexible than unions in that workers from different paths came

together from diverse levels of union membership who occupied a common geographic area." Cited in Sandra Castillo Soto, "Sociabilidad y organización popular: Cordón Industrial Cerrillos-Maipú," *Cuadernos de Historia* 32 (March 2010): 99–121 [118].

106. Mario Olivares, cited in Gaudichaud, *Poder popular y cordones industriales*, 161–215, esp. 182. See also Castillo Soto, "Sociabilidad y organización política popular," 113..

107. Faride Zerán, "'Y se llama revolución, que no se transe . . . ,'" *Chile Hoy* 34 (February 2–8, 1973): 17.

108. Faride Zerán, "Gobierno-masas: No puede esperar," *Chile Hoy* 44 (April 13–18, 1973): 17.

109. Cordero, Sader, and Threlfall, *Consejo comunal de trabajadores y Cordón Cerrillos-Maipú*, 21, cited in Castillo Soto, *Cordones industriales*, 61, 156.

110. Castillo Soto, *Cordones industriales*, 61.

111. The Cordón Cerrillos-Maipú's early attempt to establish the open cabildo as a decision-making structure remained a model for changing forms of political practice. Castillo Soto, *Cordones industriales*, 156, 183.

112. Pablo Muñoz and Luis Ahumada, interview by Franck Gaudichaud, June 24, 2002, cited in Gaudichaud, *Poder popular y cordones industriales*, 324.

113. Ibid.

114. Winn, *Victims of the Chilean Miracle*, 17.

115. Franck Gaudichaud, "Construyendo 'poder popular': El movimiento sinidical, la CUT y las luchas oberas en el period de la Unidad Popular," in *Cuando hicimos historia: La experiencia de la Unidad Popular*, ed. Julio Pinto Vallegos (Santiago: LOM Ediciones, 2005), 81–106 [95]; and Olivares, in Gaudichaud, *Poder popular y cordones industriales*, 161–88.

116. Gaudichaud, "Construyendo 'poder popular,'" 88–93, 95; see also "Crónica: JAP gran cuco de la derecha," *La Nación*, January 18, 1973.

117. Winn, *Victims of the Chilean Miracle*, 17. Thus Winn finds, "These rapid advances toward socialism owed much to the support and actions of Chile's workers and peasants, who both spearheaded and accelerated Allende's road to socialism. In the process, they transformed themselves into protagonists of their own and their nation's destinies" (15).

118. "'Poder popular' was the name given to the host of organizations . . . that are up to defend local communities, farms and factories. They organized the defense of their communities and undertook the tasks of maintaining production and supplies." Angell, "Chile since Independence," 172–73.

119. Gaudichaud here engages scholars of the carnivalesque, including Bourdieu, Bakhtin, and da Matta, and draws directly on Tomas Moulian. Gaudichaud, "Construyendo 'poder popular,'" 88. See also Julio Pinto, ed., *Fiesta y drama: Nuevas historias de la Unidad Popular* (Santiago: LOM Ediciones, 2014). On the carnivalesque, see Nancy Scheper-Hughes, *Death without Weeping: The Violence of Everyday Life in Brazil* (Berkeley: University of California Press, 1993), 480, 482; see also Roberto da Matta, "Carnival in Multiple Panes," in *Rite, Drama, Festival, Spectacle: Rehearsals toward a*

Theory of Cultural Performance (Philadelphia, PA: Institute for the Study of Human Issues, 1984).

120. Winn, *Victims of the Chilean Miracle*, 17; Gaudichaud, "Construyendo 'poder popular,'" 88–93.

121. Winn, *Victims of the Chilean Miracle*, 17.

122. Of course, we should not underestimate the role of political party representatives and union leadership in organizing labor, nor should we minimize the cordón participants' efforts to inform the shape and cadence of political change from above. Many political parties were heavily involved in the rise of cordones, comandos comunales, JAPs, Mother's Centers, and other local, neighborhood, and communal organizations. The historian Marian Schlotterbeck, for instance, offers a fascinating exploration of the ways in which the MIR encouraged and empowered workers, pobladores, and other groups to act on their everyday realities and enact change from below, beyond, and through the state. She undertakes a detailed empirical analysis of the MIR's involvement in support of the JAP in Concepción and the intricate connections that developed between different neighborhood organizations under the auspices or with the support of the MIR in the south of Chile. The MIR saw local organizations as incubators for pobladores' and workers' direct role in politics. Schlotterbeck's is a detailed account of the ways in which the October strike helped crystalize an innovative geography of political participation. Political parties and unions were still key. However, a range of new, increasingly connected political organizations created opportunities for workers and pobladores to experiment with politics, political structures, and forms of political participation, debate, and identity. Schlotterbeck, "Everyday Revolutions."

123. Cordón members often juxtaposed traditional institutions and the innovation of cordones in retrospective oral histories. As Muñoz argues in an interview with Franck Gaudichaud, "The CUT leaned more in the direction of industrial federations or municipal organizations, while the *cordón* took care of the street, in a very well defined geographic area." He continues: "Despite the CUT's strength, it was already bureaucratized and certainly controlled by Popular Unity parties (the Socialist and especially the Communist Party). At this point, however, we needed an agile, flexible, and territorial organization that could take care of problems on the streets." Cited in Gaudichaud, *Poder popular y cordones industriales*, 306. I simply suggest here that while the role that parties and unions played in Popular Unity politics has been well documented, these local institutions also and simultaneously opened spaces and opportunities for different forms of political practice and association that cannot be reduced to or connected only to party politics.

124. "Manifesto del Cordón Cerrillos," *La Aurora de Chile* 29 (June 28, 1973): 2. Reprinted in Castillo Soto, *Cordones industriales*, 272–73.

125. "Empresas al área social: Ni una menos, pero sí muchas más," *La Aurora de Chile* 8 (February 1, 1973): 1.

126. Cf. Rodrigo Baño, "Más allá de culpas y buenas intenciones: Consideraciones acerca de la Unidad Popular," in Baño, *Unidad Popular*, 307.

127. The Senate struck down the initiative that would create the Área de Propiedad Social, or APS, after a judge ordered the forceful eviction of workers from CIC and PERLAK. See Samaniego, "Octubre al rojo," 14; and Hugo Zemelman, "Sobre el significado del nuevo poder popular," *CEREN* 17 (1973): 20–21.

128. "Luis Figueroa: 'Trabajadores se jugarán enteros contra la sedición,' Intervención en el Pleno del Comité Central del Partido Comunista," *El Siglo,* July 26, 1971. See also Modinger, "Cerrillos-Maipú: El cordón de la rebeldía," *Chile Hoy* 6 (July 21–27, 1972): 10–11.

129. Garcia F. and Muñoz, *Los gremios patronales,* 37–38.

130. Phillip Oxhorn, *Organizing Civil Society: The Popular Sectors and the Struggle for Democracy* (University Park: Pennsylvania State University Press, 1995), 56.

131. "Declaración del Secretariado Nacional: Frente al Gabinete UP-Generales," in *La izquierda chilena, 1969–1973: Documentos para el estudio de su línea estratégica,* ed. Victor Farías (Santiago: Centro de Estudios Públicos, 2000), 3503–4.

132. "Trabajadores: No devolver nada y seguir avanzando," *La Aurora de Chile* 4 (November 9, 1972): 1. These workers did engage the relationship between politics "from above" and "below," but they also proposed a new way of practicing politics and envisioning political identity that did not sit unproblematically with more radical "extraparliamentary" options *or* officialist visions "from above."

133. Garcia F. and Muñoz, *Los gremios patronales,* 14–15.

134. Ibid., 58–61.

135. Ibid.

136. Ibid., 62.

137. Ibid.

138. Ibid., 58–61.

139. "Reacción de jóvenes nacionales ante el ataque a su líder: ¡Los maricones tendrán que pagarla!, dice la 'JN,'" *La Tribuna,* November 10, 1972.

140. "Enérgica advertencia del Presidente Allende: 'No aceptaremos ninguna actitud sediciosa,'" *El Siglo,* March 12, 1972.

141. *Díario de Sesiones de Senado, Sesiones Ordinarias, No. 97a,* September 14, 1972, 4561–62.

142. "Chile protestó en silencio," *El Mercurio,* October 25, 1972.

143. Fontaine elaborated a similarly complex relationship between the symbolic, material, and political when he claimed that gremios fought to intertwine "the material and spiritual well-being of the Chilean people." "Anunciaron dirigentes de la FISA: Consolidación del poder gremial," *El Mercurio,* November 11, 1972.

144. Castillo Soto, *Cordones industriales,* 317–19.

145. Winn, *La revolución chilena,* 118.

146. Ibid., 114.

CHAPTER 4

Portions of this chapter appeared in Camilo Trumper, "Ephemeral Histories: Public Art as Political Practice in Santiago, Chile, 1970–1973," in *Democracy in Chile: The Legacy of September 11, 1973,* ed. Silvia Nagy-Zekmi and Fernando Leiva (Brighton: Sussex University Press, 2005), 142–53. Reproduced with permission of SUSSEX ACADEMIC PRESS, PO Box 139, Eastbourne BN24 9BP, United Kingdom.

1. *Salvador Allende,* directed by Patricio Guzmán (JBA Studios, New York, 2004), 35mm.

2. Cf. Andreas Huyssen, *Present Pasts: Urban Palimpsests and the Politics of Memory* (Stanford, CA: Stanford University Press, 2003).

3. The Popular Unity's electoral platform, elaborated in its forty-point plan and *Government Platform,* devoted a significant section to "a new culture for a new society." This section highlighted the importance of visual media in the formation of what was claimed to be the final aim of the program, the making of "a new culture and a new person." Borrowing from Ernesto "Che" Guevara's idea of the "new man," the Popular Unity's *Platform* traced a close link between the transformation of the state, society, and culture and the creation of a new citizen. Popular Unity, *Programa de Gobierno de la Unidad Popular y las primeras 40 medidas* (Chile: Editorial 30 Años, [1969] 2003).

4. The sociologist Charles Lemert modifies Durkheim's theory that social facts (class, gender, race) are things, that these abstract concepts operate in the world as if they were real; he argues that things are also social facts, that they are informed by and code class, gender, and race. See Charles C. Lemert, *Social Things: An Introduction to the Sociological Life* (Lanham, MD: Rowman and Littlefield, 1997). Urban politics in the Popular Unity touched on a number of areas that straddled the personal and political and that could therefore be studied through a number of lenses. Public art is unique in its ability to create seemingly universal, encompassing images of national politics and citizenship and to engage or involve a wide range of people in these claims.

5. Fernando Birri, quoted in Michael Chanan, "Latin American Cinema," in *Remapping World Cinema: Identity, Culture and Politics in Film,* ed. Stephanie Dennison and Song Hwee Lim (London: Wallflower Press, 2006), 38–54.

6. Olga Grau, "Calles y veredas," *Revista de Crítica Cultural* 14 (June 1997): 18–21 [18].

7. "The brigades were formed in '68," he relates, "but people went to the streets to paint before that." Alejandro "Mono" González, interview by author. Santiago, June 2004. There was of course a much more significant array of muralist brigades than I can cover in this chapter. Eduardo Castillo Espinosa especially has traced the history of these muralist groups, including the Brigada Elmo Catalan and the Brigada Inti Paredo, among others. See Eduardo Castillo Espinosa, *Puño y letra: Movimiento social y comunicación gráfica en Chile* (Santiago: Ocho Libro Editores, 2006); Eduardo Castillo Espinosa, "Cartel

chileno, 1963–1973: Un tiempo en la pared," in *El cartel chileno, 1963–1973,* ed. Eduardo Castillo Espinosa (Santiago: Ediciones B, 2004), 4–7; Patricio Rodríguez-Plaza, "La visualidad urbana en el Chile de la Unidad Popular," in Castillo Espinosa, *El cartel chileno,* 10–12; Patricio Rodríguez-Plaza, *Pintura callejera chilena: Manufactura, estética y provocación teórica* (Santiago: Ocho Libros Ediciones, 2011).

8. The original reads: "Cobre Ya Eres Patria." Images reproduced in Castillo Espinoza, *Puño y letra,* 114. See also Mauricio Vico Sánchez, "Breve aproximación a los afiches de la Unidad Popular (1970–1973)," *Actas de Diseño* 4, no. 2 (March 2008): 67–140 [138 n. 12]; Mauricio Vico Sánchez, "Waldo González y los carteles para la Polla Chilena de Beneficiencia," in Castillo Espinosa, *El cartel chileno,* 8–9; Mauricio Vico Sánchez, *El afiche político en Chile, 1970–2013: Unidad popular, clandestinidad, transición democrática y movimientos sociales* (Santiago: Ocho Libros Ediciones, 2013); and Ana Longoni, "Brigadas muralistas: La persistencia de una práctica de de comunicación político-visual," *Revista de Crítica Cultural* 19 (November 1999): 22–29.

9. Juán "Chin Chin" Tralma, interview by author, Santiago, November 2004.

10. This is a key event in BRP oral histories. It acts as an anchor for the group's foundational myth, as a moment when Communist Party officials recognized the value of what had been hitherto an informal practice and cemented their sense of discipline and purpose.

11. Brigada members who had worked together as of the mid-1960s were drawn into the Communist Party leadership following the march as part of one of its regional subcommittees and local chapters. Alejandro "Mono" González, the BRP's original artistic director, and Juán "Chin Chin" Tralma, its central command head, participated in the PC's national propaganda committee.

12. Castillo Espinosa, *Puño y letra;* Alejandro "Mono" González and Juan "Chin Chin" Tralma, interview by author, Santiago, July 2004.

13. See Castillo Espinosa, *Puño y letra;* Longoni, "Brigadas muralistas," 22–29; Alejandro "Mono" González and Juan "Chin Chin" Tralma, interview by author, Santiago, July 2004.

14. Peter Winn, *Weavers of Revolution: The Yarur Workers and Chile's Road to Socialism* (New York: Oxford University Press, 1986), 68–69.

15. Marc Cooper, *Pinochet and Me: A Chilean Anti-Memoir* (London: Verso, 2001), 3–4.

16. In Spanish, the multiplication sign, x, is read as "for."

17. They called this concerted initiative "Triumph at Dawn." Rodney Palmer, *Street Art Chile* (London: Eight Books, 2008), 10.

18. The original reads: "x3 Allende, Venceremos, Unidad Popular."

19. "Fight, Work, Study for the Nation and the Revolution" became one brigada's motto. It appeared frequently in what David Kunzle calls "lapidary monumentality" and articulated well the BRP's choice of national and local concerns, although it reveals a slightly more bellicose bent than was usual for the BRP. See David Kunzle, "Art and the New Chile: Mural Poster and Comic

Book in 'a Revolutionary Process,'" in *Art and Architecture in the Service of Politics,* ed. Henry A. Millon and Linda Nochlin (Cambridge, MA: MIT Press, 1978), 356–81 [362].

20. The original reads: "Los Niños Nacen para Ser Felices."

21. Kunzle, "Art and the New Chile," 363.

22. The original reads: "Otro Chile Es Posible."

23. The original reads: "A Construir un Chile Nuevo."

24. Alejandro "Mono" González, interview by author, Santiago, June 2004.

25. See Alejandro "Mono" González and Juan "Chin Chin" Tralma, interview by author, Santiago, July 2004.

26. Alejandro "Mono" González, interview by author, Santiago, July 2004.

27. Declassified documents also reveal CIA support for two alternative "tracks" to prevent Allende from taking office: "Track I" sought to influence a congressional vote necessitated by the Constitution after the Popular Unity failed to secure an absolute majority; "Track II" instigated a coup against the state. See Peter Kornbluh, "Chile and the United States: Declassified Documents Relating to the Military Coup, September 11, 1973," *National Security Archive Electronic Briefing Book No. 8,* http://nsarchive.gwu.edu/NSAEBB/NSAEBB8 /nsaebb8i.htm (last accessed October 14, 2015). Kornbluh's *Briefing Book No. 8* contains two pertinent CIA declassified documents from the larger collection of the National Security Archive, Washington, DC: William V. Broe, Chief, Western Hemisphere Division, "Memorandum for the Record. Subject: Genesis of Project FUBELT," dated September 16, 1970; and "Report on CIA Chilean Task Force Activities, 15 September to 3 November, 1970," dated November 18, 1970. For a rich exploration of U.S. involvement in the Chilean coup and military regime, see also Peter Kornbluh, *The Pinochet File: A Declassified Dossier on Atrocity and Accountability* (New York: New Press, 2003).

28. See, e.g., Castillo Espinoza, *Puño y letra,* 107.

29. See, e.g., the collections of the Museo Histórico Nacional (MHN; National Museum of History).

30. Alejandro "Mono" González, interview by author, Santiago, June 2004. On the other hand, brigadistas also used the PC newspaper, *El Siglo,* and to a lesser extent radio as means of communication. *El Siglo* published a sketch of a slogan, which was then used by the brigadistas as a template for graffiti in cities throughout the country.

31. Alejandro "Mono" González, interview by author, Santiago, June 2004.

32. The trazado was also inspired at least in part by print technology. The "flat press" used a black outline as a contrast to colors that could otherwise bleed into each other. The brigada furthered the relationship between print and street practice, as we shall see below.

33. Alessandro Portelli, *The Death of Luigi Trastulli and Other Stories: Form and Meaning in Oral History* (Albany: State University of New York Press, 1991).

34. Mexican muralism, which paired public art with a definite social concern, was another important influence on Chilean popular art, although this

was a contentious issue. Brigadistas understood themselves not as artists but as workers exercising a form of political citizenship through public visual practice. Contrasting themselves with the great individual artists of the Mexican muralist movement was a means of defining themselves as an anonymous, collective group interested in political communication, not artistic innovation for its own sake. But the brigadas drew on global, historical influences that included Mexican muralism, Cuban *vallas,* and Eastern European graphic art to fashion an original form of mural art that, in their eyes, was special precisely because it had no pretensions to originality or permanence. As Alejandro "Mono" González contends, "We borrow styles, and with these borrowed styles, we build a language, we reinvent, and we work this language into a new context, into a new reality with our own commitments." Cited in Alejandra Sandoval Espinoza, *Palabras escritas en un muro: El caso de la Brigada Chacón* (Santiago: Ediciones Sur 2000), 35. Cf. Mary Coffey, *How a Revolutionary Art Became Official Culture: Murals, Museums, and the Mexican State* (Durham, NC: Duke University Press, 2012).

35. Juan "Chin Chin" Tralma and Alejandro "Mono" González, interview by author, Santiago, July 2004.

36. See David M. Henkin's masterful analysis of the written work in the city, *City Reading: Written Words and Public Spaces in Antebellum New York* (New York: Columbia University Press, 1998), 5.

37. Scholars have recently and increasingly examined the intimate relationship between continuities and radical change. Florencia Mallon's *Courage Tastes of Blood* and Lessie Jo Frazier's *Salt in the Sand* are two foundational examples. Gender historians have long examined these complexities: Heidi Tinsman's *Buying into the Regime* and Gwynn Thomas's *Contesting Legitimacy in Chile,* for instance, look at women and gendered discourse as it shifts over different political periods. Jadwiga Pieper Mooney offers a fascinating exploration of the transformation of gendered languages and practice but also the persistence of patriarchy and patriarchal inequities across political periods, either in practice or, as in the case of restrictive abortion rights, legacies of the dictatorship written into and surviving through the legal code. See Jadwiga E. Pieper Mooney, *The Politics of Motherhood: Maternity and Women's Rights in Twentieth-Century Chile* (Pittsburgh, PA: University of Pittsburgh Press, 2009). I explore this turn in periodization at the book's conclusion.

38. Castillo Espinosa, *Puño y letra,* 96–97.

39. Interview with Juan "Chin Chin" Tralma, 2004.

40. Ibid.

41. Alejandro "Mono" González, interview by author, Santiago, June 2004.

42. Ibid.

43. Mono González's statement blurs distinctions between visual and performance, image and gesture, though it does not fail to recognize the importance of these contradictory narratives. Instead, González's telling derives meaning from its ability to combine image and practice, art and politics, in new, efficient if ephemeral forms. His story is carefully crafted—plotted, told, and

retold in democracy and dictatorship as a means of honing a story of political citizenship gained, then imperiled. By "crafted," I do not mean artificial or untrue. Rather, I am suggesting that we can understand the lasting significance of visual practice in how González pieces together his narrative, in how he shapes his recollections around the memory of visual practice in situ on city streets.

44. "When we are going to paint a wall, I pass by it, I look at the street, I pay attention to movement, I pay attention to the way in which people circulate." Alejandro "Mono" González, interview by author, Santiago, June 2004. The trazador had to take into account practical and corporeal concerns about the nature of contested urban spaces. They measured the number of people who would access a particular mural, how efficiently they could work at a particular site, how expeditiously they could finish the piece, and how quickly they could escape if they were pursued. They measured these factors against the risk they ran in painting it. Technique was born out of the need to work quickly, under pressure.

45. Alejandro "Mono" González, interview by author, Santiago, June 2004. It is interesting that González claims to have learned all this through practice rather than study, further distancing himself from an artist's identity and entrenching his claim to authenticity gleaned through practice and a direct experience of the street.

46. Ibid.

47. Juan "Chin Chin" Tralma, interview by author, Santiago, November 2004.

48. Alejandro "Mono" González, interview by author, Santiago, June 2004.

49. Ibid.

50. Rodríguez-Plaza, "La visualidad urbana en el Chile de la Unidad Popular," 10–12.

51. Gonzalez highlights film as a quintessentially "modern" technology that was reshaping the ways in which Chileans understood the city in relation to political and social discourses. He argues that the brigadas' work was deeply influenced by a "different visual formulation," a way of seeing structured by exposure to the narrative techniques of film. Similarly, Martin Jay's discussion of "scopic regimes" and John Berger's analysis of "ways of seeing" offer fascinating discussions of how visual modes shape how and what we see. See Martin Jay, *Downcast Eyes: The Denigration of Vision in Twentieth-Century French Thought* (Berkeley: University of California Press, 1993); John Berger, *Ways of Seeing* (London: British Broadcasting Corporation, 1972).

52. The mural's final form "has to do with the architecture or structure of the wall," González recounts. Alejandro "Mono" González and Juan "Chin Chin" Tralma, interview by author, Santiago, July 2004.

53. The brigada's place within the Popular Unity's "new culture" was institutionalized in 1971, when parallel exhibitions of mural artists were mounted in Santiago's Institute of Latin American Art and Museum of Contemporary Art.

54. Gonzalez continued: "Our preference for the symbol of the hand comes from this. I insist: I can love, fight, receive, create, harvest, and sow with my hand. But I can also squeeze and caress with my hand. . . . In short, one element can be many things at the same time. Invoking simple yet synthetic symbols, you communicate all these codes. As a rule, we have used the face, the hand, the human body in our murals because the human body is at the center of our story. It is in everything. The human body is the foundation of our vision of society and our social commitment." Alejandro "Mono" González, interview by author, Santiago, June 2004.

55. Ibid.

56. Ibid.

57. Ibid.

58. Sontag writes, As "often as [murals and posters] convey a particular message, they simply express (through being beautiful) *pleasure* at certain ideas, moral attitudes, and ennobling historical references." Susan Sontag, "Posters: Advertisement, Art, Political Artifact, Commodity," in *The Art of Revolution: 96 Posters from Castro's Cuba, 1959–1970*, ed. Dugald Stermer (New York: McGraw Hill, 1970), xiv.

59. Alejandro "Mono" González, interview by author, Santiago, June 2004.

60. Ibid.

61. Henkin, *City Reading*, 11.

62. Daniel James and Mirta Zaido Lobato, "Family Photos, Oral Narratives, and Identity Formation: The Ukrainians of Berisso," *Hispanic American Historical Review* 84, no. 1 (2004): 5–36; Ruth Finnegan, "A Note on Oral Tradition and Historical Evidence," *History and Theory* 9 (October 1970): 195–201; Florencia Mallon, editor's introduction to *When a Flower Is Reborn: The Life and Times of a Mapuche Feminist*, by Rosa Isolde Reuque Paillalef (Durham, NC: Duke University Press, 2002), 17.

63. William E. French, "Imagining and the Cultural History of Nineteenth-Century Mexico," *Hispanic American Historical Review* 79, no. 2 (1999): 249–67 [251–53].

64. For a fascinating take on photography and oral history, see Mauricio Vico Sánchez, "Waldo González y los carteles para la Polla Chilena de la Beneficiencia," in Castillo Espinosa, *El cartel chileno*, 8–9.

65. "People took the first poster down throughout the city, took it home, and we had to triple production." Interview, Waldo González, July 2001. See also Vico Sánchez, "Waldo González y los carteles," 9.

66. Vico Sánchez, "Waldo González y los carteles," 9.

67. González Hervé's experimentation with body, class, and race is evident in the Polla series, especially in the drawings and mockups reproduced in Castillo Espinoza's beautiful *Cartel chileno*, 42–43. His play with form, skin, and color is prevalent throughout the Polla series. See, e.g., the March 25 piece, "Chile Says No to Poliomelitis."

68. Waldo González Hervé, interviews by author. Santiago, July 2001 and July 2005.

69. Ibid. Vico Sánchez, "Waldo González y los carteles," 8–9; Vico Sánchez, *El afiche político.*

70. Cf. Alessandro Portelli, *The Battle of Valle Giulia: Oral History and the Art of Dialogue* (Madison: University of Wisconsin Press, 1997); and Portelli, *The Death of Luigi Trastulli.*

71. Vicente Larrea, interview by author, Santiago, July 2001.

72. For an enthralling discussion of natural disasters and the building of political idioms and national images, see Mark A. Healey, *The Ruins of the New Argentina: Peronism and the Remaking of San Juan after the 1944 Earthquake* (Durham, NC: Duke University Press, 2011).

73. Ibid.

74. The original reads: "A Trabajar."

75. Kunzle, "Art and the New Chile," 367.

76. In a tongue-in-cheek, self-referential move, the first image in my description, a community jumbled atop a child's shoulders, features a line-drawn representation of the poster of two birds building a nest, just one example of many that illustrate how these posters form part of an interrelated series in which one image enters in complex relation to any combination of others in the set.

77. Kunzle, "Art and the New Chile."

78. "Race" has remained an unspoken foil for social relations in Chile—a "white" country in official and popular discourses, a nation marked by the persecution and decimation of indigenous peoples through colonial and national periods, the lines of difference in Chile are drawn along binary divisions between urban and rural, elite and working class, lines where the subaltern side of these relationships are touched by unspoken insinuations of indigenous "racial" background. See, e.g., Alberto Harambour, "Racialización desde afuera, etnización hacia adentro: Clase y región en el movimiento obrero de la Patagonia, principios del siglo XX," in *Historias de racismo y discriminación en Chile,* ed. Rafael Gaune y Martín Lara (Santiago: Uqbar, 2009).

79. This is what Bourdieu calls "habitus." See Pierre Bourdieu and Randal Johnson, *The Field of Cultural Production: Essays on Art and Literature* (New York: Columbia University Press, 1993).

80. Paul Groth and Peter Bressi, *Understanding Ordinary Landscapes* (New Haven, CT: Yale University Press, 1998), 1–24.

81. The concept "chain of equivalencies" comes from Kristin Ross, *Fast Cars, Clean Bodies: Decolonization and the Reordering of French Culture* (Cambridge, MA: MIT Press, 1995).

82. Michel Foucault, *The Order of Things: An Archaeology of the Human Sciences* (London: Routledge, 2002).

83. Danny Aguilar, one of Vicente Larrea's students, produced a work titled *Copper: You Are Now Nation* (Cobre Ya Eres Patria), made for the Corporación del Cobre (CODELCO) and published by the Socialist Party's Vanguardia advertising agency. The image commemorated the July 11, 1971, rally "For National Dignity" in support of the nationalization of the industry. See Vico Sánchez,

"Breve aproximación a los afiches," 138 n. 12. The Larrea and Albornoz studio pioneered the use of photography in Chilean posters, frequently introducing Antonio Larrea's photograph in high contrast and/or in montage as a central rhetorical mechanism. Their record covers featured now-iconic black-and-white photographs Antonio Larrea had taken of Nueva Canción singers like Victor Jara and Inti-Illimani, and their work in solidarity with Vietnam highlighted anonymous high-contrast images of fighters and families. See, e.g., Castillo Espinoza, *Puño y letra*, 113; and Mauricio Vico Sánchez and Mario Osses, *Un grito en la pared: Psicodelia, compromiso, político y exilio en el cartel chileno* (Santiago: Ocho Libros, 2009), 99, 106–7. Aguilar referenced but departed from his teacher's technique. In Aguilar's piece, photography plays a potently allegorical function. Black-and-white images of copper workers are interspersed with red, orange, and yellow swaths recalling melted ore and making up in block letters the words "Copper," "Popular," and "Power" among the crowd.

84. Hoover Institute Archive, Chilean Poster Collection, Stanford University.

85. See also Hernán Vidal ("Hervi"), "Viva Chile! Por fin el cobre es nuestro," (Library of Congress, Prints and Photographs Division, Yanker Poster Collection, POS 6—Chile, no. 54). Hervi's image features a grinning copper smelter extending his hand in a triumphant gesture, seemingly right into the street. This interpolates the passerby, symbolically reaching to the pedestrian and pulling him or her into this imagined national collective.

86. Sontag, "Posters," vii–viii.

87. Ibid.

88. Rodríguez-Plaza, "La visualidad urbana en el Chile de la Unidad Popular," 10–12.

89. Ibid.

90. They are also part of broader sensuous worlds. All these forms of visual imagery use color and shape, brighten the city, and express sensuous pleasure in certain concepts, ideas, morals, etc. As often as posters "convey a particular message, they simply express (through being beautiful) *pleasure* at certain ideas, moral attitudes, and ennobling historical references. . . . The Cuban posters are much less analytic than the posters from recent French revolution; they educate in a more indirect, emotional, graphically sensuous way." There is a contentious Eurocentrism and fetishization of the Caribbean here. But we can read in this fetishization Sontag's acknowledgment that emotion/pleasure has a place in an academic study. Emotion plays a large role in the interviews I conducted. Introducing *alegría*, or joy, to a gray city is part of this political commitment, a commitment to brighten run-down areas and the run-down lives of the poor. Emotion or affect here becomes political. Alejandro "Mono" González, interview by author, Santiago, 2004. Pedro Millar expresses a very similar sentiment in a conversation with the author. Pedro Millar, interview by author, Santiago, 2004.

91. Esther Gabara, "Gestures, Practices, and Projects: [Latin] American Re-visions of Visual Culture and Performance Studies," *Emisférica* 7, no. 1

(2010) (last accessed March 4, 2016). Here Gabara draws on Armando Silva, *Punto de vista ciudadano: Focalización visual y puesta en escena del graffiti* (Bogotá: Instituto Caro y Cuervo, 1987).

92. Francisco Brugnoli, cited in Ernesto Saul, *Artes Visuales: 20 Años, 1970–1990* (Santiago: Ministerio de Educación, 1991), 188. Also Francisco Brugnoli, interview by author, Santiago, November 2004.

93. This is an adaptation of Ned Blackhawk's treatment of violence as a prism of analysis. See Ned Blackhawk, *Violence over the Land: Indians and Empires in the Early American West, 1850–1930* (Cambridge, MA: Harvard University Press, 2006), 6. It is also an interpretation of Diana Taylor's arguments about performance: "Recognizing performance as a valid focus of analysis contributes to our understanding of embodied practice as an episteme and a praxis, a way of knowing as well as a way of storing and transmitting cultural knowledge and identity. Performance as a lens enables commentators to explore not only isolated events and limit cases, but also the scenarios that make up individual and collective imaginaries. . . . Performance studies can allow us to engage in a sustained historical analysis of the performance practices that both bind and fragment the Americas. As such, it plays a vital role in remapping. That's what I'm asking it to do." Taylor, *The Archive and the Repertoire*, 278.

94. Taylor, *The Archive and the Repertoire*, 26–27.

95. Ibid., 28.

96. Ibid., 29–32.

97. Ibid., 3, 31–32.

98. Ibid.

99. Ibid., 174.

100. Juan "Chin Chin" Tralma, interview by author, Santiago, July 2004.

101. On the "essential artfulness" of oral narratives, see Daniel James, *Doña Maria's Story: Life History, Memory, and Political Identity* (Durham, NC: Duke University Press, 2000), 160. See too Taylor, *The Archive and the Repertoire*, 32.

CHAPTER 5

Portions of this chapter appeared in the *Radical History Review.* Camilo D. Trumper, "Social Violence, Political Conflict, and Latin American Film: The Politics of Place in the 'Cinema of Allende,'" *Radical History Review* 106 (Winter 2010): 109–36. Copyright 2010, MARHO: The Radical Historians Organization, Inc. Republished by permission of the copyrightholder, and present publisher, Duke University Press.

1. Zuzana M. Pick, *The New Latin American Cinema: A Continental Project* (Austin: University of Texas Press, 1993), 3–4.

2. Birri was founder of the Santa Fe school of documentary film and one of the movement's pioneers. See Fernando Birri, quoted in Michael Chanan, "Latin American Cinema," in *Remapping World Cinema: Identity, Culture and Politics in Film*, ed. Stephanie Dennison and Song Hwee Lim (London: Wallflower Press, 2006), 38–54.

3. As I discuss in this chapter, these influences included but were not limited to dependency theory, Camilo Torres's and Paulo Freire's version of liberation theology, and the writings of Ernesto "Che" Guevara and Frantz Fanon. I focus here on filmmakers from Argentina, Brazil, Cuba, Bolivia, Colombia, Uruguay, and Chile.

4. Scott Baugh, "Manifesting La Historia: Systems of Development and the New Latin American Manifesto," *Film & History* 34, no. 1 (2004): 56–65. Pick, *The New Latin American Cinema.*

5. Walter Mignolo, *Local Histories / Global Designs: Colonialist, Subaltern Knowledges, and Border Thinking* (Princeton, NJ: Princeton University Press, 2000). Arturo Escobar argues that modernization and dependency theories are both discursive systems with very real consequences in global and national policy and practice. Diametrically opposed hypotheses, their arguments are nevertheless structured by a shared belief in the existence and benefits of modernity and progress. Arturo Escobar, *Encountering Development: The Making and Unmaking of the Third World* (Princeton, NJ: Princeton University Press, 1995).

6. Baugh, "Manifesting La Historia," 57.

7. Glauber Rocha, reproduced in Zuzana M. Pick, *Latin American Film Makers and the Third Cinema* (Ottawa: Carleton University Press, 1978), 154–55.

8. Ibid.

9. Glauber Rocha, reproduced in Fundación Mexicana de Cineastas, ed., *Hojas de cine: Testimonios y documentos del nuevo cine latinoamericano* (Mexico City: Secretaría de Educación Pública, 1988), 166–67.

10. Baugh, "Manifesting La Historia," 56, 59. See also Chanan, "Latin American Cinema," 41.

11. The New Latin American Cinema's founding manifestos are subtle, powerfully written analyses of contemporary political and social realities.

12. Paul Schroeder Rodríguez, "After New Latin American Cinema," *Cinema Journal* 51, no. 2 (Winter 2012): 87–112.

13. In Zuzana Pick's words, "The first step toward consciousness of under-development is through a cinema that presents a national and social reality . . . [which has often been] falsified, deformed or hidden." Pick, *Latin American Film Makers*, 4–7.

14. Nelson Pereira dos Santos, cited in Ana M. Lopez, "Towards a 'Third' and 'Imperfect' Cinema: A Theoretical and Historical Study of Filmmaking in Latin America" (PhD diss., University of Iowa, 1986), 305.

15. Miguel Littín, reproduced in Pick, *Latin American Film Makers*, 169; and Glauber Rocha, reproduced in Pick, *Latin American Film Makers*, 120.

16. For an interesting discussion of music and politics, see César Albornoz, "Los sonidos del golpe," in *1973: La vida cotidiana de un año crucial*, ed. Claudio Rolle (Santiago: Planeta, 2003), 161–98.

17. Pick, *Latin American Film Makers*, 10.

18. Reproduced in Pick, *Latin American Film Makers*, 13.

19. Pastor Vega, "Cuba: Cinema, National Culture," reproduced in Pick, *Latin American Film Makers*, 216–31 [221–25].

20. Pick, *Latin American Film Makers*, 10. In Spanish: *toma de conciencia*.

21. Ibid., 12.

22. Cf., e.g., Miguel Littín's *El chacal de Nahueltoro*.

23. The screen was, for them, "the crossroads of a certain set of geographies ... which gains its resonance because the world in which such a place is located is multi-layered and multi-dimensional." Chanan, "Latin American Cinema," 48–49. Chanan also described the screen as an "amalgam of space and place" in which these filmmakers were able to reinscribe "the periphery as a site of counter-narrative[,] ... a new type of historicism" (49).

24. Schroeder Rodríguez, "After New Latin American Cinema," 87–112. See also George Yudice, "Audiovisual Educational Practices in Latin America's Peripheries," in *The Education of the Filmmaker*, ed. Mette Hjort (New York: Palgrave Macmillan, 2013), 239–59.

25. Schroeder Rodríguez traces a historical chronology that touches on early European cinematic influences, Latin American revolutionary movements and their significance for aesthetic innovation, and the relationship between militant filmmaking on the Left and their transformation in response to the rise of authoritarian states. He charts a relationship between the phases and forms of filmmaking that is not a simple or linear one but rather a sort of Deleuzian "unfolding" that connects the general to the particular in surprising ways: "Many other Latin American directors who did not follow this particular evolution in its entirety also helped define specific phases and transitions in the NLAC[,] ... [including] Miguel Littín, whose *El chacal de Nahueltoro* combined documentary-style reenactments and traditional narrative forms in a scathing critique of the justice system in Chile." Schroeder Rodríguez, "After New Latin American Cinema," 92–94.

26. Ibid., 91.

27. Lopez, "Towards a 'Third' and 'Imperfect' Cinema," 357–61.

28. Michael Chanan, *Chilean Cinema* (London: British Film Institute, 1976), 19–20.

29. Sergio Bravo, cited in John King, *Magical Reels: A History of Cinema in Latin America* (London: Verso, 1990), 169.

30. See Baugh, "Manifesting La Historia," 58.

31. Sergio Bravo, cited in King, *Magical Reels*, 169–170.

32. This included Violeta Parra's recovery of folk melodies and musical traditions, which greatly influenced the nueva canción movement; it also included Parra's own work with traditional, popular *arpillerería*, or patchwork embroidery, and Victor Jara's engagement with popular music and theater.

33. King, *Magical Reels*, 170.

34. Douglas Hübner, interview by author, Santiago, 2005.

35. Lopez, "Towards a 'Third' and 'Imperfect' Cinema," 364–65. Fiction and documentary filmmakers signed a revealing manifesto in favor of the Popular Unity in which they sought to define their interrelated role as proponents of a

"new" Latin American cinema and a national revolution. Their manifesto succinctly expressed a desire to define the relationship between artist and revolutionary and the role of the filmmaker in state formation: "We are men engaged with the political and social realities of our people before we are filmmakers. We are engaged in their great task: the construction of socialism. . . . What we mean by revolutionary is that which is realized in conjunction between the artist and his people, united in a common objective: liberation. The people are generators of action and finally the true creators; the film maker is their instrument of communication." Reprinted in Pick, *Latin American Film Makers*, 13.

36. Chanan, *Chilean Cinema*, 19–20.

37. King, *Magical Reels*, 172.

38. Roberto Tejada examines the relationship between the city, body, and camera in a very different context. Studying Manuel Alvarez Bravo, Tejada concludes that the "subject's relation to space is constitutive of the image environment in that it structures the site and setting for representation." Roberto Tejada, *National Camera: Photography and Mexico's Image Environment* (Minneapolis: University of Minnesota Press, 2009), 95, 117.

39. Federico Salzman, interview by author, Santiago, June 2005.

40. Ibid.

41. For him, Pedro Chaskel and Héctor Ríos's documentary short *Venceremos* is an example of this drive, inspired by "a strong desire to take to the streets . . . to find . . . as realistic an aesthetic as possible." Francisco Gedda, interview by author, Santiago, May 2005.

42. Gedda, interview by author, Santiago, May 2005.

43. Roland Barthes, *Camera Lucida: Reflections on Photography* (New York: Hill and Wang, 2010), 26.

44. Salzman, interview by author, Santiago, June 2005.

45. Recent literature on visual studies and visual practice, which emphasizes a rich, historically contextualized understanding of systems and practices of production, projection, and reception, can offer important insights into the role of cinema and politics.

46. Carlos Flores Delpino, interview by author, Santiago, May 2005.

47. Ibid.

48. Flores tells this story in a "tragic" mode, a show of force doomed to fail: "Three hundred thousand workers, with *colihues* and flags don't mean anything concrete . . . when it comes time to confront the power of the coup and the military." In other words, the coup serves as the fulcrum on which turns Flores's memory of political power lost. Yet it is urban conflict that frames the tragic narrative. Flores, interview with the author, Santiago, May 2005.

49. Carl Fischer, "Temporalidades y masculinidades frágiles en la UP de *La batalla de Chile*," in *Enfoques al cine chileno en dos siglos*, ed. Mónica Villarroel (Santiago: LOM Ediciones, 2013), 215–22 [215].

50. Anne Marie Stock reminds us that this was a practice common in the Cuban NLAC. Ann Marie Stock, *On Location in Cuba: Street Filmmaking during Times of Transition* (Chapel Hill: University of North Carolina Press, 2009).

51. Sergio Trabuco Ponce, *Con los ojos abiertos: El Nuevo Cine chileno y el movimiento del Nuevo Cine latinoamericano* (Santiago: LOM Ediciones, 2014), 274–75.

52. Patricio Guzmán, "Mi encuentro con Jorge Müller," *El Desconcierto*, December 2, 2013, http://eldesconcerto.cl/mi-encuentro-con-jorge-muller/ (last accessed July 29, 2015). Cited in Trabuco Ponce, *Con los ojos abiertos*, 315–16.

53. Douglas Hübner, interview by author, Santiago, May 2005.

54. Baugh, "Manifesting La Historia," 62.

55. Ana M. Lopez, "*The Battle of Chile:* Documentary, Political Process, and Representation," in *The Social Documentary in Latin America*, ed. Julianne Burton (Pittsburgh, PA: University of Pittsburgh Press, 1990), 273.

56. Ibid.

57. Lopez, "Towards a 'Third' and 'Imperfect' Cinema"; Jorge Rufinelli, *Patricio Guzmán* (Madrid: Cátedra, 2001).

58. Lopez, "*The Battle of Chile*," 273.

59. The team worked with Marta Harnecker, a leading left-wing intellectual in the tradition of Louis Althusser and key contributor to *Chile Hoy*. See, e.g., Marta Harnecker, *Los conceptos elementales del materialismo histórico* (Mexico City: Siglo XXI, 1971).

60. See Ruffinelli, *Patricio Guzmán*, 130.

61. Ruffinelli, *Patricio Guzmán*, 130–31.

62. Guzmán, in Ruffinelli, *Patricio Guzmán*, 131.

63. Lopez, "*The Battle of Chile*," 271. Lopez is one of the first scholars of Chilean film to analyze Guzmán's documentary as both a film (with an important aesthetic language) and a historical document (a means of articulating a complex argument about the period that it visually and aurally commemorated).

64. Jorge Sanjines, in Pick, *Latin American Film Makers*, 73.

65. Lopez, "*The Battle of Chile*," 267.

66. I have argued that those who marched with empty pots and those who occupied city streets during the truckers' strike were aware that their engagement with public space instigated a new relationship between the language of politics and discourses of gender and citizenship that revolved around food and hunger. The city's muralists and poster makers were aware that they articulated a visual language that could marry the power of representation with the politics of public space. These are all related critical practices brought together around politics and the street.

67. As we shall see below, *Venceremos* follows in the tradition of recentering the body in hunger as the focus of an intelligible "idiom" of politicized outrage, and *Unos pocos caracoles* examines the relationship between political sentiment, grassroots mobilization, and the city.

68. Nelly Richard, *Cultural Residues: Chile in Transition* (Minneapolis: University of Minnesota Press, 2004), 73–74.

69. Here I draw on Bourdieu's foundational conceptualization of embodied practices or "habitus." Pierre Bourdieu, *Distinction: A Social Critique of the Judgment of Taste* (Cambridge, MA: Harvard University Press, 1984).

70. Or, in Guzmán's words, their cinematic style gives them the ability to "probe reality for a narrative [hidden within]." Ruffinelli, *Patricio Guzmán.* See also Pick, cited in Lopez, "*The Battle of Chile*," 272.

71. "Momio" is a colloquial term for a right-wing person, which literally translates as "mummy" and refers to conservatism, ossification.

72. This sequence echoes the film's inaugural moments, in which the sound of these planes, laid over black, fed into the initial images of La Moneda as it was bombed.

73. These explicit and implicit references to the relationship between democracy and dictatorship occur throughout. For instance, the army officers presiding over the electoral process that was taking place in the National Stadium ominously prefigure the images of the stadium-as-internment-camp that define the building after the coup.

74. This, again, is the subject of Fischer's "Temporalidades y masculinidades," 215.

75. Thomas Miller Klubock, "History and Memory in Neoliberal Chile: Patricio Guzmán's Obstinate Memory and *The Battle of Chile*," *Radical History Review* 85, no. 1 (2003): 272–81.

76. Ibid., 277.

77. I am here drawing on and modifying Martin Jay's concept of "scopic regimes" and broader visual studies methods. Drawing on visual studies methods, I argue that we must examine processes of production, circulation, and consumption in order to fully understand just how these films are analyses of local landscapes that simultaneously map alternative methods and geographies of cinematic expression. Throughout Latin America, this methodology relies on the study of where these films were shown—in theaters, factories, plazas— alongside their aesthetic and visual language. See Martin Jay, "Scopic Regimes of Modernity," in *Vision and Visuality*, ed. Hal Foster (Seattle, WA: Bay Press, 1988): 3–23; and Martin Jay, *Downcast Eyes: The Denigration of Vision in Twentieth-Century French Thought* (Berkeley: University of California Press, 1993).

78. John Urry, "Sensing the City," in *The Tourist City*, ed. Dennis R. Judd and Susan S. Fainstein (New Haven, CT: Yale University Press, 1999), 71–86.

79. Allende often invoked "History" in a Marxist vein, as an inexorable force whose movement forward is spurred by the political and class conflict in which he is embroiled. Allende's own, modernist view centered on dialectic resolutions—on a belief in the ultimate progress of History spurred on by the clash of apparent paradoxes, of politics from above and below, government and opposition, of the inevitable opening of political spaces even in the face of military repression and his imminent demise. His modernist and Marxist conception of History as defined by progress is evident too in his final words on the radio before dying in the presidential palace. At 9:03 A.M., Allende reasserted his belief in the trajectory of History and the potential of the people and the nation in the face of military violence, predicting that the city's boulevards, its great alamedas, would soon be opened, the coup turned back.

80. Lopez, "*The Battle of Chile*," 271. Among others, Álvaro Ramírez examined the issue of infant malnutrition in *Desnutrición infantil* (1969); and Douglas Hübner analyzed the problems of the landless in *Herminda de la Victoria* (1969), as did Carlos Flores Delpino and Guillermo Cahn in *Casa o mierda* (1970) and Ignacio Aliaga in *Campamento Sol Naciente* (1972). *Venceremos* fits into this tradition.

81. Lopez, "Towards a 'Third' and 'Imperfect' Cinema," 385.

82. See Pick, cited in Lopez, "*The Battle of Chile*," 272.

83. *Venceremos*, like *La batalla*, highlights the political and representational power of sound. Similarly, César Albornoz charts how Ricardo Garcia, a central figure in the distribution of the nueva canción, had a radio show, *El sonido de la história*, in which he attempted to present historically significant moments through sound, mapping a soundscape that interlocked crucial, world-changing moments and everyday aural experiences: "They presented tapes that showed events or some specific periods . . . such as power transfers from one president to another, etc. The goal was to educate the mass public in history through sound, a public who daily listened to tunes, lyrics in English, love stories, the honking of buses, street demonstrations." These are part of an even wider array of often-ignored sounds that were nonetheless infused with deep political significance. Albornoz, "Los sonidos del golpe," 180–81.

84. This was a hallmark of some of the NLAC's most prominent members. The influence of Santiago Alvarez's newsreels and Solanas and Getino's *Hora de los hornos* is evident in this practice.

85. Walter Mignolo examines the dialectical, mimetic relationship between the "modern" and its "others." Mignolo, *Local Histories / Global Designs*.

86. Lopez argues that the NLAC "sought to provide spectators with different consciousnesses of their worlds, ones which would disturb the apparently natural order of things and which would break down rationalizations and preconceived ideas." Lopez, "*The Battle of Chile*," 267–88.

87. Lopez, "Towards a 'Third' and 'Imperfect' Cinema," 291, 397.

88. Richard, *Cultural Residues*, 50.

89. Robert Stam, "Beyond Third Cinema: The Aesthetics of Hybridity," in *Rethinking Third Cinema*, ed. Anthony Guneratne, Wimal Dissanayake, and Sumita S. Chakravarty (London: Routledge, 2003), 31–35, 41–45.

90. Here I am borrowing from Pratt and Vernon's insights into the ways in which even radically anticolonial efforts, such as Gandhi's fasts against British colonial policy and the Indian caste system, draw from a bank of shared ideas and therefore become politically coherent to people across the political spectrum. Looking closely at British press readings of Gandhi's fasts and paying particular attention to a key shift in their coverage, Pratt and Vernon show how the body can be interpreted differently in relation to an array of discursive systems and to a complex, slippery, and malleable set of social and political idioms. Tim Pratt and James Vernon, "Appeal from this fiery bed . . . ': The Colonial Politics of Gandhi's Fasts and Their Metropolitan Reception," *Journal of British Studies* 44, no. 1 (2005): 92–114 [92–93].

91. The conversations on the street, in factories, and in homes that Guzmán's crew fashioned and then filmed in *La batalla* are a perfect example of this process. As I have indicated, a number of scholars have recently studied poblaciones as sites of auto-construction and the building of political citizenship (see chap. 3, n. 5). I have examined cordones along the city's industrial ring as political incubators grounded in place. Each of these sites emerges as a laboratory of alternative political practices; each also roots the transformation of citizenship in the everyday conflicts and the changing landscape of grassroots mobilization.

CONCLUSION

1. Edward Murphy, *For a Proper Home: Housing Rights in the Margins of Urban Chile, 1960–2010* (Pittsburgh, PA: University of Pittsburgh Press, 2015), 136.

2. Already consolidating his authority in 1974, Pinochet formed the Dirección de Inteligencia Nacional (DINA), the secret police responsible for multidudinal internal acts of disappearance and torture and spectacular international murders that included those of constitutional officer Carlos Prats in Buenos Aires and former ambassador Orlando Letelier in the heart of Washington, DC. Peter Winn, "The Pinochet Years," in *Victims of the Chilean Miracle: Workers and Neoliberalism in the Pinochet Era, 1973–2002*, ed. Peter Winn (Durham, NC: Duke University Press, 2004), 19–21.

3. Steve J. Stern, *Remembering Pinochet's Chile: On the Eve of London 1998* (Durham, NC: Duke University Press, 2004), 31. These sources include a range of North American and Chilean scholarship; interviews and conversations with victims, witnesses, and perpetrators; analysis of the evidence compiled in two national reports on terror and torture produced by the Truth and Reconciliation Commission and Corporation of Repair and Reconciliation; original research in public archives like those of the Catholic Church's Vicariate of Solidarity; and engagement with those dedicated to recording memories of short- and long-term detention in and beyond Santiago. Stern builds on the reports, which while understating the number of victims were a "remarkable achievement . . . [and] sufficed to demonstrate the systematic and massive quality of repression" (31, 157–61). It should be noted that Teresa Meade, by expanding the scope of analysis to "political" and "economic" exile in the 1970s and 1980s, proposes that the number of exiles was as high as one million, almost 10 percent of Chile's population at the time, Teresa Meade, "Holding the Junta Accountable: Chile's 'Sitios de Memoria' and the History of Torture, Disappearance, and Death," *Radical History Review* 79 (Winter 2001): 123–39 [138 n. 7].

4. Luis Hernán Errázurriz and Gonzalo Leiva Quijada, *El golpe estético: Dictadura military en Chile, 1973–1989* (Santiago: Ocho Libros, 2012), 25.

5. Steve J. Stern, *Remembering Pinochet's Chile: On the Eve of London 1998* (Durham, NC: Duke University Press, 2004), xxiii.

6. Mary Louise Pratt, "Overwriting Pinochet: Undoing the Culture of Fear in Chile," *Modern Language Quarterly* 57, no. 2 (June 1996): 152–63 [155]. See too Giselle Munizaga, "El sistema comunicativo chileno y los legados de la dictadura," in *Cultura, autoritarismo y redemocratización en Chile*, ed. Manuel Antonio Garretón, Saúl Sosnowski, and Bernardo Subercaseaux (Mexico City: Fondo de Culutra Ecónomica, 1993), 89–99.

7. *El Mercurio*, September 15, 1973, cited in Errázurriz and Leiva Quijada, *El golpe estético*, 15.

8. *El Mercurio*, September 11, 1974.

9. Errázurriz and Leiva Quijada, *El golpe estético*, 14, citing *El Mercurio*, April 29, 1974.

10. Bando no. 30, September 17, 1973, cited in Errázurriz and Leiva Quijada, *El golpe estético*, 14.

11. Murphy, *For a Proper Home*, 149.

12. Ibid., 143.

13. Winn, *Victims of the Chilean Mircle*, 19.

14. Murphy relates a fascinating example of the tensions involved in policing intersecting gender and class comportment in the immediate aftermath of the coup. Murphy, *For a Proper Home*, 142. This so-called Operation Cut was heavily commented on in the pro-dictatorship press, which proposed that short, carefully groomed hair as a "new style" arose for "non-capillary reasons." See *Paula* 153 (November 1973): 89, cited in Errázurriz and Leiva Quijada, *El golpe estético*, 24; also see Errázurriz and Leiva Quijada, *El golpe estético*, 24–25, for the various articles compiled from *El Mercurio* and other publications under dictatorship.

15. I remember being puzzled by the sight of my parents' copies of Marx's *Capital*, required reading for economics students at the University of Chile in the late 1960s and early 1970s, wrapped in wallpaper and sitting conspicuously on my grandmother's bookshelves when I first lived in Chile as a young child in the early 1980s.

16. "La Alcaldía ha decretado hoy," *El Mercurio*, September 18, 1973, cited in Errázurriz and Leiva Quijada, *El golpe estético*, 20.

17. Errázurriz and Leiva Quijada, *El golpe estético*, 12, 28. Errázurriz and Leiva Quijada also analyze the first issue of the magazine *Orden Nuevo* (New Order), which referenced the Brigada Ramona Parra iconography to envision not a "new man" but a new social and political order as the root of a "unified" Chile achieved either by "restoration" or "creation" (17).

18. "Aseo exterior de todos los edificios," *El Mercurio*, July 10, 1975, cited in Errázurriz and Leiva Quijada, *El golpe estético*, 20.

19. See "Gigantesca operación Limpieza," *El Mercurio*, September 19, 1973, 29; "Con gran entusiasmo cientos de jóvenes han proseguido la tarea de limpiar los muros de la ciudad," *El Mercurio*, September 22, 1973, 17; and "Toda la ciudad—especialmente la juventud—colabora entusiastamente en el nuevo rostro de Santiago," *El Mercurio*, September 14, 1973, cited in Errázurriz and Leiva Quijada, *El golpe estético*, 24.

20. Murphy, *For a Proper Home*, 141.

21. Ibid.

22. Explorations of the gendered violence of state terror in the Southern Cone include Margarite Feitlowitz, *Lexicon of Terror: Argentina and the Legacies of Torture* (New York: Oxford University Press, 1998); Alicia Partnoy, *The Little School: Tales of Disappearance and Survival* (San Francisco: Cleis Press, 1998); Marcelo M. Suárez-Orozco, "The Treatment of Children in the 'Dirty War': Ideology, State Terrorism and the Abuse of Children in Argentina," in *Child Survival: Anthropological Perspectives on the Treatment and Maltreatment of Children*, ed. Nancy Scheper-Hughes (Dordrecht: D. Reidel, 1987), 227–46.

23. Murphy, *For a Proper Home*, 141.

24. Elizabeth Q. Hutchinson, Thomas M. Klubock, and Nara B. Milanich, eds., *Chile Reader: History, Culture, Politics* (Durham, NC: Duke University Press, 2013), 459. The commission contextualized the testimony received thus: "This Commission received testimony from 3,399 women, which corresponds to 12.5 percent of those who offered testimony. More than half of these women were detained in 1973. Almost all of these women reported being victims of sexual violence regardless of their age, and 316 testified that they were raped. However, we believe that the number of raped women is greater [because it is so difficult to talk about] and because many who were arrested have testified that they witnessed rapes at a large number of detention facilities. The torture that under-aged or pregnant women suffered highlights the brutality of these acts and the grave consequences that they live with. . . . The testimonies speak for themselves" (460). Many women were assaulted in the presence of family members, friends, or other prisoners in an attempt to play upon, fracture and retrench identities of proper femininity and masculinity that shaped political activism.

25. Julieta Kirkwood, in Hutchinson, Klubock, and Milanich, *Chile Reader*, 484.

26. Grandin, in Murphy, *For a Proper Home*, 139. For a rich discussion of these scholars' work in one place, see Nancy Scheper-Hughes and Philippe Bourgois, *Violence in War and Peace: An Anthology* (Oxford: Blackwell, 2002).

27. See Michael Taussig, "Terror as Usual: Walter Benjamin's Theory of History as a State of Siege," *Social Text* 23 (Autumn–Winter 1989): 3–20.

28. Camilo Trumper, "The Politics of Public Space: Santiago de Chile's *Estadio Nacional* through a Historical Lens," *Brújula* 4 (December 2006): 45–59. The phrase "rituals of rule" references William H. Beezley, Cheryl English Martin, and William E. French's fascinating *Rituals of Rule, Rituals of Resistance: Public Celebrations and Popular Culture in Mexico* (Wilmington, DE: SR Books, 1994).

29. Taussig, "Terror as Usual," 3–20.

30. Suárez-Orozco, "The Treatment of Children in the 'Dirty War.'"

31. Stern, *Remembering Pinochet's Chile*, 31, 180 n. 27. Murphy, in turn, finds in terror the means by which the regime formulated "an ambitious, total-

itarian effort to reshape social [and political] life." Edward Murphy, *For a Proper Home*, 135.

32. For a compelling argument regarding the fruitful potential of placing cultural history at the heart of our studies of the 1960s, the 1970s, and the Cold War, see Eric Zolov, "Introduction: Latin America in the Global Sixties," *The Americas* 70, no. 3 (January 2014): 349–62 [351].

33. I am indebted to Peter Winn for suggesting that I analyze the relationship between Ritoque and the Ciudad Abierta.

34. Ana Maria León, "Prisoners of Ritoque: The Open City and the Ritoque Concentration Camp," *Journal of Architectural Education* 66, no. 1 (2012): 85–97.

35. Ibid., 89, 90, 94. See also Miguel Lawner, *Isla Dawson, Ritoque, Tres Alamos: La vida a pesar de todo* (Santiago: LOM Ediciones, 2003), 75.

36. León, "Prisoners of Ritoque," 91. See also "Óscar Castro llegará al cine con su historia en campo de concentración Ritoque," www.cooperativa.cl. October 14, 2014 (last accessed August 27, 2015).

37. León, "Prisoners of Ritoque," 91.

38. Brian Loveman, for instance, has recently traced deep continuities between the "serious *permanent* limitations on civil liberties and political rights, freedom of association, inclusive representation, freedom of the press and mass media, rule of law, and accountability of government officials to citizens" and the eruption of violence on September 11, 1973. Brian Loveman, "The Political Architecture of Dictatorship: Chile before September 11, 1973," *Radical History Review* 124 (January 2016): 11–41 [12]; original emphasis. In this context, he concludes, the armed forces' "violent confrontation with miners, industrial workers, shantytown dwellers, and peasants was not a novelty," or an imposition from outside, but was instead "identifiably rooted in Chile's own authoritarian political culture and institutions" (31).

39. Florencia Mallon, *Courage Tastes of Blood: The Mapuche Community of Nicolás Ailío and the Chilean State, 1906–2001* (Durham, NC: Duke University Press, 2005), 236.

40. Ibid., 238–39.

41. Gwynn Thomas, *Contesting Legitimacy in Chile: Familial Ideals, Citizenship, and Political Struggle, 1970–1990* (University Park: Pennsylvania State University Press, 2011); Jadwiga Pieper Mooney, *Politics of Motherhood: Maternity and Women's Rights in Twentieth-Century Chile* (Pittsburgh, PA: University of Pittsburgh Press, 2009); Julieta Kirkwood, *Ser política en Chile: Las feministas y los partidos* (Santiago: LOM Ediciones, 1982); Julieta Kirkwood, *Chile: La mujer en la formulación política* (Santiago: FLACSO, 1981).

42. Thomas, *Contesting Legitimacy*, 142–43. See also Margaret Power, *Right-Wing Women: Feminine Power and Struggle against Allende, 1964–1973* (University Park: Pennsylvania State University Press, 2002), 229, Appendix E.

43. Carmen Saenz, interview, in Margaret Power and Lisa Baldez, "Women Lead the Opposition to Allende: Interview with Carmen Saenz." Reprinted in Hutchinson, Klubock, and Milanich, *Chile Reader*, 408.

44. Thomas, *Contesting Legitimacy,* 143.

45. Pratt, "Overwriting Pinochet," 153.

46. Gobierno de Chile, *República de Chile,* 194; and Augusto Pinochet, "Mensaje presidencial 11 septiembre 1973–11 septiembre 1974," 2, cited in Thomas, *Contesting Legitimacy,* 143–44.

47. Lisa Baldez, *Why Women Protest: Women's Movements in Chile* (New York: Cambridge University Press, 2002), 120–21.

48. Thomas, *Contesting Legitimacy,* 142.

49. Pieper Mooney, *Politics of Motherhood,* 135.

50. Kirkwood, in Hutchinson, Klubock, and Milanich, 406–8.

51. Baldez, *Why Women Protest,* 129. See too the pioneering work of Patricia M. Chuchryk, "From Dictatorship to Democracy: The Women's Movement in Chile," in *The Women's Movement in Latin America,* ed. Jane S. Jaquette (Boulder, CO: Westview Press, 1994), 65–108; Patricio Orellana and Elizabeth Quay Hutchinson, *El movimiento de derechos humanos en Chile, 1973–1990* (Santiago: Centro de Estudios Políticos Latinoamericanos Simón Bolívar, 1991); Elsa Chaney, "The Mobilization of Women in Allende's Chile," in *Women in Politics,* ed. Jane Jaquette (New York: John Wiley, 1974): 267–79.

52. Baldez, *Why Women Protest,* 129–30.

53. Ibid., 130; Marjorie Agosín, *Tapestries of Hope, Threads of Love: The Arpillera Movement in Chile, 1974–1994* (Albuquerque: University of New Mexico Press, 1996); Steve J. Stern, *Battling for Hearts and Minds: Memory Struggles in Pinochet's Chle, 1973–1988* (Durham, NC: Duke University Press, 2006); Steve J. Stern, *Reckoning with Pinochet's Chile: The Memory Question in Democratic Chile, 1989–2006* (Durham, NC: Duke University Press, 2010).

54. Pieper Mooney, *Politics of Motherhood,* 154.

55. Ibid., 135.

56. Ibid.

57. Ibid., 154–56.

58. Ibid., 158. Women often organized public resistance to the military regime precisely by appropriating or reclaiming anti-Allende gendered symbols, especially the empty pot. MOMUPO's leader, Marina Valdez, claimed that the banging on empty pots "was to demonstrate your opposition to the [military] government . . . because there was massive unemployment, because your family didn't have food to eat." Baldez, *Why Women Protest,* 122.

59. Pieper Mooney, *Politics of Motherhood,* 158–62.

60. Jorge Pinto Rodríguez, "Ser hombre en el Norte Chico: El testimonio de un historiador," in *Diálogos sobre el género masculino en Chile,* ed. Sonia Montecino Aguirre and María Elena Acuña (Santiago: Universidad de Chile, Facultad de Ciencias Sociales, Programa Interdisciplinario de Estudios de Género, 1996), 83–96. See also Thomas M. Klubock, *Contested Communities: Class, Gender, and Politics in Chile's El Teniente Copper Mine, 1904–1951* (Durham, NC: Duke University Press, 1998). See too Mallon's incisive summary of this tradition in Florencia Mallon, "*Barbudos,* Warriors, and *Rotos:* The MIR, Masculinity, and Power in the Chilean Agrarian Reform, 1965–74," in

Changing Men and Masculinities in Latin America, ed. Matthew C. Gutmann (Durham, NC: Duke University Press, 2003), 179–215 [181].

61. Mallon, "*Barbudos,* Warriors, and *Rotos,*" 181, 194.

62. Ibid., 211.

63. Ibid., 210–11.

64. Winn, "The Pinochet Years," 21. See also Mario Garcés and Sebastián Leiva, *El golpe en la legua: Los caminos de la historia y la memoria* (Santiago: LOM ediciones, 2005), 27.

65. See, e.g., the second book of Stern's trilogy on memory, Steve J. Stern, *Battling for the Hearts and Minds: Memory Struggles in Pinochet's Chile, 1973–1988* (Durham: Duke University Press, 2006).

66. Mallon, "*Barbudos,* Warriors, and *Rotos,*" 211.

67. On "structures of feeling," see Raymond Williams, *The Long Revolution* (New York: Columbia University Press, 1961).

68. "Las clases de marchas," *Documentos Gráficos* 1, no. 3 (1972).

69. Ibid.

70. Ibid.

71. Ibid.

72. As its editorial comment read, "Depending on their interests the newspapers may change the official numbers, may make positive or negative comments for or against the march, but most important, it should not be forgotten that photographs do not lie." *Documentos Gráficos* 1, no. 3 (1972): n.p.

73. "Las clases de marchas."

74. Ibid.

75. Ibid.

76. Ibid.

77. *Documentos Gráficos* 1, no. 3 (1972): n.p.

78. Ibid.

79. Ibid., 39.

80. "Despite their intended function as evidence, or even more recently as aesthetic objects to be looked at, there is something inscrutable about these pictures that oblige us to account for not only the history of an archive but also 'the history of a *concept in general.*'" This point regarding the interrelation between photographs' transparency and the invention of the concept of objectivity is particularly salient in relation to the Casasola collection because the images have long been used as an evidentiary base for the writing of the history of revolution. Roberto Tejada, *National Camera: Photography and Mexico's Image Environment* (Minneapolis: University of Minnesota Press, 2009), 40; original emphasis.

81. In short, it reveals that the archive, performance, and photographic practice are intertwined arenas in which political narratives were engaged and remade in democracy and dictatorship.

82. Taylor here establishes the repertoire of embodied performance not just as a legitimate object of study, but "an episteme and a praxis, a way of knowing as well as a way of storing and transmitting cultural knowledge and identity."

Diana Taylor, *The Archive and the Repertoire* (Durham, NC: Duke University Press, 2003), 278. Cf. Michel-Rolf Trouillot, *Silencing the Past* (Boston: Beacon Press, 2005).

83. Ángeles Donoso Macaya, "Arte, documento y fotografía: Prolegómenos para una reformulación del campo fotográfico en Chile (1977–1998)," *Aisthesis* 52 (2012): 407–24 [408].

84. Nelly Richard, "Márgen e institución," in *Arte en Chile desde 1973: Escena de avanzada y sociedad,* ed. Nelly Richard (Santiago: FLACSO Chile, 1987), 2–11.

85. Donoso Macaya, "Arte, documento y fotografía," 408.

86. In their influential study of photography, John Berger and Jean Mohr find that the paradox of the photographic image is that it enjoys a strong claim to objectivity, truth, and transparency but is weak in inherent meaning. Because photographs are necessarily decontextualized, a depiction of a frozen moment in time whose frame excludes much more than it contains, photographs can and must be recontextualized—named, captioned, paired with other images, and thereby made to mean a number of different things in a number of different ways. Simultaneously, Chilean photographers used the authority of the lens to create powerful, creative, meaningful works; but they also consciously and creatively played with the discourse of objectivity surrounding the lens and the multivalent, aesthetic potential of photographic practice. In short, Berger and Mohr here establish a close connection between objectivity and open-ended meaning-making. John Berger and Jean Mohr, *Another Way of Telling* (London: Granta Books, 1989), 92.

87. Taussig argues that terror works itself into the very fabric of social interaction and introduces a debilitating uncertainty and anxiety that results from the particular combination of ubiquity and secrecy that defines "state of siege," when terror is at once the rule *and* the exception. Taussig, "Terror as Usual." See also Michael Taussig, *The Nervous System* (Oxford: Routledge, 1992), 2.

88. This is an interpretation of Klubock's trenchant, critical, yet optimistic stance vis-à-vis Guzmán's *Obstinate Memory*: The film's "focus on personal, rather than collective, memory reflects profound changes in Chilean society since 1973 and the difficulty of making the past relevant to the present in the contemporary context. But the film also has another function. As a 'memory place,' it may produces a dialogue between history and the memories of the UP and the 1973 coup. *Memoria obstinada* may 'fan the spark of hope' of the Allende years and the memory of those who died struggling to build a socialist society." Thomas Miller Klubock, "History and Memory in Neoliberal Chile: Patricio Guzmán's *Obstinate Memory* and *The Battle of Chile*," *Radical History Review* 85 (Winter 2003): 272–81 [279].

89. Antonio Larrea's personal photographic archive charts a parallel, equally telling trajectory that straddles the Popular Unity and the dictatorship, with the coup and bombing of the presidential palace as the crucial event and turning point. Larrea's collection of photographs and contact sheets juxtaposes images

of the September 4 celebration of the Popular Unity's third anniversary (which features images of BRP members carrying the Larrea brothers' posters through the streets) to photos of the aftermath of the coup (images that present the bombed-out remains of the presidential palace and the cars that had been parked near it). Antonio Larrea, Personal Archive.

90. Marcelo Montecino, Personal Archive.

91. These photographic campaigns enjoyed a measure of success, as evidenced by the fact that international solidarity campaigns used the stadium as the visual linchpin in their calls for action. The solidarity group of the German Democratic Republic, for instance, created a poster that featured barbed wire molded into the shape of a stadium, encompassing a Chilean flag that bleeds out through a crack in the barbed-wire fence. Peter Stobinski, Catherine Gittis, and Bernd Rückert, *Internationale Solidarität im Spiegel des Plakats / Chile en el corazón* (Berlin: Solidaritätskomitee der DDR, 1980).

92. Cf. Martin Jay, *Downcast Eyes: The Denigration of Vision in Twentieth-Century French Thought* (Berkeley: University of California Press, 1993); W.J.T. Mitchell, "Showing Seeing: A Critique of Visual Culture," *Journal of Visual Culture* 1, no. 2 (2002): 165–81.

93. Alicia Partnoy, "Cuando Vienen Matando: On Prepositional Shifts and the Struggle of Testimonial Subjects for Agency," *PMLA* 121, no. 5 (October 2006): 1665–69 [1665–68].

94. Partnoy responds to what she reads in Sarlo's call to "go beyond the overwhelming predominance of the testimonial account of the repression by the military dictatorship and to engage with more strength in theoretical reflections to be able to understand what has happened," by highlighting the theoretical or analytical in the testimonial. Ibid., 1665.

95. Ibid., 1665–69.

96. Calirman proposes that "as incidents of censorship of visual art accumulated, innovation became a necessity, with artists developing more indirect modes of expression to circumvent censorship, often appropriating the strategies of urban guerrilla groups (which were being crushed by the military regime at the time) and performing quick actions or momentary interventions outside museums and art institutions." Claudia Calirman, *Brazilian Art under Dictatorship: Antonio Manuel, Artur Barrio, and Cildo Meireles* (Durham, NC: Duke University Press, 2012), 2.

97. "Far from paralyzing the creative production of the country, as many believed would happen, a period rife with suspicion and censorship stimulated newly anarchic practices, at times aggressive and at other times disguised in subtler modes of artistic intervention." Ibid., 2.

98. Ibid., 4.

99. Richard, "Márgen e institución."

100. Richard defines the Avanzada above all as avant-garde. In her view, the movement derives its significance from radical innovation rooted in the practices developed in response to dictatorship. Her chronology begins with the 1973 coup, which emerges as a discrete "event" and a foundational break that inaugurates a

new moment in, and narrative of, history. The coup is here a protracted moment of violence that shatters political, social, and aesthetic worlds and the modes and languages of representation that traditionally support these worlds. Ibid., 2, 4–5, 7, 11. Her writing gives shape to this historicity, which revolves around the coup as complete and total rupture that ultimately sets the stage for the unprecedented "emergence," in her words, of the avanzada on an already extant "arena of catastrophe [where] sense has been shipwrecked" (2). Thus does Richard place the avanzada project temporally (as a post-coup product born seemingly free of precedent and historical connection) and spatially (in an urban field defined by repression and censure). Prefiguring theorists of violence like Elaine Scarry, Richard argues that radical violence ultimately undermines the legitimacy and credibility of extant languages of representation, thereby rending the subject from that reality. See, e.g., Elaine Scarry, *The Body in Pain: The Making and Unmaking of the World* (Oxford: Oxford University Press, 1985); and Nancy Scheper-Hughes, "Bodies, Death, and Silence," Veena Das, "Language and Body: Transactions in the Construction of Pain," and Giorgio Agamben, "The Witness," in *Violence in War and Peace: An Anthology*, ed. Nancy Scheper-Hughes and Philippe Bourgois (Malden, MA: Blackwell, 2003), 186–95, 327–33, 437–42.

101. Nelly Richard, "The Photographic Condition," *Art & Text* 21 (1986): 35–36; Richard, *Arte en Chile desde 1973*, 44.

102. Nelly Richard, conversation with Idelber Avelar. See Idelber Avelar, "La Escena de Avanzada: Photography and Writing in Postcoup Chile—A Conversation with Nelly Richard," in *Photography and Writing in Latin America: Double Exposures*, ed. Marcy E. Schwartz and Mary Beth Tierney-Tello (Albuquerque: University of New Mexico Press, 2006), 259–70 [261].

103. Ibid., 261.

104. Ibid.

105. Ibid.; Donoso Macaya, "Arte, document y fotografía," 422.

106. See also Luis Ernesto Cárcamo Huechante, "MEDIAted Memory: Writing, Photography, and Performativity in the Age of the Image," in *Beyond the Lettered City: Latin American Literature and Mass Media*, ed. Debra Castillo and Edmundo Paz-Soldán, Hispanic Issues Series (New York: Garland, 2000), 103–16 [111].

107. Ibid. Here, Richard turns to an evocative literary and visual figure—the ellipsis—as emblematic of the necessity and potential of fracture in the context where dislocation cannot be remedied by relocation (3, 5, 11). Ellipses is simultaneously noun and verb, simultaneously semiotic and visual metaphor that marks the significance of the "fragment" or "fragmentary" and "absent" for her theory of the avanzada under dictatorship. The ellipsis supplants yet retains the overall outline of a presumably once-coherent totality, highlighting fracture and absence while suggesting at least the possibility of unity.

108. Many struck spoons together in workplace lunchrooms or banged pots and pans in their homes late into the night, an appropriation of the symbolism of the empty pots protest reinterpreted as an aural remonstration against military repression and curfew.

109. Pedro Araya, *"El Mercurio miente* (1967): Siete notas sobre escrituras expuestas," *Revista Austral de Ciencias Sociales* 14 (2008): 157–71.

110. "Muestra: Panfletos en la Biblioteca Nacional," *El Periodista* 3, no. 50 (December 7, 2003).

111. Roberto Aguirre Bello and Juan Pablo Rojas Schweitzer, *Panfletos: Poniendo el grito en el suelo* (Santiago: Biblioteca Nacional de Chile, 2003).

112. Kena Lorenzini, *Marcas crónicas: Rayados y panfletos de los ochenta* (Santiago: Ocho Libros, 2010), 20.

113. Ibid., 104.

114. Ibid., 9.

115. Ibid., 71.

116. Ibid., 61.

117. David Henkin's first monograph is a fascinating exploration of the written word in public. David M. Henkin, *City Reading: Written Words and Public Spaces in Antebellum New York* (New York: Columbia University Press, 1998).

118. See Henkin, *City Reading*, 11.

119. Guadalupe Santa Cruz, "Ciudad Pizarra," in Lorenzini, *Marcas crónicas*, 8; emphasis added.

120. Ibid.

121. Lorenzini, *Marcas crónicas*, 174–75.

122. Santa Cruz writes: "It is also possible, as Gustavo Boldrini suggests, to 'construct a flexible paradigm [*una planta movediza y volante*] of the city' through an analysis of 'street paper,' in which the temporality of the flyer is the temporality of a city always in the present." Santa Cruz, "Ciudad Pizarra," 10.

123. Cited in "'Marcas crónicas' de Kena Lorenzini: Recados callejeros de los 80 se juntan en libro fotográfico," *El Mercurio*, June 22, 2010.

124. Lorenzini, *Marcas crónicas*, 105.

EPILOGUE

1. Patricio Rodríguez-Plaza, "La visualidad urbana en el Chile de la Unidad Popular," in *El cartel chileno, 1963–1973*, ed. Eduardo Castillo Espinosa (Santiago: Ediciones B, 2004), 10–12; Patricio Rodríguez-Plaza, *La peinture baladeuse: Manufacture, esthétique et provocation théorique latino-américaine* (Paris: L'Harmattan, 2003), 220.

2. Pedro Lemebel, *Zanjón de la Aguada* (Santiago: Seix Barral, 2003), 222, cited in Pedro Araya, *"El Mercurio miente*: Siete notas sobre escrituras expuestas," *Revista Austral de Ciencias Sociales* 14 (2008): 157–72 [169].

3. Alessandro Portelli, *The Battle of Valle Giulia: Oral History and the Art of Dialogue* (Madison: University of Wisconsin Press, 1997).

4. Steve Stern articulates a theory of "competing selective remembrances." Steve J. Stern, *Remembering Pinochet's Chile: On the Eve of London 1998* (Durham, NC: Duke University Press, 2004), xxvii.

Index

women *(continued)*
51–52; in the March for Democracy,
59–61; political participation of,
63–64; protests by, 13, 43–44;
resistance by, 173, 254n58; violence
against, 50–52, 165, 252n24. *See also*
gender
Women's Studies Circle, 172–73
Wong, Jorge, 17–18
workers: in the cordones industriales,
79–80, 81–82, 86; in films, 131;
in the truckers' strike, 81–82,
91–92
working class: design for, 40; in the
empty pots protest, 50–51; in Popular
Unity, 66–67; in urbanization, 5;
urban planning for, 23

Yarur textile mill, 80, 81, 200–201n17
youth brigades/groups, 6, 50, 86

Zerán, Faride, 84